Also by Arthur F. Wright

STUDIES IN CHINESE THOUGHT, *editor (1953)*
CONFUCIANISM IN ACTION,
    co-editor with David S. Nivison (1959)
BUDDHISM IN CHINESE HISTORY *(1959)*
THE CONFUCIAN PERSUASION, *editor (1960)*
CONFUCIAN PERSONALITIES,
    co-editor with Denis C. Twitchett (1962)
PERSPECTIVES ON THE T'ANG,
    co-editor with Denis C. Twitchett (1973)

The
Sui
Dynasty

The
Sui
Dynasty

Arthur F. Wright

 Alfred A. Knopf   New York   1979

THIS IS A BORZOI BOOK
PUBLISHED BY ALFRED A. KNOPF, INC.

Grateful acknowledgment is made to the following for
permission to reprint previously published material:

   Cambridge University Press: Excerpt from The
Cambridge History of China, Volume 3, reprinted
by permission of Cambridge University Press.

   N.V. Boekhandel 7 Drukkerij voorheen E. J.
Brill, Leiden: Excerpt from Family Instructions for
the Yen Clan.

   Yale University Press: Selections from The Poetry of the Early T'ang, by Stephen Owen. Copy-
right © 1977 by Yale University.

Library of Congress Cataloging in Publication Data
Wright, Arthur F   1913–1976.
The Sui dynasty.
Bibliography: p.
Includes index.
1. China—History—Sui dynasty,
581–618. I. Title.
DS749.2.W74   1978   951'.01   78-54898
ISBN 0-394-49187-4
0-394-32332-7 (pbk.)

Manufactured in the United States of America
Published December 11, 1978
Second Printing, June 1979

When Arthur F. Wright died on August 11, 1976, he had completed and revised the first six chapters of this book. The remaining portion has been edited from a shorter version of the history of the Sui Dynasty originally written by him for publication in *The Cambridge History of China*, to be published in 1979. Robert M. Somers, formerly a student of Professor Wright's at Yale and now assistant professor of history at the University of Missouri-Columbia, contributed the concluding chapter.

Contents

The
Sui
Dynasty

CHAPTER 1

The Sui Challenge

In the history of any civilization there appear times of relative stability, relative quiescence. And scattered through the record are periods of rapid change, of momentous innovation when old institutions are swept away and new solutions to old, intractable problems are found and put into effect. Such periods strike the historian, surveying the whole record of that civilization, as having been decisive for the distinctive shape which that civilization assumed. For the historian of Chinese civilization the Sui period, 581 to 617, is one of these. The Sui swept away the anachronistic institutions which had developed over the four centuries of disunion that preceded it. It replaced them with institutions that were the bone and sinew of the second great Chinese empire, the T'ang, that was to last until 906. And many of those same institutions were to be found in the infrastructure of all the dynasties of later imperial China—a China that endured until February of 1912. More than this, the Sui found ways to end the long centuries of separate political and cultural development in the four main regions of China, ways to ameliorate the cultural dissonance and disharmony, the mutual suspicion that had grown up in those separate regions. Thus the building of new institutions and the achievement of political unity were inseparable from a whole galaxy of measures designed to achieve an empire-wide community of culture and of values. The measures to accomplish these things and the men who devised them are the central subject of this book.

But first some preliminary questions must be answered if we are to assess the accomplishments of the men of the Sui: what was the geographic and cultural scale of their enterprise, and what models did they look to for help? When we have sketched out the answers to these questions we shall look into world history for achievements sufficiently similar to give us a comparative perspective on the Sui accomplishment.

The geographic scale is subcontinental. Areas affected by the Sui, though unevenly occupied, stretched north and south, from Peking to Hanoi (as far as from Philadelphia to Havana), east and west, from the East China Sea to the Jade Gate (as far as from New York to the Rockies). The climate was as varied as these dimensions suggest—from the dry but fertile North China Plain to the well-watered subtropical area of the Yangtze Valley, to the full tropics at the fortified entrepôt of Chiao-chou near modern Hanoi. The land was interlaced with mountain ranges, from the Wu-t'ai shan in the north, which had live glaciers in Sui times, to the great T'ai-hang range running north and south and dividing the alluvial plain of the Yellow River from the piedmont regions to the west of it—from the craggy spine of the Shantung peninsula across to the towering east-west Ch'in-ling range that contains the dramatic peaks of the Hua-shan, and the Chung-nan shan dividing the Wei River Valley from Szechwan in the southwest.

The two great river systems that articulate this great landscape had known human settlement from the earliest times. Each river in its way was unique. The Yellow River rose in the far western highlands, made a U-shaped turn near the northern deserts, which left it flowing swiftly from north to south through the hilly area of loess— fine, wind-driven yellow earth. At the southern end of the loess highlands, it turned abruptly eastward and northeastward and spread out, yellow with silt, between banks a mile or more apart. Finally it traversed the whole of the alluvial plain and emptied into the sea north of the Shantung peninsula. The traveler en route to China by steamship in recent times will remember seeing the water turn yellow a full day out of North China ports.

The Yangtze rises in the Tibetan highlands, makes its way swiftly, taking in the water of many tributaries, across the mountain-girt basin of Szechwan. Then, some fourteen hundred miles from the sea, it enters the Yangtze gorges, famed for their spectacular scenery and for the hazards of their rapids and sand bars. Sheer cliffs rise one and two thousand feet above the river, and sometimes its course narrows to less than three hundred yards. Finally, some thousand miles from the sea, it flows out of its gorges and meanders through lush and beautiful lands to its mouth. This great river each day pours an average of one-half cubic mile of water into the ocean. In Sui times the Yangtze Valley was more sparsely settled than the Yellow River Plain. Arable lands south of the Yangtze lay along the valleys of its tributaries—each valley separated from the next by formidable mountain ranges. In the sixth century, Chinese settlement was just beginning here, and most of the valley land and all the upland were still in the hands of aborigines.

The Pacific was the eastern boundary of this vast land. North China had few satisfactory ports, and the Yellow Sea was inhospitable to navigation. To the south there were thriving port cities along the lower Yangtze, but along the coast there was, at that time, no major port between Hangchow—whose development into a major city began in Sui times when it was made the southern terminus of the Grand Canal—and Canton, at the mouth of the Pearl River, whose hinterland was at the beginning of its great period of settlement and development. The western boundary was ill-defined. In the south, it was somewhere in the mountains—mountains that stretch from what is now Burma to the wild areas west of the Szechwan Basin that are part of the Tibetan massif—an area that is even today largely aboriginal. Proceeding north, these mountains give way slowly to plateau and steppe-land, unsuitable for Chinese agricultural settlement. This land is intersected by a long finger of territory running from the upper Wei River Valley northwestward through the modern province of Kansu toward the Jade Gate (Yümen in Chinese) that in turn leads to the trade routes across Central Asia. The northwestern and northern frontier was marked then, as it is now, by long reaches of the fifteen-hundred-mile-long Great Wall, which traverses mountains, hills, and deserts until it finally ends in the sea at the modern Shanhaikwan. This was, in Sui times, the critical frontier, the boundary between settled Chinese farmers and their natural enemies, the nomadic peoples of the steppe. Along it were garrison towns and trading posts where the Chinese carried on a lively barter trade with the steppe peoples. As one approached this frontier from the Chinese side, the terrain changed slowly and subtly from that of intensively cultivated farmland to the dusty pasture-lands of the steppe.

Given the longitudes and latitudes of this subcontinental area, cultural diversity was very great. We shall return to this in the next chapter when we describe the cultures of sixth-century China. But it is worth noting here some gross contrasts—contrasts that began long before the Sui and persisted long after it. The people who lived nearest the Great Wall frontier had intermarried and interacted for centuries with various raiders and invaders from the steppe land. Their culture and their physical type was different from their cous-ins' further south. The northerners were taller, bigger boned, some-what fairer than the people of the south. They grew millet and wheat in the alluvial plain of the Yellow River, and they had less—and less regular—rainfall to depend on than people in the south. Northerners took pride in living relatively close to the shrines of early Chinese civilization: the centers of the Shang civilization (c. 1765–1060 B.C.), the tomb of Confucius, the twin early capitals of China—Ch'ang-an, in the piedmont area west of the passes, and Loyang, in the Yellow River Plain. The south was inhabited by three different groups: im-migrants from the north who had been at one time or another refu-gees from invasion or civil disturbance in the north; people of old southern families whose culture went back to the pre-imperial states of Ch'u, Yueh, and Wu—states that lay athwart the Yangtze and contended for supremacy with the northern states in the fourth and third centuries B.C.; the aborigines, people of primitive culture—hunters, food gatherers, intermittent farmers—who had once occu-pied all the valleys, hills, and mountains of the south but who were, by Sui times, gradually being converted to Chinese culture or driven further back, a process that today is still incomplete. In the sixth century the aborigines occasionally "converted" a Chinese official sent to control them, and they were capable at times of organized military action against Chinese governments in the south. They in-termarried with Chinese settlers and contributed their beliefs and folkways to the stream of southern culture. The east-west contrasts are as striking as the north-south ones. Contrast a hypothetical fish-ing village on Hangchow Bay—with its boats, fishing, and rice cul-ture, having annual rainfall of about sixty inches—with a horse-trading and garrison town on the edge of the steppe, eleven hundred air miles west-northwest. Here there may be less than fif-teen inches of rain a year, intensely cold winters and all the commu-nity's attention focused on what tribes will appear from the steppe with what horses and other animals and at what prices. Here the merging of steppe and Chinese cultures by intermarriage and the borrowing of folkways back and forth is as common as the mingling of aboriginal and Chinese cultures far away on the southeast coast.

The Chinese had long called this entire area with its diverse climates, peoples, and cultures *T'ien-hsia*, "all under Heaven." It is scarcely surprising that they regarded it as the vast stage on which the whole human drama was enacted. Nor is it surprising that they regarded the struggles for control of all or part of it as *the* decisive events in the history of civilization—events that at once measured the stature of those who succeeded or failed in the great enterprise and determined the future of all civilized men for decades or centuries to come. This then, in rough terms, is the scale, geographic and cultural, of the Sui undertaking. This is the scale which we must keep in mind in assessing the degree of their success.

The Sui leaders were aware of the challenges that faced them. They knew the vast and rugged land; they knew about the repeated failures of efforts at reunification during the three centuries that preceded them. But they also knew a great deal about the first dynasties that succeeded in establishing a unified and centralized empire in the third and second centuries B.C. These were the dynasties of Ch'in (221–207 B.C.) and of Western Han (206–6 B.C.). The Ch'in, they knew, had, by the relentless use of military force and terror, destroyed what was left of the old order: its system of independent states, its great families, and the local networks of power and loyalties that supported them. Once in unchallenged control, the Ch'in had taken the most draconian measures to consolidate their power. They had torn the leading families from their local bases of power and transported them to the Ch'in capital in the west; they had destroyed the city walls in every part of their new empire and, abolishing ancient state boundaries, had put the empire under a rational system of local administration, staffed by Ch'in-appointed bureaucrats. They had proscribed ancient traditions of thought, outlawed those who spread such traditions, and destroyed their books. They made the laws of the empire supreme, and they terrorized their subjects by decreeing brutal punishments for even minor infractions. The men of Sui knew that the Ch'in had brought the period of the Warring States to an end and established the First Sovereign Emperor to rule over "all under Heaven." But they also knew that the Ch'in had gone too far too fast too ruthlessly and that their empire exploded into rebellion shortly after the death of the First Emperor. Thus the accomplishments of the Ch'in undoubtedly excited their admiration while that dynasty's short life and violent end made it a dubious model for those seeking to reunify the empire seven centuries later. The model they took was rather the Former or Western Han, which was the beneficiary of the Ch'in unification, the Han that subtly incorporated many useful Ch'in innovations while allowing local cultures to revive and thinking men to have some limited intellectual choice and a role in policy formation. The Han preserved the concept of empire, of a supreme autocrat, and of rational units of local administration. It continued the Ch'in system of codified law— though with something less than faith in its total efficacy. It drew from many schools and developed a state orthodoxy—which scholars call "Han Confucianism"—and made that orthodoxy the basis of a rudimentary but significant examination system for the recruitment of a meritocracy. Externally the Han extended its hegemony over vast reaches of Central Asia, over the Liao River Valley and northern Korea, over northern Vietnam in the far south. And, for all its foreign adventures, the Han presided—for many decades of its life—over a growing population spreading into previously aboriginal land, over a developing economy that filled the imperial coffers and made possible an opulent life for the fortunate. The second Han Dynasty, which began in A.D. 25 and lasted until A.D. 220, was not as centralized or as successful as the first, but it perpetuated the basic institutions of the first Han, the imperial ideology and much else. From a sixth-century vantage point, looking back across three and a half centuries of foreign invasion, political disunion, and cultural fragmentation, the great Han must have appeared a model for the Sui to follow, a model of unity and stable power. So it seemed to the men of Sui, who in considering policies or policy priorities, court ritual, or local administration always had the Han experience in mind. Historical precedent had, for the Chinese, a power not found in other societies; this led Sui statesmen to turn to history for guidance and, within the long history of China, to turn to the Han Empire for a model.

We now turn to the comparative dimension, seeking in world history an example of an attempt at unification roughly comparable to the Sui's in order to elucidate the character of challenges met and to measure the degree of success achieved. To identify such a comparable effort we should look for a historical situation presenting all or most of the following elements: a subcontinental area, an area once under an ecumenical empire but for centuries split into separately evolving cultures and polities; a major effort at reunification, an effort that evokes or revives institutions and symbols of the previous but long dead empire. The example that, despite many differences—notably in population and resources—seems to fit most closely is the Carolingian Empire. Charlemagne, like the Sui founder, was a product of the culturally mixed societies that had developed, as a result of barbarian invasion, on the marches of the previous empire. In the Chinese as in the European case, those invaders had dealt a death blow to the ancient empires; the sack of Rome by the Goths in 410 is comparable in its devastating psychological shock to the sack of Loyang by the Huns in 311. And, in the wake of both these catastrophes the institutions of the ancient empires were preserved by weak legitimist regimes located far from the original centers of empire: the European at Constantinople, the Chinese at the Yangtze Valley city that, in modern times, we know as Nanking. Both Charlemagne and the Sui founder resorted to the old empire's tradition of codified law, Charlemagne first in the cumulative capitularies of old German law and later in an attempted revival of Roman codification. The Sui were able to draw on the codes of many of the successor states of the long-vanished Han and to weave from many strands a new synthetic code applicable to all its subjects. Both Charlemagne and Sui Wen-ti faced, when they came to power, a great diffusion of central authority: Charlemagne the crazy quilt of claimants to local power—hereditary mayors of the palace, dukes, counts, and bishops—and Wen-ti the long-entrenched great families of the northeast, the northwest, and the south, people who regarded hereditary access to office as a right and the official appointment function as an inheritable privilege. Both took strong measures to reverse the centrifugal flow of power, but Sui Wen-ti strove to restore the administrative rationality of the ancient Han Empire while Charlemagne resorted mainly to the ties of sworn fealty and to gifts of land and serfs as means of insuring loyalty. Charlemagne did appoint his own official inspectors and his own dukes along the borders, but he consistently followed no one pattern for the civil administration of his empire; indeed the legacy of trained officials which the Sui inherited was lacking in eighth-century Europe.

When we consider what might be called "cultural policy," we again find many similarities in the measures taken by the two reunifiers. Charlemagne made his court the focus of science, art, and literature. He made efforts to revive Latin studies and to restock the libraries of Europe. Sui Wen-ti issued decrees on the purification of Chinese literary style, and both he and his son carried out large projects of recovering and recopying books, both secular and Buddhist, that had been scattered in the chaotic years since the fall of the Han. Toward their weak legitimist rivals the two reunifiers had different policies. Charlemagne at one time contemplated marriage with the Empress Irene who reigned in Constantinople, and he would by this act have united Christendom. But this plan was soon abandoned, and the East Roman Empire was proclaimed illegitimate because it was ruled by a woman! By contrast, once Sui Wen-ti had proclaimed himself Son of Heaven he laid claim to "all under Heaven," and that included the last of the legitimist dynasties at Nanking which, a few years later, he forcibly extinguished. "All under Heaven" was less ambiguous than the term "Europe," which in Charlemagne's time was just beginning to be used to designate a political entity, or than "Christendom," in which there were both western and eastern spiritual and political centers, not to mention uncertain and ever-shifting boundaries. Though Charlemagne's advisors spoke of "Europe" as a political unit, this usage seems not to have had wide currency nor much effect on his decisions. Toward the end of his life he divided the "Empire of the Franks" among his sons as their patrimonies. All the sons but one died, and in his hands the empire gradually disintegrated.

In their policies toward religion we find superficial similarities but crucial differences. Both monarchs insisted on the priesthood following strict disciplinary rules, and both took strong measures against monastic vagrancy. Both were men of profound piety, and both ordered the churches in their realm to invoke divine aid regularly for the well-being of themselves, their empires, and their subjects. The moral and religious sanctions of both monarchs' right to rule were challenged by their legitimist rivals: Charlemagne's struggle with Constantinople lasted his lifetime, while Sui Wen-ti, after eight years, ended legitimist challenges from Nanking first by crushing the southern regime and thus silencing the voices that made them, and second by incorporating in his own regime some of the ancient traditions that had in fact been preserved in the south. But here the parallels and near-parallels end. Charlemagne was crowned by Pope Leo III in the Church of St. Peter on Christmas Day, 800, and was there given the title of Emperor and Augustus and acclaimed by the people of Rome. Charlemagne in this action and in all matters of faith conceded to the Pope and the bishops' authority as God's intermediaries on earth. Sui Wen-ti never conceded the realms of faith, morals, or legitimation to any religious hierarchy. The Confucian ritualists saw to the symbols and enactments of legitimation according to traditions going back to the Han and before. The Buddhist and Taoist "churches" received munificent imperial patronage, and particularly saintly or eloquent monks were the object of special favors, but the organizations of both religions were kept under strict imperial vigilance and control.

What are we to make of these comparisons and contrasts? Certainly that two men with comparable ambitions for unification gained power for a time over two areas of subcontinental scale within roughly two centuries of each other. But fundamental contrasts underlie the comparisons we have just noted. Sui Wen-ti had manpower and versatile specialists in a number that Charlemagne would have envied (though Wen-ti found them barely adequate for the tasks he set them). Wen-ti presided over an agricultural economy that, with strict management, was able in a short span of years to produce vast surpluses, while agriculture in Carolingian Europe was at a poor and primitive level. Wen-ti could, with luck and tenacity, establish himself as Son of Heaven, presiding over "all under Heaven" in a manner that substantiated his claim to be the heir of the great emperors of the long-vanished Han. Charlemagne and his advisors sought their models in "Christian antiquity," an age when imperial omnipotence was already diluted by the claims of Christianity and its establishment. Whereas Wen-ti and his son after him could blandly disguise the fact that their ancestors had partaken of the "barbarian" culture of North China, Charlemagne could not and would not disguise his Germanic inheritance, and was restrained by it, in ways great and small, from "acting out" the part of Roman Emperor. Again, while Wen-ti and his advisors knew, from their knowledge of Chinese history—particularly the history of the Chou Dynasty (1050–247 B.C.)—that blood ties and bonds of fealty could not sustain a stable political order, Charlemagne had no such historical perspective. So, in the end, we have found many specific policies for the reconstitution of empire that are comparable, in whole or in part, but such comparisons must be seen as lying above a substratum of contrasts that help us to understand the Sui achievement in proper perspective.

Shall we speculate beyond these comparisons and contrasts? A great historian of Carolingian Europe wrote the following lines which might serve as a kind of epitaph of Charlemagne's empire:

> Decline was at the same time a gathering of forces for the future; and the foundations were being laid for the independent life of the succession states. . . . Europe has never since formed a political unity, and all later attempts to bring about political unity have ended in failure. But, because of the common historical and cultural inheritance from the Carolingian age, the resulting disunity has never dissolved into complete anarchy.*

It seems to me that if the Sui reunification had not succeeded, the Sui's epitaph might have read much like this. The Chinese world might well have been divided into independent successor states, perhaps four of them. And, given the separate and distinctive cultures of the four geographic areas of sixth-century China, there might well have developed, in succeeding centuries, states with their own institutional structures, their own vernacular languages and literatures, their own prides and chauvinisms. China, which Michelet once characterized as "une autre Europe au bout de l'Asie," would have become another Europe in a far more literal sense. In this speculative realm, argument and counter-argument could continue without end, but what I wish to suggest is that the Sui period may well be one of those times of decision, suggested at the beginning of this chapter, in which a civilization is given a distinctive shape, when—as in this case—a unity of culture and polity is reestablished as the norm, a norm that has endured to this day.

In a shorter perspective, Chinese historians have often likened the Sui to the Ch'in nearly eight hundred years before, in that both swept away a decayed old order, introduced drastic change, lasted only two generations, and were succeeded by the great empires of T'ang and Han, respectively. There seems little to be argued with in this comparison, for in both cases the need for sweeping changes in an anachronistic older order seems obvious. And the needed changes set up widespread resistance among those who have been dispossessed or deprived of power. Then, when the renovating dynasties weaken, if only a little, the forces of those they deprived or oppressed rise against them. But in the cases of the Ch'in and the

---

* The sources of factual information and quotations appear in the Notes, beginning on page 215.

Sui, the succeeding great dynasties are the beneficiaries of harsh measures taken by their predecessors. The T'ang builds on the foundations laid by the Sui, and the Han on those put down by the Ch'in. This is as tidy a parallel as one can find in Chinese or any other history. And perhaps the Sui gains in importance by being the "ground-clearer" for the great age of T'ang.

The parallels just mentioned raise the question of cycles in Chinese history. Did the Chinese world pass through recognizable stages of evolution or did its history repeat itself in such uniform cycles that to understand the whole record one need only look at one cycle? Perhaps enough of Sui history has already been touched upon to suggest part of my answer. The Sui period was one of violent change, of striking innovation—a period in which decisions were made that affected the subsequent history of China. Such an assertion can be made only in the context of an evolutionary view of the history of Chinese civilization. But while we must dismiss the notion of a cycle that implies the literal reenactment of similar sequences of events, there remain, in contemplating Chinese history, certain patterns of recurrence that it would be foolish to ignore. I refer to the strength of certain traditions and patterns of behavior that tend to move the later actors on the scene, when faced with a problem, to find the position or take the attitude that someone in comparable circumstances had taken in the past. This tendency is reinforced by certain continuities, down the centuries, in the education of the élite and by the power that past exemplars and historical precedent had over the minds of educated men. This power has no parallel in any other civilization, and it is attributable in part to the relative isolation and self-sufficiency of the Chinese world and in part to the unique continuity of the Chinese language and of Chinese literary and intellectual traditions beginning a millennium before the Christian era. So we should notice past exemplars and previous sequences of events when we contemplate the behavior of an actor in the Sui or any other period of Chinese history. But in doing so, we at the same time should realize that the problems peculiar to that figure's own time as well as the prevailing climate of opinion will modify the total pattern of behavior and rule out any crude repetitions of past models. What we see instead are, rather, configurations recognizably similar to those that have occurred in the past. If we ignored them, we would miss many of the subtleties, not to mention the ironies, of history.

Aside from such configurations, there are striking continuities, geographic and cultural, that affect our story at many points. For example, the Sui founder seized power in a plain that had witnessed the rise and fall of dynasties for eighteen hundred years, and there were tombs to remind him of dead monarchs, both the wise and the foolish, the successes and the failures. There were ruined palaces as well as tombs, to summon up the glories of the Han which had perished there nearly four hundred years before him—the last dynasty to have centralized and gained effective control of all of China. And if the Sui founder did not think of restoring the ecumenical empire, the historians in his entourage were there to urge the example of Han upon him. And, when it came time to proclaim the founding of the Great Sui, the founder turned to his scribes and ritualists who were versed in the ancient precedents and procedures of establishing one's claim to universal dominion. Ritual step after ritual step was executed according to these precedents, and edicts were drafted proclaiming, in time-honored phrases and metaphors, the signs that the new dynasty had Heaven's mandate to rule, that it was taking the steps necessary to bring the new political order into consonance with cosmic forces and with the needs of the people. For the Sui founder and his advisors, the Chinese past was almost palpable, an ever-present thing which influenced all decisions, attitudes, and behavior.

The past was known to the Sui leaders through an ancient and continuous tradition of written histories and works of other kinds: classics from the distant past, literary collections, legal and ritual codes, treatises and descriptive works on every subject of human interest. When we write about the Sui today, we cannot make use of all the books that were in the Sui imperial library, for many have disappeared, but we have at our disposal a formidable body of materials.

First in importance is the *Sui History* (*Sui-shu*) in eighty-five chapters compiled under imperial auspices early in the succeeding dynasty. The bulk of this work was completed in 636 by Wei Cheng, the tough Confucian counselor to T'ang T'ai-tsung; he had the collaboration of a group of distinguished scholar-officials; ten monographs were completed later by other hands, and the whole was presented to the throne in 656 and ordered placed in the imperial library. The monographs are different in focus from the rest of the *Sui History*, for they were commissioned to cover their subjects—such as law, administrative geography, political economy, bibliography—for five northern and southern dynasties in the period 502–617. They are of great importance, but they are opaque to anyone not familiar with state policies, personalities, and events of the period covered. To make intelligible his translation of the "Monograph on Law," the late Étienne Balazs required 315 long footnotes and nine appendixes—this for a Chinese text of only twenty-five folio pages!

The tradition of a dynasty's compiling the history of its predecessor was an old one, but having the work done by commissions headed by high-ranking officials was instituted by the T'ang. The *Sui History*, like most of its predecessors and successors, was divided into three parts: basic annals (*pen-chi*), a chronological year-by-year account of main events as seen from the court; "biographies" (*lieh-chuan*) largely made up of the lives, with emphasis on their official careers, of leading figures of the dynasty; the monographs (*chih*) just discussed. Certain sections of the history were followed by postscripts (*lun*) in which the historians expressed their judgments on the preceding accounts of events or groups of biographies. For the *Sui History*, Wei Cheng wrote those judgments and with a pronounced Confucian moral bias. But for the most part the history is in an anonymous third-person style and, like its counterparts in earlier and later times, was pieced together from selected segments of the raw sources available. In the case of the *Sui History*, what were these raw sources? The basic annals were derived from several types of records kept at the Sui court. The system of recording was not as elaborate as it was to become under the T'ang and subsequent dynasties. But there were officers compiling regular detailed records of imperial and official acts. For the Sui the principal record was the "account of imperial activities" (*ch'i-chü chu*); this may have been supplemented by "dynastic histories" (*kuo-shih*) that pulled together from time to time a synoptic record of one period of the dynasty's life. Only odd fragments of these raw records survive as quotations in other books, for many of the records, together with the Sui imperial library, were lost when a barge in which they were being moved capsized. But it should be remembered that Wei Cheng and many of his associates had lived under the Sui, knew its leading figures, and possibly interviewed survivors; they probably also had access to earlier unofficial writings of all sorts. The texts of the *Sui History's* biographies were based in large part on funerary documents submitted by surviving family members of the subject and checked, whenever possible, against official files.

The *Sui History* is the most complete single work on the period, but a wide variety of other sources may be used to check and supplement it. Among these are the histories of the preceding dynasty, the *History of the Northern Chou*; the history of the last of the southern dynasties, which the Sui extinguished in 589, *History of the Ch'en*; and a synoptic account of four northern dynasties down to and including the Sui, the *History of the Northern Dynasties*. Another kind of work is the monumental *Tzu-chih t'ung-chien* by the Sung historian Ssu-ma Kuang (1019–1086). It is a stately chronicle-style history of the Chinese world from 403 B.C. to A.D. 959, and it represents both the new standard of criticism and the new moralism characteristic of its day. The Sui is covered in chapters 175 through 184, and Ssu-ma Kuang made use of valuable primary sources, many of them no longer extant.

One problem is that all the written sources, particularly the official, are focused almost exclusively on the capital and on the élite. Little is heard of the vast majority of the people unless they create an administrative problem—rise in revolt, are so drought-stricken as not to be able to pay their taxes, die in large numbers from pestilence or starvation, and so forth. We are allowed an occasional glimpse of common life from a legal fragment, from a short story, and from some of the manuscripts found at Tun-huang, far in the west, early in this century. But there is by no means enough to present a coherent picture of the lives of commoners.

Histories such as that of the Sui were written by officials assigned for the term of the project and, when completed, were presented to the throne for approval. Thus not only the interests but also the ideology of the ruling group were reflected in their contents. What then are some of the elements of this ideology that are reflected, consciously or unconsciously, in the histories? First of all, the values which the historians hold are Confucian. They have a deep-seated belief in the moral value of history, believing that history, when properly recounted, will show the working of a moral dynamic in the affairs of men. Those who wrote histories were anxious to be recognized as "good historians" (*liang-shih*), truthful, not introducing interested or partisan biases or yielding to pressure and wielding what was called a "crooked brush" (*ch'ü-pi*). At the same time they were under an obligation, which they saw as going back to Confucius himself, to make moral judgments of the events and the people they wrote about. And Confucius, they believed, sanctioned what is called "appropriate concealment" (*hui*), that is, the suppression or burial in another place in the history of particulars which might blur the consistency or a moral point. For example, in the *Sui History*, the authors in their role as "good historians" did not wish to give full authority to the story that the second Sui emperor had had a hand in his father's death. On the other hand, they were writing in the service of a new dynasty concerned with making the point that the second Sui emperor was so morally derelict that the T'ang did not represent a rebellion, but a "raising of the banner of righteousness" (*ch'i-i*) in order to overthrow him. So the historian placed this damaging particular about the first emperor's death not in the basic annals but in the less important section later in the history devoted to the biographies of imperial women.

In the *Sui History*, biographies fill fifty of the eighty-five chapters, and the distinctive features of the Chinese biographical tradition limit in various ways what we can know. Biography was seen as providing exemplary and minatory figures for posterity; it was consistent with this view to group biographies in largely moral categories and to place particulars that spoiled the moral consistency of a given life elsewhere in the history. The order in which the categories of biographies appeared reflected the working of two criteria of judgment: one was how powerful, how important a person had been; the other was moral, that is, the good came first, the bad and disreputable at the end. As we have noted, many of the materials for a biography came from surviving relatives of the subject. They thus tended to be cast in the set laudatory phrases of the various kinds of funerary writings. More than this, the phrases used in funerary writings and in biographies had tended, over a period of a thousand years and more, to become standardized, formulaic. For example, "When young, he was precocious. The elders of the village questioned him for hours on the classics, and he startled them with his broad knowledge." Or, "He was versed in ancient literature and so proficient in composition that he had no sooner put brush to paper than the piece was finished without a mistake." Biographies place heavy emphasis on official careers, and behind the career data and the set phrases it is exceedingly difficult to glimpse the personality of the subject. But the biographies often contain *extenso* quotations from the subject's official writings and from his literary works, and these may not have survived in any other form.

The historians were all men experienced in the political arena, and it would be natural for them to give a little extra attention to subjects whose descendants, when the history was written, were politically powerful, certainly to be extremely circumspect in handling such subjects. There is evidence that they did: the author of a history written a few decades earlier was roundly denounced by more than a hundred members of powerful families for what they thought was demeaning treatment of their immediate ancestors.

Ideology and political pressures obviously had their influence on the historians. Equally significant were the feelings they had about the position and prerogatives of the privileged official class to which they belonged. Historians of the Sui, like others in the Chinese tradition, were extremely sensitive to anything that seemed a threat to the official class to which they belonged. Though some were themselves Buddhists, they saw organized Buddhism as a power center that had continually to be watched, lest it encroach upon their privileged functions of advising the emperor, pronouncing on all moral issues, formulating state policies, and performing all major administrative functions in a bureaucratic state. Political monks, both Buddhist and Taoist, always got a "bad press" from the historians, particularly if they gained entry to the palace or the privilege of audience with an emperor. Eunuch servitors in the imperial palace were, of course, the natural enemies of the official class, and if one of them enlarged his sphere of influence, he could be sure of the implacable hatred of the officials and of historical notices that reflected it. More subtly expressed was the natural antipathy between the official style and the style of the emperors: this was always present but was most pronounced when the emperor was aggressive, flamboyant, and extravagant, as was the second Sui emperor. One can see the contrasting styles and standards of judgment very clearly in a valuable book which records discussions on moral and political subjects between the great T'ang emperor T'ai-tsung and his ministers. When the talk turns to the last Sui emperor, the officials pull all the stops in condemning his extravagance, his flamboyant schemes, and so forth. T'ai-tsung at one point asks, in effect, if all this is so, where were the officials who should have been admonishing Yang-ti and bringing him back to the path of caution, frugality, and virtue? Thus he says very plainly that emperors are not solely responsible for bad policies and that officialdom must take its share of the blame. The officials, in their role as historians, always had the last word. They knew this and used it in ways both subtle and unsubtle to win a point with the emperor; the emperor knew this, and his concern for his posthumous "image" often led him to yield on a point that had aroused official opposition. Other factors aside, one hardly needs to be reminded that the authors of the *Sui History* were not immune to the usual human weaknesses, notably strong likes and dislikes. Wei Cheng, for example, had nothing but contempt for the man who had served twenty years as official historian at the Sui court and had indeed compiled the first history of the Sui (now lost). This official, Wang Shao, appears in the *Sui History* as a shameless sycophant; worse than that, in Wei Cheng's view, he was a Buddhist, who catered to the Buddhist piety and the credulity of the first Sui emperor. So Wei Cheng concludes his postscript to the biography of Wang Shao in the *Sui History* with a stinging denunciation: "He loved strange stories and valued devious and misleading talk. His written style was base and vile, the organization of his work confused; he brought dishonor upon the [historical] tradition."

Perhaps these brief remarks on the historiography of the Sui are enough to suggest the skepticism and wariness which we must employ in using the standard sources. It is often difficult to judge the truth of a statement found only in a single text. Yet the difficulties in using one genre of historical writing as a source can often be mitigated by reference to other genres. For the whole period of Buddhist dominance in China, from the fourth to the tenth centuries, Buddhist historical works provide valuable supplements to secular histories. And so they do for the Sui period. Although such works are religiously inspired and aim both to glorify Buddhism and exalt the great monks and lay adherents, they adopt the sober tone of the Confucian histories and provide a wealth of credible particulars on a variety of subjects: the building of temples and reliquaries, Buddhist activities at court, the history of the translation of Buddhist scriptures and their exegesis, the lives of the monks and the nuns. Occasionally a Buddhist chronicle will quote at length from an official historical document that is otherwise lost. There are also Taoist historical works that refer to the Sui, but, in general, these are much poorer in historical particulars and emphasize the internal and doctrinal history of religious Taoism.

Works of pure literature of the Sui era include essays, letters, and a modest amount of poetry, both occasional and otherwise. Thus, while there does not come down from the Sui period the overwhelming volume of writings that survive to document the ages after the invention of printing—roughly from 900 onward—the variety is still great enough to make it possible to cross-check on a large number of points of fact and interpretation. Finally there are the results of archeological discoveries of several kinds: collections of inscriptions from the time of the Sui whose subject matter is mainly but not exclusively Buddhist; the wall paintings and the manuscripts of Sui times discovered, early in this century, at Tun-huang on the northwest border of China—these, too, largely associated with Buddhism; the sculptures, ceramics, and bronzes in Chinese and foreign museums which help us to visualize the life of that distant age; Sui sites, particularly those excavated since 1949, which include a number of Sui tombs and the foundations of its capital city. On problems which are not to be solved by reference to any of these materials, the historian of China—like his colleagues in other fields—must rely on what Marc Bloch termed "the master quality of a historian," namely, the sense of what cannot have happened.

CHAPTER 2

Sixth Century China

The world that the Sui leaders aspired to unite once more into a single political and cultural order was immensely complex, comparable, as I have suggested, to that of Charlemagne's Europe, with the orthodox and legitimist pretensions of the East Roman Empire thrown in. Sharp geographical differences from region to region went far toward determining the different cultures of sixth-century China. And, as these cultures developed, their institutions, their customs, their ways of thinking and behaving became sharply divergent. These contrasts in turn generated mutual suspicion, hostility, and all manner of chauvinisms and snobbisms. Barriers, both physical and psychological, as they persisted for decades and centuries, became ever more formidable. All these obstacles faced by one who aspired to reunify sixth-century China were compounded by an imperative of Chinese political tradition: that no one can reestablish lasting political unity without reasserting an ecumenical moral order setting common standards of belief, of values, and of behavior. Despite all these problems and conflicts, it would be mistaken to say that a would-be unifier had nothing to work with. There was a common written language, a more or less uniform political ideology, certain ideas and values, drawn from different religious traditions, that found acceptance throughout the land.

The North China Plain, the great stretch of alluvial earth built up and nourished for aeons by the Yellow River, ran southward—interrupted only by occasional hills and scarps—from the borders of the steppe-land to the area of the Huai River where dry farming gave way, throughout historic time, to rice culture. In this plain, and near the Yellow River's course, were the ancient capitals of the Shang Dynasty in which were centered China's first civilization and the first elements of a stable political order. The entire plain had been settled under the Shang's successors, the Chou, and it was dotted with ancient cities, many of them the capitals of the independent states that flourished and fought with one another in the last centuries of the Chou period. These were the places that had witnessed, in the fifth and fourth centuries B.C., the first great flowering of China's creative thought and of literature, and, in these same years, the rapid development of statecraft and of governmental institutions. By the time of the imperial orders of Ch'in and Early Han (221 B.C.–A.D. 6) the North China Plain was not only by far the most populous and richest area within the empire, it was also, in symbols and in established rituals, the sacred heartland of China. Here was the birthplace and the tomb of the "peerless sage of ten thousand generations," Confucius. Here was Mount T'ai which emperors ascended, with solemn ritual, to report to Heaven on their success in governing "all under Heaven." Here too were many places which claimed to be the birthplace of the shadowy founder of the Taoist tradition, Lao-tzu. Near the western edge of the plain was the ancient city of Loyang, first a citadel built by the conquerors of the Shang (in the twelfth century B.C.), later a major city under the early empires and then principal capital of the Later Han and of its successors. By the sixth century the traditions of Loyang stretched back nearly two thousand years. Its glories and its tragedies figured in hundreds of poems and prose pieces. It was, by historical and cultural standards, the principal city of what the Chinese have long called the "chung-yüan," or Central Plain. It was indeed one of those places where the collective memory of a civilization is focused.

The plain's western limit is formed by an immense mountain range which begins near modern Peking and continues south and southwest, eventually meeting an eastern extension of another great mountain chain projecting out from the Tibetan massif. At the convergence of those two enormous ranges of mountains, about one hundred miles west of Loyang, the Yellow River makes its famous right-angle bend eastward and flows steeply through a rugged defile between the two mountain barriers before it comes out into the plain. The mountain chains have been key strategic and political factors in Chinese history, making passage difficult from the plain into the northwestern regions. One principal pass and a few lesser defiles allow passage from the plain through those barriers. The principal pass is at an altitude of nearly thirteen hundred feet, and leads westward among the mountains into the very different terrain of Kuan-chung—"the land within the passes"—a high-lying plain watered by the Wei River and its tributaries, surrounded on three sides by mountains, and for two thousand years the staging area for conquest of the populous plain to the east. A great Chinese historian of the end of the first century A.D. said of Kuan-chung:

> In abundance of flowering plants and fruits
>   it is the most fertile of the Nine Provinces
> In natural barriers for protection and defense
>   it is the most impregnable refuge in heaven and earth
> This is why its influence has extended in the six
>   directions
> This is why it has thrice become the seat of imperial
>   power.

It was from this area that the Chou—more than a thousand years before the Christian era—moved eastward to conquer and replace the earlier Shang power in the plain. From it the King of Ch'in, after more than twenty years of relentless war, finally crushed the independent states of the plain; here, in 221 B.C., he proclaimed himself First Sovereign Emperor and ruled all China from his capital in "the area within the passes." When, a few years later, the Han supplanted the Ch'in, they too established their capital here and called it Ch'ang-an. Thus the history of this area was less rich in cultural memories—of great thinkers of many schools, of literature and the arts—than the North China Plain. It was, rather, resonant with the sounds of marching men, of war chariots, of the echoes of cavalry columns making their way to the passes or westward to engage the forces of the peoples of the steppe, the natural and perennial enemies of the Chinese. Thus, in the mid-sixth century, the ethos of these two areas were quite different.

But the cultures of Kuan-chung and the North China Plain had also been deeply affected by the vicissitudes of their histories during the three centuries before this time, and the effects of these centuries were visible, indeed palpable in both the plain and in the area within the passes. The Han's successors, all of whom had aspired to universal dominion, proved weak and quite unable to maintain effective government throughout the vast empire. Between A.D. 281 and 302 a frightful sequence of natural disasters—famine, plague, locusts, floods—devastated the north. There was no effective government to provide relief or to repair flood control works or suppress the widespread "banditry" that came in the wake of these disasters. A contemporary witness who had made a tour of inspection reported that previously rich farmlands were covered with weeds and that only 20 percent of the Chinese population remained—mostly the old and the weak.

This was bad indeed, but it was made infinitely worse by the policy successive governments had pursued for many decades of allowing "barbarians" to settle within China proper, a policy founded on the firmly held principle that all those who settled within China would gradually but inevitably adopt Chinese culture and be naturalized into hard-working, tax-paying tillers of the soil. But the policy did not work in these bitter times, and the Chinese struggled with enclaves of foreign peoples for ever-diminishing means of subsistence. Still worse, these peoples made common cause with their cousins from the steppe-land, and the once-great Chinese empire was subject to subversion from within compounded by military intervention from beyond the borders. Finally, in 311 a coalition of these forces attacked Loyang, sacked the city, and carried the Emperor off into captivity. A contemporary letter written by a Sogdian merchant to his home office puts it laconically but well; he expresses astonishment that "those Huns who were yesterday the Emperor's vassals" should now have overthrown the empire. "And Sir," he writes, "the last emperor—so they say—fled from Saragh [Loyang] because of the famine, and his palace and walled city were set on fire. . . . So Saragh is no more . . . !"

Thus Loyang and the whole North China Plain, the heartland of Chinese culture, fell under the control of alien peoples. Six years later, old Ch'ang-an, the capital within the passes, also fell, and the last Chinese political foothold in the north was gone. Surviving members of the imperial house and of the aristocratic élite fled south and east and took refuge in the lower Yangtze Valley. This began the long-lasting division of the Chinese world into two parts, with aliens in control of the north and a feeble Chinese power maintaining itself in the Yangtze Valley and further south. But political division was

only one of the consequences of the debacle in the north. The other
was a profound traumatic shock to the Chinese people. The fall of
Loyang has been likened, in its immediate effect and long-term consequences, to the sack of Rome by the Goths. But the sack of the ancient capitals of Loyang and Ch'ang-an brought with it the loss of the
whole of the north—of every monument, of all the places sacred or
memorable in the history of Chinese civilization: the tombs of emperors and culture heroes, the shrines of Confucius and Lao-tzu, the
sacred mountains, guardian symbols of the Chinese universe, the
Great Wall, built and manned down the centuries as a deterrent to
alien incursions into the Chinese world.

The broad alluvial plain of the lower Yangtze, which had received millions of refugees from the sequence of natural disasters
that had struck in the north in the late third century, now had a fresh
influx, this time of members of the imperial house and of those
northern aristocratic families that had so long misused the power
they monopolized. The newly arriving immigrants found a physical
environment that contrasted sharply with that of their homeland in
the north. Here the rainfall was abundant, and the land was not
brown and dusty in winter but green through all the seasons. Here
the growing season lasted most of the year, and rice cultivation was
the prevailing form of agriculture, in contrast to the millet, wheat,
and bean crops that were typical of the north. The landscape was
dramatic: the wildness of the Yangtze gorges, wide stretches of
shimmering lakes and, along the seacoast, craggy mountains rising
sharply from the narrow coastal plain. The human landscape was
stranger still, for the Chinese of the Yangtze Valley spoke dialects
the northerners often could not understand at all, and these people
had traditions and all manner of customs that the northerners had
never encountered. Moreover, beyond—and often surrounding—the
centers of southern Chinese settlement were aboriginal people, "barbarians" who led a primitive life as yet unaffected by Chinese influence. To the northerners this new environment at first seemed
strange and hostile; they behaved at first like émigrés—homesick
and nostalgic, willing to stay only until the north could be reclaimed.
Meanwhile they complained of the southern diet and longed for the
wheat flour delicacies, the dumplings and pancakes they had enjoyed in the north. They looked upon the southerners with disdain.
At Chien-k'ang, the site of modern Nanking, the northern refugees
established a new capital and there enthroned a relative of the last

emperor to rule in the north. In the beginning the capital was most unimpressive, low-lying and easily flooded when the Yangtze waters rose. But the northerners maintained their old court ritual and insisted on using the dialect of Loyang, their lost capital, as a court language and scorned the regional Wu dialect. A fourth-century poet of southern origin, when asked why he did not recite his poems in the dialect of Loyang, said: "Why should I make a noise like an old serving-maid?"

In the decades following the northern influx, there were many other areas of friction between the newcomers and the southerners. The same great families that had contributed so much toward the loss of the north now claimed the high offices at the southern court. They accumulated large landholdings and thousands of semi-servile people to work them. In the provinces the northerners, like the settlers of North America, often transplanted the names of their northern districts. But, as the years passed and as efforts at military reconquest of the north failed, abrasive relations between southerners and the northern immigrants gave way to accommodation. The year 364 may be seen as symbolic of the end of a period of sharp cultural conflict, and of self-delusion on the part of the northerners. In that year the emperor at Chien-k'ang ordered taxpayers to cease and desist from the practice of listing their original northern domiciles on the tax rolls and thus claiming tax-exempt status as recent immigrants. Rather, everyone was ordered to give his actual southern place of residence. By this time immigrant families had developed substitutes for their favorite northern dishes, they had learned to speak the regional Wu dialect—a necessity for the day-to-day business of life—and intermarriage with southern families became commonplace.

There is yet another side to southern history in this period. Beyond the capital and the few other centers of high culture lay the virgin lands of the south, well-watered, fertile, and potentially of very high yield. The obstacles to development were formidable: the backbreaking work of clearing the land; the need to channel and control the waters; disease; the harassments of aborigines. Yet work parties went out, many of them sponsored by great families, and they gradually brought this land under cultivation. Slowly, the areas won attracted more Chinese settlers. First stockaded camps and then walled towns became centers for governing the settlers and for military control of the aborigines. This steady development enriched the south and added to the affluence of the major centers and the leading families. The Liang Emperor Wu-ti became alarmed at the scale of exploitation by some of these families and issued an edict:

> [Many officials and local magnates] have enlarged and se-
> cured their estates, crossing boundaries, cutting roads and
> waterways, seizing crops and game and even collecting fire-
> wood, so that the poor peasants are without recourse. From
> this time on, those crossing boundaries . . . will be pun-
> ished by military law. Nor may officials . . . set up estates
> of their own, competing for private profit against the state in-
> terest. . . . Those disrespecting this order will be executed!

There is no evidence that this decree was heeded. Instead the power and wealth of the great families continued to increase; the capital they accumulated was put to work in further land settlement and in commerce; the number of their semi-servile dependents, aug-mented by a continuing flow of immigrants, steadily grew. For all the social inequities and political instability, the south prospered; this was the beginning of the centuries-long process that was to make the Yangtze delta the richest and most populous area of China. By the beginning of the fifth century, inhabitants of the region, whether of immigrant or native stock, were referring to themselves with pride as *nan-jen,* or southerners. The ruling families were the arrogant and self-conscious perpetuators of all the cultural traditions passed down from the last Chinese empire of Han and the rightful heirs of its po-litical hegemony. But southerners as a whole had developed a mixed culture made up of strands of northern and of native traditions and a style of life that was distinctly their own.

As this was taking shape the unification of North China under alien Turko-Mongol rule was nearing completion, and the two areas adopted mutually hostile policies and attitudes: continuous military hostility (in which the south was at a great disadvantage), the main-tenance of trade barriers and restrictions on travel from one area to the other, cultural chauvinisms of many varieties that naturally throve in an atmosphere of mutual hostility and isolation. From this period onward the northerners habitually referred to the southerners as *tao-i,* island-dwelling barbarians (a contemptuous term long-used for the uncivilized aborigines of the south), while the southerners spoke of the northerners as *su-lu,* servile people with their hair tied in a braid, sometimes translated "caitiffs." This terminology of contempt was used by northern historians to refer to members of the southern ruling élite, and vice versa.

North-south hostility was deeply affected by developments in the north immediately following the division of the country in 317, in the period traditional Chinese historians refer to as "the sixteen kingdoms of the five barbarians." It was a time of incessant war between and among the rival states dominated by alien minorities of diverse racial and geographic origins: those from the northwest frontier area—people later called Tibetans and Tanguts—and those descended from the steppe nomads of the north and northeast who spoke languages classified as Turkish, Mongol, or Tungusic. We need not follow the fortunes of these regimes which rose by violence and soon disappeared in murderous wars, coups d'état, and occasionally in racial pogroms. But certain trends, with long-term effects on the history of the sixth and later centuries should be noted. Nearly every northern prince of whatever racial or cultural origin aspired to unify North China and ultimately to preside, as Son of Heaven, over the Chinese world. With that ultimate ambition, he would inevitably call on Chinese advisors who commanded the traditions of statecraft and administration as well as the complex ritual-symbolic process that had to be followed to give his regime legitimacy in Chinese eyes. The Chinese monopoly of all these gave them a chance to influence their rude masters and gently but firmly lead them in the direction of Sinicization. Sometimes their work was undone by a sudden access of atavism, a violent move by one segment of the ruling group to return to their own ancestral ways, their own language, their own cults. One among the many arguments favoring the old ways states the case for the old nomadic life with great clarity. The speaker is a general in the service of a tribal chief who has just given himself a splendid new Chinese title. He argues as follows:

Long ago our ancestors came out of the northern borderlands. With hair streaming down their backs and clothes buttoned on the left they were free of ceremonial regulations. They moved about irregularly and were without the institution of the walled town. . . . Now it seems to me fitting that we establish the Chinese in their walled towns and encourage their agriculture and silk production to provide for the needs of our martial house. We then will be free to practice our military arts, so as to crush those who have not yet submitted to us. . . .

But with the rise to power of a Turko-Mongol people—the Hsien-pei who founded the Northern Wei Dynasty—North China's agriculture gradually revived and prospered. And, as the Turko-Mongols came to dominate a population of Chinese peasants, they adopted more and more of the methods of taxation and administration that were characteristic of the Chinese tradition. As they prospered from the taxes of their peasant subjects, their upper class was more and more drawn to the material culture, the arts, and the style of life of the Chinese, and this tendency was given further impetus by intermarriage between the alien minority and the Chinese. By the early fifth century a culture had emerged in North China that was a complex amalgam of Chinese and alien elements. And when, in 439, the Tartar Toba had brought political unification to the north, they pushed further toward the full consolidation of regional power. The Northern Wei Dynasty, like the great Chinese dynasties of the past, defended the northern frontiers against steppe invaders and launched military expeditions that gained control of the Central Asian oasis kingdoms and the western routes of access to China proper. They established firm control of the two great centers of Chinese imperial power: the North China Plain and the northwest. In the course of their rise they had developed a formidable army, and they must have seemed well on their way toward becoming masters of the whole Chinese world.

In 494 they took another step toward that goal. They moved their capital from its old location near the northern steppe frontier to Loyang, a site full of the resonances of Chinese imperial history. There, according to traditional Chinese capital plans, they built a splendid new city. And, at the same time, the Wei Emperor issued sweeping orders for Sinicization. The Hsien-pei were ordered to give up their own language and to speak only Chinese at court; they were ordered to give up their own surnames and take Chinese names instead (here the imperial family led the way by taking the surname Yüan); their own tribal rituals were to be given up and only Confucian and Buddhist observances followed. The Hsien-pei style of dress was outlawed in favor of the Chinese style, and intermarriage between the Hsien-pei and Chinese upper-class families was actively encouraged.

This sequence of moves created deep resentment among the Hsien-pei who still lived by their ancient ways—tough nomads and soldiers who guarded the northern and western frontiers and who came to hate their Sinicized cousins leading sedentary and self-indulgent lives in the thoroughly Chinese atmosphere of Loyang. Moved by their grievances and led by Hsien-pei nobles who shared their views, this group, a million strong, exploded into the North China Plain in 523. A vast bloodletting ensued: the sack of Loyang and the massacre of two thousand courtiers including an empress dowager and her puppet child-emperor. This was followed by ten years of civil war; out of it emerged two military men who, in 534, divided the Wei into two parts: a western part with a capital at Ch'ang-an "within the passes" and an eastern part with a capital at the city of Yeh in Honan. In the most general terms, the western empire represented a reassertion of elements of the Toba heritage, while the eastern empire had a Toba ruling élite obliged to work closely with the Chinese upper class in the administration of a Chinese peasant population. The violent disruption of the Toba drive toward dominion over the whole Chinese world and the subsequent struggle between the western and eastern Toba successor states for control of North China gave the "legitimate" power at Nanking a new lease on life.

In 502 a new dynasty was founded at Nanking with the usurpation by yet another descendant of a prestigious clan. This was Hsiao Yen, who ruled as Emperor Wu of the Liang Dynasty from 502 until 549. Liang Wu-ti began, as so many of his predecessors at Nanking had, by trying to curtail the overweening power of the great clans which, from the beginning of the Period of Disunion, had dominated the southern dynasties—controlling the economy, monopolizing all high offices, excluding others from all but the lowliest positions, and forcing commoners into their service. These clans grouped and regrouped into clique after clique; they made and unmade emperors, expanded regional governorships into personal satrapies and built up their own military forces. For a short period early in his reign Liang Wu-ti had some success in reclaiming power for his dynasty. He appointed people of lower social standing to office, and he tried to get men into palace service and into regional military commands who were loyal to him. His armies recaptured substantial areas previously lost to the north. In the latter part of his reign, however, his political powers waned, eroded by the rapaciousness of his own relatives, whom he never tired of forgiving and rewarding, and by his increasing preoccupation with Buddhist observances. But, in the early 500s Liang power was by no means negligible, and the northern empire of Wei had not yet been forcibly partitioned.

Mutual hostility and isolation had, of course, produced stereotypes of all kinds. In most general terms, southerners considered the northerners uncivilized, tainted by the lower cultures of their alien masters, and the northwesterners even more so. For their part the northerners—and even more violently the northwesterners—considered the southerners lazy, effeminate, and pretentious. Another theme that runs through all levels of antagonism is the southerners' claim that they were the true heirs of the great empire of Han, the legitimate guardians of all the traditions and symbols of Chinese imperial authority. The northerners scoffed at the idea that an effete regime in the lower Yangtze Valley was a legitimate successor to the proud dynasties that had for centuries dominated all China from Ch'ang-an and Loyang.

There survives an account by a northern contemporary of a heated exchange of views between northerners and southerners that dramatizes the deep-seated chauvinisms on both sides. The occasion was a dinner party given in Loyang by a southerner who had, some time before, defected to the Northern Wei and served as an official in Loyang. The guest of honor was an official from the southern court who had come to Loyang on a diplomatic-political mission, but the party also included two aristocrats from the North China Plain. The guest of honor got very drunk and addressed the company with these remarks:

> Though the Wei Dynasty is indeed prosperous, it is still one of the Five Barbarians. The correct New Year's Day [i.e., the calendar] has been passed down from one generation to the next, and this surely exists only south of the Yangtze. The jade seals of the First Sovereign Ch'in Emperor now belong to the Liang Dynasty.

One of the northern grandees had this to say in reply:

> You are only using the area of the lower Yangtze as a temporary refuge, and there you live meanly in a corner of the empire. Much of the land has a fetid dampness that nurtures all manner of insects. This border area is malarial, a place where frogs and turtles share the same lairs, where men and birds cohabit. Among your close-cropped gentry, there are none with strong and healthy looks, and your tattooed people are endowed with bodies that are small and weak. They float about on your three rivers, row about on your five

lakes—unaffected by ritual or music, not to be improved by laws and ordinances. Although the prisoners transported to the South under the Ch'in and Han dynasties brought in and intermixed the true Chinese speech [of the north], still the difficult southern languages of Min and Ch'u were not changed for the better. Although you set up rulers and ministers, those above were harsh and those below were violent. This is why Liu Shao first murdered his father and Liu Chün later violated his mother [two vicious southern princes of the fifth century]. Thus to turn one's back on proper human relationships—wild beasts are no different! And to these one must add the Princess of Shan-yin [a fifth-century precursor of the equal rights movement who demanded a number of lovers in proportion to the emperor's concubines] who, in asking for lovers, betrayed her husband and brought her licentious relations into the household without regard for jeers and ridicule. You are steeped in these inherited ways; you have never felt the transforming effects of proper ritual; you are like the people of Yang-t'i [a notorious goiter area] of whom it is said that they don't know that a tumor is a deformity.

Our Wei Dynasty, having responded to the Lo Writing and the River Plan (two harbingers of legitimate rule), established the ancient tripods of universal dominion at Mount Sung and the Lo River. The five sacred mountains became our protectors, the area within the four seas our residence. Our models for improving the social tone and changing the customs were in accord with the precedents of the five emperors of antiquity. The splendors of our ritual and music, of our codes and regulations, surpass those of a myriad monarchs and stand preeminent. Is it that you fisher-folk would emulate your moral betters and come to pay court and, like animals, drink water from our ponds, and, like fowl, peck at our grain? How can the presumptuousness of the likes of you reach such a point as this?

The northern recorder tells us that this diatribe left the audience speechless, which we can well imagine.

Southern contempt for northern culture could be illustrated by many quotations. But let us take the judgment expressed by Yü Hsin, a noted southern poet captured by northwesterners and carried off to live in their capital at Ch'ang-an; there he is said to have overawed the northwesterners with his literary virtuosity and to have been deluged with commissions from noble families to write the texts of funerary inscriptions. The poet was once asked by a southern visitor about the literary scene in the north. Yü mentioned three writers as having some merit, but added: "With these exceptions, northern literary production is simply like the braying of donkeys and the barking of dogs."

Diatribes and jabs of the kind just quoted might be multiplied, but we are fortunate in having a contemporary work that offers relatively more judicious contrasts between the cultures of north and south. This is a book of family injunctions written by Yen Chih-t'ui, who was first an official in the south, then served the Northern Wei successor state in the North China Plain and ended his life in the service of the Sui in the northwest. He says in his famous chapter on manners and customs: "Formerly, when I lived south of the Yangtze, I could learn the best manners by direct experience. But you, having been born in a military atmosphere, don't understand much of what you see and hear. Therefore I have made a rough account of these matters for the perusal of my sons and grandsons." Yen's judgments of northern literary and classical studies echo those of Yü Hsin. Save for a few scholars, he finds "the rest . . . mostly rustic persons whose speech is rough and manners unrefined. If you ask them of their special fields, they have clearly mastered nothing; ask them a simple question, and they will answer you with several hundred words in which there is no main idea." Then he tells a story current in the city of Yeh: "A doctor of literature or an erudite man bought a donkey and wrote three documents in which [the complicated character] lü for donkey does not appear once!"

When it came to everyday manners, Yen was nostalgic for the punctiliousness observed in the south but rather admiring of the more casual and informal ways of the northerners. Speaking of the contrast, he says:

> The ancients stressed that parting is easy while meeting is difficult. South of the Yangtze, on seeing off a guest, one wept at the words of farewell. A certain imperial prince, a younger brother of the Emperor Wu [was setting out for a distant post and] was taking his leave of the Emperor. The latter said "I am very old and deeply affected by being separated from you," and tears streamed down his face. The prince, though

his countenance was gloomy, shed no tears but blushed as he went out. For this he was punished. . . . Northern customs, on the other hand, disregard such things. It was customary to say good-bye at any crossroad and to separate with a merry laugh.

In another passage Yen outlines for his sons the proper rituals to be followed to show respect to a father's friend. Then he says:

I have noticed that northerners pay little attention to these matters. Strangers meeting on a public road immediately call each other "brother," guessing ages without considering whether it is a correct form of address or not.

Yen Chih-t'ui was also a fascinated observer of the differences in the status and behavior of women in the societies he had lived in. He remarked on the extremely sheltered lives of the southern women, on the superior skills in weaving, sewing, and embroidery of northern wives, on the prevalence in the south—especially in families with many concubines—of female infanticide. He disapproved of the amount of concubinage in the south, and particularly of the custom of widowers marrying a concubine or maidservant from their own households; he found the northern practice of formal remarriage of widowers more desirable, though not without its own sources of discord. Northern women impressed him not only as stern monogamists but also as extremely "managing":

In the city of Yeh it was the custom for women to handle all family business, to demand justice and to straighten out legal disputes, to make calls and curry favor with the powerful. They filled the streets with their carriages, occupied the government offices with their fancy dresses, begged official posts for their sons and made complaints about injustices done their husbands. Were these customs handed down from the Toba Wei Dynasty?

In this last surmise he was surely correct, for in steppe traditions everywhere, and certainly among the Hsien-pei before they invaded China, women had carried a large share of the responsibility in tribal life.

Finally, in this sketch of culture contrasts and cultural disso-

nances, we might touch on a serious and vexing problem that faced
Chinese officials in the service of alien rulers—the problem of collaboration and modes of collaboration, the problem of how far one
should go in self-defense or to gain favor with those one despised.
Yen Chih-t'ui tells this story:

> There was a court official who once said to me, "I have a son
> who is seventeen and has quite a good epistolary style. I shall
> teach him the Hsien-pei language [spoken by the alien em-
> perors and their courtiers] and to play the *p'i-p'a* [a favored
> foreign instrument, a kind of lute], in the hope that he will
> gain a certain degree of proficiency in these. With such ac-
> complishments he is sure to gain favor with men in high
> places. This is a matter of some urgency." At that time I hung
> my head and made no reply. Strange indeed is the way this
> fellow teaches his son. Even if, by such means, you could be-
> come a minister, I would not wish you to do so.

As the sixth century advanced, tensions within these societies
increased, and political intrigue and military conflict between the
rival states became ever more bitter. Perhaps the sharpest hostility
existed between the two states which had split the Northern Wei
into western and eastern empires. We remarked that the western
tended to perpetuate more of the Hsien-pei heritage and the eastern
a mixed inheritance of Hsien-pei and Chinese elements. The western
had its center in Kuan-chung, the eastern in the heart of the North
China Plain. They thus occupied the two main geopolitical areas of
the north, areas with a millennial history of mutual hostility. The
military campaigns between the successor states of the Northern
Wei were fought on the same battlefields where control of the whole
north had been contested century after century.

The Western Wei had been founded by an able Hsien-pei general, Yü-wen T'ai, who was supported by nobles of Hsien-pei and
mixed-blood descent. Backed by formidable military force, particularly in cavalry, Yü-wen T'ai ruled autocratically, and one of his first
steps was to reverse the hated measure of 496 that required everyone
to have Chinese surnames and to order the reestablishment of
Hsien-pei surnames. In 556, the Wei puppet emperor was deposed,
and the Yü-wen proclaimed themselves rulers of the "Chou." This
ancient dynastic name was freighted with meaning: it was the name

of the dynasty that had first swept out of the northwest and conquered the civilization of the North China Plain; at the hands of later Confucian ideologues, the Chou had been elaborated into a symmetrical model of ideal government, and this idealization was expressed in a Han compilation known as the *Rituals of Chou (Chou-li)*. Thus we find the Yü-wen—rough warriors who spoke the Hsien-pei language at their court—laying the groundwork for claiming universal dominion in China. But they went much further.

Yü-wen T'ai appointed as his chief advisor a Chinese scholar named Su Ch'o (498–546), who was instructed to take steps necessary to establish the Chou's claim to universal rule. One step was to rename all the offices of the government using the highly artificial nomenclature found in the *Rituals of Chou*. A related step was Su Ch'o's composition of an announcement in the archaic style of one of the most revered Chinese classics, the *Classic of History*; then came an order that all officials (few of whom could have been literate in Chinese!) were to write their communications in this archaic style rather than in the looser, "decadent" style common in the south. This experiment failed, but on a more practical level Su Ch'o was given wide powers to build up civil government along highly authoritarian lines. He pushed through sweeping changes, improved the collection of taxes, regularized the recruitment of militia to support the strong cavalry. He composed a sort of catechism known as the "Six Articles" which officials were obliged to know by heart if they wanted to keep their posts or be promoted. These articles, a blend of paternalistic Confucianism and hard-headed Legalism, were to give every official general guidance in the conduct of civil government, skills which the Yü-wen anticipated would be needed when their war machine finally crushed their rival to the east and administration of the conquered territory became a practical necessity. Thus the long-term ambitions of the Yü-wen softened their Hsien-pei atavism and led them to adopt Chinese institutions and ideological elements necessary to the realization of their ultimate objective—the control of North China and then of all China. These Chou experiments cast a long shadow forward on the Sui effort, for the Sui founder served them as an official and usurped their power in the same northwestern region that had been their power base.

The Eastern Wei Empire was established in the wake of the ruinous uprising of Hsien-pei malcontents that had devastated the North China Plain from 523 until 531. In that year the Hsien-pei leader Kao Huan reached an agreement of mutual assistance with the

great Chinese landholding families, and on this basis in 534 established the Eastern Wei with a capital at the city of Yeh in Honan. He
maintained a puppet emperor for a time, but in 550, Kao Huan's heir
and successor disposed of the puppet and proclaimed himself Emperor of the Ch'i Dynasty. (Ch'i in ancient times had been the most
powerful of the states in the North China Plain.) Kao Huan had come
to power as mediator between the Hsien-pei and the Chinese, peoples whose mutual contempt and hatred had been deepened by
years of civil war. His son and successor Kao Yang turned out to be
one of the most frightful tyrants in the history of China. His blood-
lust, insatiable cruelty, and megalomania made his regime one of
unrelieved horror. One example will serve to illustrate his monstrous sadism. On one occasion he visited the Terrace of the Golden
Phoenix at his capital to receive the lay vows of a Buddhist. He ordered condemned prisoners to be brought, had them equipped with
wings made of bamboo matting, and ordered them to fly off the terrace. This was a savage travesty of the Buddhist custom of "lib-
erating living creatures" (fang-sheng). All those who jumped off the
terrace were smashed by their fall. The Emperor viewed this specta-
cle as so amusing that he laughed uproariously.

His court was a snake pit of violent intrigue, especially between
factions of Hsien-pei and Chinese officials. Yet, despite pathological
monarchs and an extravagant and totally unstable court, the North
China Plain gradually regained its ancient productivity, partly by the
establishment of military colonies whose task it was to bring land
back into cultivation and provide a reservoir of self-supporting soldiers. An elaborate system of land allotment and taxation in kind
was set up, and regional granaries established to provide emergency
relief and to stabilize supply and demand. The Chinese gentry and
Chinese officials representing them at the court were largely responsible for these policies and their implementation in the provinces.
Special excise and commercial taxes were proposed by Chinese officials and levied in the capital area to defray the spectacular extravagances of the monarchs.

The Northern Ch'i had inherited many of the military institutions of the Wei, and these were reorganized for their own purposes:
an imperial guard of 120,000 Hsien-pei soldiers at the Emperor's disposal; four garrisons strategically placed to protect the capital at Yeh;
a military headquarters at what is now the city of T'ai-yüan in
Shansi—traditional staging area for the defense of the northwestern
frontier; garrisons stationed along the Great Wall (part of which had

been reconstructed by the Ch'i) as protection against fresh outside attacks.

Despite the follies of the emperors who succeeded Kao Huan, uneasy *de facto* cooperation between Chinese and Hsien-pei maintained, for a time, the Ch'i Empire, and during this time Chinese agricultural management and taxation were restored, and distinctively Chinese institutions—schools, Confucian learning, and much else—were slowly reestablished. With its far richer and larger territory and with a population greater than that of its western rival, the Northern Ch'i was economically the strongest among the rival states that aspired to reunify China. But the racial tensions we have noted undermined its political strength. This weakness was early diagnosed by Kao Huan. He remarked in 537 that the families of many of his military officers had moved west to the land of his rival, and others continued to be enticed. Then he says sarcastically: "Beyond the Yangtze there is that aged denizen of Wu, Hsiao Yen [disrespectful way of referring to the Emperor Wu of the Liang], who concerns himself exclusively with ritually approved clothing and caps, with rites and liturgical music. Yet the Chinese aristocracy of the North China Plain regarded him as the reincarnation of legitimacy." He went on to say that if he did not behave with great circumspection, his military officers would defect to his western rival, and his Chinese gentry would flee to the Liang. Then, he asks, with such a dispersal of talent, how would he be able to run a state?

The third state aspiring to reunify all of China was the Liang, with its capital at Nanking. In land under cultivation and in population it was greatly overshadowed by its two northern rivals. Throughout the first half of the sixth century its ruler and dominant figure was Emperor Wu, so contemptuously referred to by Kao Huan as a doddard obsessed with the fine points of Chinese ritual paraphernalia. But Emperor Wu, as we noted earlier, was by no means a negligible figure. His early years on the throne were marked by strenuous efforts on many fronts to accomplish what his southern predecessors had consistently failed to do: reduce the overweening power of the entrenched immigrant clans and achieve a real measure of centralized power. To this end, he decreed, in 509, that "all those with talent may advance along the road of success. If they desire office, after they have been tested, the Board of Civil Office will assign them tasks in accordance with their ability. Even if they come from cattle pens or sheep markets (or low-ranking families), only their talent will determine the post assigned." And he personally appointed

to office, in the palace, the bureaucracy, and the army, men of low
social origin, men he hoped would be loyal to him. For example,
Ch'en Ch'ing-chih—the Liang's most famous general who in 529
briefly captured Loyang from the Wei—had been the Emperor's
personal servant. And, in the first years of his reign Wu-ti took, in
rapid succession, many of the steps traditionally expected of a full-
fledged "Son of Heaven." He attempted to reduce peasant vagrancy
and rebuild a tax base for the central governments; he ordered the
codification of the laws and the rituals; he encouraged the study of
the Confucian classics in the prefectural centers and in the capital; he
became a knowledgeable and renowned patron of learning; he improved and embellished his capital.

But the promise of his early years was short-lived. He gave far
too much power and autonomy to his own family members who
served as regional governors, built up their own armies, and plotted
against one another and against the throne. One imperial prince actually sought help against the Emperor from the dynasty's deadly
enemies, the Northern Wei. Even though the Emperor might appoint
lesser people to important substantive posts, the great aristocratic
clans claimed their ancient privileges and emoluments, their hereditary rights to the highest offices. Powerful families in the provinces,
many of them recent immigrants from the north, engrossed great
tracts of virgin land—legally the property of the Emperor—and
opened it up with thousands of semi-servile dependents. And, as
wealth accumulated, some of the great families became interested in
trade and amassed further wealth and power. The older aristocratic
clans set the tone of life at the court and capital, and our astute observer Yen Chih-t'ui was an eyewitness. He has nothing but contempt for them; here is one characterization:

> In the most prosperous period of the Liang, the descendants
> of the nobility were usually unlearned. . . . There was not
> one of them who did not perfume his garments, shave his
> face, use powder and rouge, ride in a carriage with long aw-
> nings, wear elevated clogs, sit on square cushions . . . lean
> on soft silk bolsters arranged with curios or trinkets on each
> side. Moving in and out with cultivated grace, they put on the
> airs of holy immortals. When they sought a rank in an exam-
> ination, . . . they hired others to answer the questions and
> write the essays. When attending official feasts for high state
> officials, they commissioned others to write the poems ex-
> pected of them.

In a more analytical vein, but still bitterly censorious, he writes:

> The ancestors of southern high officials took advantage of
> the restoration of the Chin Dynasty [at Chien-k'ang, in 318],
> came south across the Yangtze and became immigrant offi-
> cials at the court. It is now eight or nine generations later and
> they have never done manual work in the fields but have all
> simply lived off their official stipends. If they have anything,
> it is all thanks to what their slaves did for them. They have
> never seen the turning of a furrow or soil, nor weeded out a
> blade of grass. They don't know the month in which to plant,
> nor in how many months one should reap. How can they
> know about other practical matters? Hence, in office they
> could do nothing and at home they could manage nothing,
> and these are both the result of a surfeit of leisure.

Unbearable social strain was caused in the Liang by the combined effects of these descendants of the nobility, with their feckless
pretensions, the more active (and more rapacious) of the later immigrant families, provincial officials who used their offices to loot and
oppress their people, imperial princes who reversed Emperor Wu's
measures of centralization, and the Emperor's increasing absorption
in Buddhist observances (stressed as a cause by all Confucian historians). The increasing strain is reflected in the popular rebellions recorded in the historical sources (the frequency increases as the Liang
continues); in the year 504 and again in 511, 516, 529, 530, 533, 541,
542, and 544. And the rebellions later in the Liang were larger in
both area covered and people participating. The 533 rebellion in one
prefecture had an army of dissidents numbering one hundred thousand. By 547, we are told, "the people's lives were bitter and sad. Everyone thought of rebellion."

The spark which ignited this tinderbox of discontent might have
come from anywhere. As it turned out, the catalyst was Hou Ching, a
soldier of fortune from the far northwest who, after many efforts to
set himself up as a warlord, and by treachery and deceit, as a greater
warlord, finally had to flee south. He arrived on the north bank of
the Yangtze with only eight hundred men, the remnants of his once
substantial forces. Emperor Wu, now really in his dotage, went
against all advice and appointed him governor of a key prefecture
just north of the river. But the Emperor soon betrayed him and attempted to use him in an exchange of high-level captives between
the Liang and their enemies, the Northern Ch'i. Hou Ching, a rene-

gade northerner with no southern connections, turned to the masses
of the disaffected and to some disloyal princes and generals and
began to assemble a force. He went into open rebellion in August of
548, and in a series of surprise moves, he was soon at the walls of
Chien-k'ang. The siege was long and bitter, marked by great brutal-
ity on the part of Hou Ching. He openly wooed the poor and the oppressed, who fled the besieged city in large numbers, and as openly
showed his deep contempt for the long-established aristocracy. After
a siege of four months the city fell. Its defending force had been
decimated and the population starved into submission. Many members of the great families, still clad in their magnificent robes but deserted by their retainers, simply starved to death in their mansions;
the Emperor was captured but shortly thereafter was left by Hou
Ching to starve to death in his palace. Hou Ching's forces continued
to loot and pillage the lower Yangtze area, and he made only feeble
efforts to restore order or stability. Finally, in 552 he was defeated
and killed. Meanwhile, two of the Liang princes had tried to continue the dynasty elsewhere. One proclaimed himself emperor in
distant Szechwan, another at the ancient city of Chiang-ling in the
Central Yangtze. But both fell victim to powerful armies of the
northwestern state of Chou. One of its armies made its way through
the high mountain passes south into the heart of Szechwan, besieged
and captured its capital city, and annexed the whole vast area to the
Chou. Another army descended upon Chiang-ling, took the city, executed the emperor, massacred many of the inhabitants, and took
thousands of captives north to their capital "within the passes."
They left a member of the Liang house as governor of a puppet state
centered on Chiang-ling, one that could be extinguished at their
pleasure.

The southern dynasty of Liang had lost heavily in these upheavals. Their vast western territories and the upper reaches of the
Yangtze had fallen to their northwestern rival; so had control of the
central Yangtze area. War and massacre had ruined their capital and
laid waste some of their most productive lands. A large proportion of
the old southern élite had been exterminated, and for the first time
since "legitimate" Chinese power had set up its "government in
exile" at Chien-k'ang, there was no scion of a great northern immigrant clan to start another dynasty. Instead, one of a group of tough
uncultivated southern generals who had finally disposed of Hou
Ching eliminated his rivals and proclaimed the dynasty of Ch'en.
The territorial losses that followed the Hou Ching rebellion greatly

reduced the area over which he could claim control; and, in the years of civil disturbance, local strong men had, with their own armies, gained control of many prefectures. The Ch'en ruler could do no more than confirm that control by appointing them governors.

Despite their weakness, the Ch'en emperors maintained a measure of authority, mainly because of the constant struggles between their northwestern and northeastern rivals who fought each other for control of all of the north. The fourth Ch'en emperor, who ruled from 569 to 582, was victimized by a clever diplomatic plot generated by the Northern Chou state in the far northwest. The Chou sent an embassy to Chien-k'ang with the proposal that, if the Ch'en would attack the Northern Ch'i from the south, the Chou would attack from the west; if they were victorious, the allies would divide the Northern Ch'i lands—all of the North China Plain—between them. The Ch'en, for their participation, were promised the rich agricultural area north of the Yangtze but south of the Huai that had once been governed from Chien-k'ang. The Ch'en ruler agreed, moved his armies north and, in 575, defeated the Northern Ch'i forces then under simultaneous attack from the west by the Chou. The Ch'en then occupied the promised territory. But they had little time to glory in their spoils, for in 577 the Chou—having overrun the Ch'i—turned their formidable war machine against their erstwhile allies and totally defeated them. The Ch'en armies were routed or captured, vast quantities of war matériel were lost, and so was all the newly regained territory. In the wake of this debacle, southern power was at low ebb, and, to any northern statesman in the years after 577, the Ch'en must have looked like an easy conquest. It was northern politics and a large measure of luck that delayed such an outcome for another twelve years.

Surveying the decades of military and political conflicts tends to obscure the underlying strands of common culture and common tradition that persisted throughout the whole vast land. In this substratum, of course, are the elements that could be used eventually by someone with sufficient luck and acumen to restore political unity. (There was nothing inevitable about such an outcome; as I have argued, but for the Sui's success, political disunity and increasingly divergent regional cultures might have been the norm for succeeding ages.)

The most obvious element in this common substratum is a written language that permitted communication across all manner of political and cultural barriers. A letter, a poem, a pronunciamento could be written in one corner of the Chinese subcontinent and be read and understood in the opposite corner. Written Chinese, thus described, would seem to resemble Esperanto—a language which indeed makes possible communication between men separated by distance and by culture. But the Chinese written by men of the sixth century communicated much, much more than the bare content of the message. By that time it had been continuously used and developed over a period of two millennia. And, as a result, almost every word and certainly every phrase carried with it from repeated historic use a rich freight of allusive meaning: echoes of men and events, references to places and times, to archetypal situations and much else. In all formal writing, specific historical allusions were omnipresent—used as argument to drive home a point or to refute one. Thus, tribal chiefs fresh from the steppe—once they had Chinese scribes to write communications for them—began to imbibe little by little the whole historic culture of China; and when their sons began to learn Chinese for themselves, the learning process was accelerated, and the moral and aesthetic appeal of the Chinese written heritage began to work upon them. Often the older generation would take alarm at this slow and subtle undermining of their ancient tribal ways and decree a return to their native languages and their ancestral way of life. But such efforts were always abortive, and for very practical reasons: if a leader of non-Chinese origin wanted to rule all or part of China (and they always did), Chinese writings contained the political values of the people the invader sought to dominate, all the statements that might be used to legitimate his rule *plus* the discussions of all the policies and ways of governing that might bring success to his rule.

The ever-present Chinese advisors to alien rulers were fully aware of the ways in which the Chinese language could, in the course of time, prove to be a powerful instrument of acculturation. They knew when to exercise patience and when to make strategic retreats. By the mid-sixth century the Chinese language and much of the written heritage was the common property of the upper classes, of whatever ethnic origin, in the whole of China. There were sharp differences among sixth-century writers in the different regions as to what the proper style should be for both practical and literary writing, but that it should be Chinese was not a matter for debate.

Chinese political ideas backed by the authority of the ancient classics and exemplified by successes and failures known from Chinese history—these provided a common stock of political formulae; there were no other traditions with competing formulae, and within the Chinese there was rich variety. The reader may recall the torrent of references to Chinese legitimacy that poured from the lips of a Northern Wei aristocrat upon the head of a presumptuous visitor from the south. The Wei spokesman was representative of a state established by aliens, but without knowing the context one could not detect it: *our* dynasty was sanctioned by immemorial harbingers of universal rule, the Lo Writing and the River Plan; *our* models for improving the social tone and changing the customs were in accord with the sage emperors of Chinese antiquity: *our* ritual and music, *our* codes and regulations surpass those of countless monarchs of Chinese history.

Again, when we consider the Wei successor state in the Northwest—the Chou—and its efforts to establish a claim to universal dominion, we find its Hsien-pei–speaking military leadership drawing on many strands of the same Chinese political tradition: renaming all offices in accordance with a political classic that purported to reflect ancient Chou practice; adopting the governmental model outlined in the same classic—that of a harmonious and cosmically consistent hierarchy rising to a supreme autocrat at its apex; decreeing an official style patterned on the archaic prose of one of China's most ancient classics.

The Chinese dynasties with their capitals at Chien-k'ang in the Yangtze Valley never ceased reiterating their guardianship of the legitimate Chinese political traditions, everything from such tangible relics as the seals of the First Sovereign Emperor of China to the nomenclature of offices, to the elaborate rituals (with their musical accompaniments) that celebrated and symbolized the centrality of the true Son of Heaven not only in the "all under Heaven" but also in the cosmos. Governments in the South were more often feeble than not, and their political institutions bore little resemblance to those of the long-vanished Han. But, century after century, the sonorous pronunciamentos poured forth asserting the dynasties' rightful claims to all China, their government's sole right to establish a proper lunar calendar, to confer proper titles and nomenclature of all kinds, to receive tributary missions from barbarian satellite states and so forth. All this in the light of contemporary political realities strikes many a note of pure make-believe. But southern pretensions, like their counterparts in the north, testify to the fact that ancient Chinese political tradition—its ideas, its nomenclature, its symbolism—was very much alive throughout the land and was there to be put to use by some ultimate reunifier.

Interwoven with strands of this political tradition was a set of moral values generally associated with the name of Confucius. They consisted, at their more abstract level, of the cardinal virtues of benevolence (*jen*), righteousness (*i*), adherence to the proper norms of behavior (*li*), understanding (*chih*), and faithfulness (*hsin*). These values had the authority of the classics behind them, yet this tumultuous age was notable neither for abstract moral thought nor classical study. Thus these values were translated down into proverbs and maxims, homely guides for the education of the young. And through all these, there runs a strong authoritarian strain: let the young submit to their elders; let women, in the various stages of their lives, submit to their menfolk; let everyone show proper respect for superior rank and social status. As in earlier Confucianism, the family was seen as the microscosm of the state, and the cornerstone of the education of the young was the *Classic of Filial Submission* (*Hsiao-ching*), which preached absolute submission to the authority of one's parents and one's family elders.

Yen Chih-t'ui, whose family admonitions we have so often quoted, speaks of many aspects of this stern code. Here is a typical passage:

> Manners and breeding are transmitted from the upper to the lower classes and bequeathed by earlier to later generations. So if a father is not kind, the son will not be filial; if an elder brother is not friendly, the younger will not be respectful; if a husband is not just, the wife will not be obedient. When a father is kind but the son refractory, when an elder brother is friendly but the younger arrogant, when a husband is just but a wife cruel, these are the bad people of the world; they must be controlled by punishments; teaching and guidance will not change them. . . . If punishments are not properly meted out, the people will not know how to act. The use of clemency and severity in governing a family is the same as in a state.

Throughout his admonitions Yen often stresses the virtue of wisdom or prudence, especially important when one is a Chinese in the service of alien rulers. Here he generalizes from his own experience:

The rise and fall of a dynasty and the success and failure of an army should be discussed when wide learning has been attained. To enter into a general's tent or to participate in a court audience and be unable to advise the ruler so as to plan for the benefit of the country would be a cause for shame to a man of honor. Yet I have often seen scholars who have read some military books but possess little experience in strategy . . . take the lead in revolt, cheating and injuring good people. . . . They cannot foretell who will survive and who will fall, but will impulsively give support to any leaders. Such practices are the root of personal ruin and family destruction. Take warning. Take warning.

The great range of formal observances by which educated people expressed the values in this ethical system was noted by Yen in South China and in the north. Such observances, indeed, constituted one of those values—namely *li*, which may be interpreted as the norms of proper behavior. There are endless canonical prescriptions that should be followed in paying respects to one's elders, one's betters, and one's ancestors—indeed prescriptions for every kind of encounter between people. These prescriptions, though backed by canonical authority, were variously interpreted. Yen found the southerners in most cases overpunctilious, the northerners too informal. Yet neither he nor his peers in north or south would have denied that such a body of codified norms defining the niceties of social relations was an essential of civilized life; adherence to such a code was one of the crucial things that separated Chinese and Sinicized aliens on the one hand from "barbarians" on the other.

In this sixth-century Confucianism, the way to understanding (*chih*) was study. Yen Chih-t'ui never tires of urging this upon his sons, nor does he neglect the practical argument that a family which does not maintain a tradition of study will lose its place in the upper class and sink back into the anonymous helpless mass of the peasantry. Here is a portion of his more abstract argument:

The reason for reading and studying is primarily to open the mind and clarify the vision in order to improve one's conduct. Those who do not know how to care for parents are expected to observe how the ancients anticipated their parents' wishes, watching their facial expressions . . . etc. Those who do not know how to serve their ruler are expected to

observe how the ancients adhered to duty without interfering
with others, preparing in the face of danger, to give up their
lives, not forgetting to give the ruler earnest admonitions in
order to benefit the country. . . .

Although its principles were flouted on every hand in the volatile
and predatory societies of the age, they were asserted and reasserted
in the formal education of the sons of the élite; they were kept alive
in Chinese families both as guides to day-to-day conduct and as part
of the precious Chinese classical heritage that might one day be restored to predominance. Thus, this common body of values was yet
another tradition that transcended regional differences; if not flourishing, it was alive, and it was there for the would-be unifier to put to
use.

The Confucian values had their strength in the upbringing of
children, in setting norms of conduct for daily life in society, and in
providing the ethical bases for a political order. And as the roots of
these values went deep into the core of Chinese civilization, their
appeal was first to the Chinese population and second to other peoples in the various stages of adopting that civilization. Buddhism, by
contrast, was a universal religion, a religion appealing to all sorts and
conditions of men everywhere in the world. And its strength was less
in teaching men standards of behavior in society than in allaying
men's fears of the unknown, in promising that the ills one might suf-
fer in this life could be redressed in lives to come, in teaching that all
creatures might one day find blissful release from all suffering. By
the sixth century, Buddhism—some five hundred years after it appeared in China—had become an all-pervasive religion. In north and
south alike, its shrines and monasteries dotted the landscape, and
stately temples and pagodas embellished the cities. These were the
centers of all the magnificent ceremonies that marked special occasions and the feast days of the Buddhist calendar. Perhaps the grand-
est of all were ceremonies connected with the ruling houses: ceremonies of dedication of temples built by princes and nobles; solemn
masses for the repose of the imperial ancestors; feasting of great
numbers of clergy on the birth of an imperial heir; chanting of the
sacred texts, accompanied by the burning of incense, to bring rain, to
end a plague, to protect a dynasty against its enemies. The birthday
of the Buddha in April was everywhere celebrated, usually with
a solemn ceremony called "washing the Buddha," in which an

image—symbolizing the new-born baby—was washed in scented waters.

Buddhism had brought to the Chinese subcontinent a new vision of time and eternity, a vast pantheon of divinities, new ideas of salvation and, accompanying those ideas, a whole range of activities and observances meant to advance oneself and one's fellow creatures along the road to salvation. If we turn again to Yen Chih-t'ui, we find a not untypical kind of Buddhist faith blended with his profound commitment to the Confucian tradition:

> Would it be that the sage rulers Yao, Shun, the Duke of Chou, and Confucius himself sacrificed their own happiness for nothing? Consider it carefully: for one man who pursues his spiritual cultivation, how many living beings will be saved and freed from the effects of the evil deeds of their several lives? If you, my sons, want to make plans for a worldly life, having set up a household you won't be able to leave your wives and children. But even if you cannot become monks, you should nevertheless practice the Buddhist abstinences, attend to the chanting and reading of the sacred books and thereby provide for passage to your future state of existence. Incarnation as a human is difficult to attain. Do not pass through yours in vain!

But the formula Yen recommends to his sons is only one of dozens or hundreds of ways people expressed their Buddhist faith. The construction of monuments to the Buddhist divinities, the building and endowing of monasteries, was a way of accumulating spiritual merit that appealed to the rich and the powerful. For example, the city of Loyang had, by 534, no less than 1,367 Buddhist establishments—pious endowments by the nobility and officialdom. And just outside the city were the famous cave-temples of Lung-men. There a great complex of shrines had been carved out of the living rock and filled with sculptures depicting scenes from the Buddhist scriptures and figures from the vast pantheon of Buddhist divinities. The Lung-men complex was a continuation of what the Northern Wei had built outside their former capital in northern Shansi, the magnificent cave and temple complex known as Yün-kang. At Chien-k'ang, capital of the southern dynasties, Buddhist building was on a lesser but still impressive scale. Indeed the lavish use of labor and materials for Buddhist building projects was criticized by officials in north and south alike. One pious but ruthless official of the Northern Wei built seventy-two temples as well as financing the copying of sixty sets of the Buddhist scriptures and providing living expenses for famous monks. A monk rebuked him for bringing about the death of men and oxen in his building projects; he replied that posterity would see and be impressed by the buildings and would know nothing of the men and oxen who had perished.

Ordinary people could gain merit by less lavish projects. Often the people of a village would pool their donations and commission an image of a favorite divinity, and the list of donors on surviving images shows that they came from all strata of local society. Again at the local level, cooperatives were founded to finance feasts on Buddhist holy days or to pay for a pilgrimage that the villagers might make to one of the great temples that became known as the dwelling place of a particularly benign and potent Buddhist god.

Some people gave themselves to a monastery as slaves, thus contributing, as it were, the rest of their mortal lives for their future spiritual welfare. Emperor Wu of the Liang did a variation on this theme when he offered himself thrice to a monastery and thrice ordered his courtiers to give the monastery huge amounts of treasure for his release. But the supreme act of spiritual commitment to one's own salvation and to the salvation of all living creatures was to become a monk or a nun. Against a background of Chinese social and ethical values—however attenuated these may have become in the sixth century—the sacrifice was staggering: renounce one's surname and thus one's place in the continuity of the dead, the living, and the unborn that was the essence of the family cult; take the vow of celibacy and thus deny to one's parents any offspring to continue the blood line and the sacrifices to its dead; take the tonsure and thus disfigure the body that, in the cult of filial piety, was to be returned to the grave as it had been received from one's parents—complete and unblemished; give up all the time-honored ways to success and self-fulfillment in public office and elect instead a life of poverty, meditation, and the spread of Buddha's word among the deprived.

A class of celibate clergy following a life governed by religious rules was a constant source of friction with state authority in all the regions of China. The clergy was free of the obligations to pay taxes and perform forced labor for the state. The "idleness" of the clergy was denounced by court officials under every monarch. And, inevitably, there were thousands of taxpayers who declared themselves clergy to escape the obligations of an ordinary subject. These were the "wild clergy" (su-seng or yeh-seng), and they would not only evade their just dues to the state but go among the hard-pressed peasantry and foment rebellion. Between 402 and 517 nine peasant rebellions led by Buddhists are recorded for North China alone.

The inherent conflict between absolute imperial power and a Buddhist clergy living according to its own rules was argued at both northern and southern courts. The clergy's relation to imperial power was ingeniously solved in the north. The first general administrator of Buddhist clergy appointed by the Northern Wei produced the following formula:

> He [i.e., the Emperor] loves the Way. He is the Tathāgāta of our time; it is right that monks should pay him homage. . . . He who has the power to spread the Teaching is the master of men. I bow down, not before the Son of Heaven, but before the Buddha himself.

The southern solution was different. There the clergy maintained, with the help of powerful aristocratic lay adherents, considerable independence of the power of the state. And the southern monks were inclined to sneer, somewhat uncharitably, at their northern colleagues for what appeared to the southerners as a blatant political compromise.

For all these points of friction, Buddhism was interwoven with the preexisting life patterns of all manner of people in all parts of the land. Buddhist monasticism offered an alternative for those who were world-weary and sought a place of retreat. Buddhist nunneries, some of them of extraordinary opulence, became the usual place of retirement for highborn widows or for whole harems of a dead prince. Great families would often donate one of their mansions to be converted into a monastery together with land to support it; such establishments then assumed special responsibilities for keeping the donor-family's records and for saying masses for the spiritual felicity of the family's dead members. Scholarly monks were devoted to Buddhist variations on the traditional Confucian scholarly concerns: study of a particular sutra and writing a commentary on it; writing biographies of the monks, bibliographies of Buddhist books, histories of famous temples. There were times when a great preaching monk would bring large congregations, in city and country alike, under his spell, and perhaps lead them to adopt a new path to salvation. And there were times when religious fervor gripped a city or a province, and monks might immolate themselves "for the salvation of all living creatures," while the wealthy would be inspired to make lavish gifts to match the monk's sacrifice. In country villages the monks took over many of the functions long performed by local adepts of the ancient folk religion: exorcism, healing, in-trance communication with the dead.

These few paragraphs on the role of Buddhism in sixth-century China have pointed to some of the ways that Buddhism had entered into the lives and the thinking of people at all levels of society and in all corners of the land. As it did so, it became perhaps the most powerful of the traditions that an aspiring reunifier might make use of.

The spread of Buddhism throughout the land did not go unchallenged. Naturally, stiff-necked Confucian officials would and often did oppose it at every point where it invaded one of the spheres of authority that they claimed for the state and emperor. Their efforts would often be checked by a group of influential Buddhist courtiers, or by the palace women or eunuchs who were usually pro-Buddhists, or again by the personal sympathies of the emperor himself. Within the population generally, opposition came from another quarter. The beginnings are still unclear, but, after the religiously inspired rebellions at the end of the second century were forcibly crushed, many of their characteristic beliefs and practices lingered on among the people in Szechwan, Kiangsu, Shantung, and elsewhere. From such centers there gradually developed a set of practices and beliefs which we can identify as those of a Taoist religion. These were at first amorphous, but a succession of religious leaders shaped them by the content of their revelations and by judicious borrowings from Buddhism. The first of these in the north was K'ou Ch'ien-chih (365–448), who claimed to be a "Heavenly Master" in the line that began with the Yellow Turban rebel leaders at the end of the Han. K'ou's visions directed him to purify and reform the Taoist religion, and he was successful in administering lay vows (in the Buddhist manner!) to the Northern Wei Emperor Hsiao-wu, who was later to order the first proscription of Buddhism. The principal formulator of religious Taoism in the south was T'ao Hung-ching (455–536), and he settled at Mao-shan, near the southern capital, the seat of the Taoist "Sect of Supreme Purity." T'ao was an educated man, from a Buddhist family, and he borrowed heavily from Buddhism as he pulled together these borrowings and Chinese alchemical and longevity traditions. His main work was a collection of the revelations of "men of truth" (*chen-jen*) which he called the *Chen-kao* ("Proclamation of Truth"). He maintained that these revelations were divinely inspired, just as were the preachings of the Buddha found in the Buddhist sutras. The borrowings from Buddhism were at first mainly on the doctrinal level, but gradually the Taoist religion took on the features of a religion in the Buddhist manner; centers for living and worship which they termed *kuan*, similar to the Buddhist temples (*ssu*); a special habit similar to the monkish frock of the Buddhists, censers, and much other Buddhist paraphernalia. In the middle of the sixth century a Taoist master imposed celibacy on his followers, and this gradually became the norm. Conventual Taoism, with its growing canon of scriptures, its monasteries and nunneries, its vast pantheon of gods and spirits, and its yoga-like practices for transcending ordinary existence marked the beginning of a full-fledged native religion which was to compete with Buddhism for the adherence of people of all classes. From the mid-sixth century onward the two religions were competing on a number of levels. They vied for the emperors' favor; they wrote bitter polemics against one another, competing for the attention of educated Chinese; they spread their influence into city and countryside in outright competition for influence with ordinary people. They claimed to have better spells, better hygienic practices, more control over more potent spirits than the Buddhists. Thus the Taoist religion began its rise to formidable influence. In the sixth century it was far less powerful, its adherents far less numerous than Buddhism, but it too was widespread enough throughout the land that a reunifier would be foolish to ignore it.

CHAPTER 3

The
Rise of
Yang Chien

Yang Chien, the founder of the Sui Dynasty, was born into an old and respected family which had its ancestral seat near the western extremity of the Yellow River Plain. For six generations his ancestors had been officials under the non-Chinese dynasties of the north, and they had maintained their power and their position by intermarriage with families of the dominant Turko-Mongol élite. Yang Chien's father, Yang Chung, first served the Northern Wei and when, in 534, that kingdom split into the Western and the Eastern Wei, Yang Chung chose to give his loyalty to the founder of the Western Wei, Yü-wen T'ai. For his military and administrative services Yang Chung was rewarded with exalted titles and enfeoffed as Duke of Sui (*Sui-kuo kung*). And, when Yü-wen T'ai restored to his own people the Turko-Mongol (Hsien-pei) surnames taken from them in the sweeping Sinicization of the late fifth century, he conferred similar surnames on those with Chinese names who had achieved military distinction under him. Yang Chung was given the surname of P'u-liu-ju, which may be a transcription of Mongol *bur-qasun*, meaning a kind of willow.

In 541 Yang Chung was on duty a short distance northeast of the Western Wei capital, and there his wife bore him a son whom they called Chien. In the histories, the birth of a future Chinese emperor is always surrounded by prodigies—auspicious animals appear, a purple vapor fills the room, he shortly manifests physical traits which wise men interpret as signs that he will one day become "Lord of Men." Much of this appears in the accounts of Yang Chien's birth and early childhood. But beyond this standard emperor lore, the records tell us something of the particular circumstances of his birth. His mother gave birth to him in a local Buddhist temple; perhaps some soothsayer had advised her to do so to gain for herself and her child the protection of Buddhist gods. As was customary at that time the baby was given a Buddhist childhood name—Na-lo-yen, transcription of the Sanskrit name Nārāyana, which may mean "firm and stable" or "hero of divine power." Such names were meant to invoke the protection of the gods against evil influences, illnesses, and all the other hazards of childhood. About the time of his birth a Buddhist nun appeared on the scene—a nun known for her practice of meditation and for her prowess in foretelling the future. The nun, who had the clerical name Chih-hsien, told the mother that the child was most extraordinary and should not be brought up in lay quarters. Whereupon the nun began looking after the baby in a special apartment, separated from the family residence. She was apparently in charge of his upbringing until he was twelve years old, and he is said to have referred to her fondly in later life as his *a-she-li*, a transcription of the Sanskrit ācārya, "mentor." The content and quality of Yang Chien's early education can only be a matter of speculation, but it is certain that he was strongly indoctrinated with the Buddhist scheme of values and with the Buddhist view of the universe. This was to have effects on his behavior and outlook throughout his whole life.

In 553 Yang Chien took leave of his Buddhist teacher, returned to his father's house, and, we may assume, took up the ways and the occupations of other young aristocrats of his time: horseback riding, hunting, falconry, archery, and martial exercises. At this time he was also admitted to the academy (*T'ai-hsüeh*) set up in the capital by the Emperor to give the sons of his nobility a degree of literacy and at least a smattering of Confucian writings on statecraft and morality. At school Yang Chien is said to have been stern and withdrawn, so much so that even his own young kinsmen did not dare treat him with impropriety. We do not know what he may have learned in his brief attendance at the academy, but his interest in the art of letters and in Confucian writings was distinctly limited. The only Confucian work he later referred to with approval was the most authoritarian moral catechism, the *Classic of Filial Submission* (*Hsiao-ching*). And, in his first year as emperor, we find him rebuking an old friend who had failed to rally to him in his bid for power. The friend, with head bowed, brings forth two historical allusions in his own defense. At which point Yang Chien, in a rage, says: "Although I am not versed in bookish language, I know full well by what you've said that you have not been obedient to my will." The anti-intellectualism that is so often the accompaniment of a deep religious faith appeared early and characterized each stage of his career.

At the age of thirteen he was appointed to a minor post by the prefect of the capital. Thereafter, no doubt on the strength of his father's influence, he was promoted year by year, and his personal fiefs were steadily upgraded until he was made Duke of Ta-hsing. In retrospect the most important event of these early years was the marriage arranged for him in 557 to the seventh daughter of Tu-ku Hsin, a long-time friend of his father's. The Tu-ku's were a high ranking non-Chinese clan which had a vast network of influential connections, powerful from the fourth until well into the eighth century. The girl's mother was a Ts'ui of Ch'ing-ho—perhaps the most prestigious of all Chinese clans in the north. Despite his family's influence, Tu-ku Hsin was forced to commit suicide by a powerful and vicious capricious prince of the ruling Yü-wen house. In the same year his daughter was married to Yang Chien. We can imagine that the young woman's feelings toward the Yü-wen were profoundly affected by her father's tragic death. She was in many ways a typical northern woman of her class and time; she was extremely able in practical matters, she was literate and cultivated, and she was of course a devout Buddhist whose every day had its periods for Buddhist observances. She was also a firm believer in monogamy; she and her young husband, then thirteen and sixteen, swore on oath that neither would have offspring by a different spouse. She bore Yang Chien five sons and at least five daughters. As time went on she became his constant companion and trusted advisor in matters great and small.

After 568, when his father died and Yang Chien succeeded to his title and became Duke of Sui, he became increasingly important at the court. But in the peculiarly volatile and poisonous atmosphere of such courts, prominence meant frequent periods of jeopardy. Envy was but thinly disguised, and a well-calculated and well-timed slander would often move an emperor to wrath and bring death to the victim and extermination to his family. Yang Chien survived several such attacks, for the able Emperor Wu—reigned 561 to 577—knew the value of his high court officials and was not moved by repeated slanders whose motives were quite transparent. Nevertheless Yang Chien at times took the precaution of making himself as inconspicuous as possible in the interests of his own and his family's survival. In 561 Yang Chien's eldest daughter, Li-hua, then only an infant, had been betrothed to the Crown Prince. This appeared at the time as a signal honor, a mark of the dynasty's high regard for the house of Yang. It was, in the end, to have incalculable consequences for their lives and fortunes.

As a ranking military commander, Yang Chien played an active role in the bitter and almost continuous war between the states of northwestern and northeastern China—the two successor states of the Northern Wei, now known as the Northern Chou and the Northern Ch'i. On one occasion he is said to have led a water-borne force of thirty thousand men to attack a Northern Ch'i army in Honan. In 577 he accompanied the Emperor Wu on the final and victorious campaign which overwhelmed the Northern Ch'i and made the Northern Chou the masters of all North China. As a reward for his service in the high command of the victorious army, Yang Chien was given the exalted title of "Pillar of the State" (*Chu-kuo*). He was appointed to military and administrative posts in the conquered area, first as commandant of a key prefecture in the north-central part of the Great Plain and then in a similar post in the southern part. These assignments gave him a brief exposure to two areas of the Great Plain and perhaps some feeling for its distinctive culture, an experience which would stand him in good stead when he usurped the power of the Northern Chou and, in so doing, inherited the problems they had faced in integrating the two distinctive and mutually hostile areas of North China.

Yet, at this stage of his career it is hard to imagine that thoughts of usurpation were in his mind. He and his wife must have deplored the Emperor Wu's heavy-handed proscription of Buddhism, and indeed Yang Chien's childhood mentor, the nun Chih-hsien, hid out in the Yang house to escape laicization. Yet in the summer of 578 the Emperor was basking in the glory of his victory over the Northern Ch'i, and he was about to lead his seasoned troops to curb Turkish depredations in the vicinity of modern Peking. It must then have seemed likely that this capable ruler and general, now thirty-six years old, would go from victory to victory and would succeed where others had long failed, destroy the weakened dynasty at

Nanking, and bring China once again under one rule. But on the eve of his departure from Ch'ang-an he fell ill, and in the sixth month of 578 his death was announced.

Yü-wen Pin, the Crown Prince and Yang Chien's son-in-law, succeeded and soon showed himself to be in the terrible tradition of pathological power holders that had been the curse of the northern dynasties. When he scheduled an audience—to be held in the "Palace of Heavenly Virtue"—he ordered all those attending to fast for three days and abstain from sexual intercourse for one day. When they faced him, he sat on a platform colored in five hues to symbolize earth and he referred to himself as "Heaven." He stripped the ornaments off all nobles and officials in attendance so as to emphasize his own magnificent hat and other ornaments. Those who remonstrated, or gave the slightest offense, were put to death. In his private apartments he committed the ultimate impropriety: he feasted and drank from the vessels used in the imperial ancestral hall. He is pictured as lascivious and capricious in his treatment of the palace women; he beat them unmercifully, humiliated them, and maintained a reign of terror. For what basic reason we do not know, Pin, in the second month of 579, went through the ritual of abdication in favor of his six-year-old son, but he continued to hold all the reins of power. Beginning with Pin's accession, a bare eight months earlier, Yang Chien was given the exalted titles and offices appropriate to the father-in-law of the Emperor, and he was left in charge at the capital when the Emperor went on progress. Yet tension quickly developed between Yang Chien and his new master. Yang Chien's policy recommendations were rejected, and he must have sensed that he could expect little but trouble from the harsh and capricious young Emperor. The *Sui History* puts it succinctly: "As Yang Chien's position and reputation rose ever higher, the Emperor more and more regarded him with jealous dislike." Events at court in the early summer of 580 brought matters to a crisis.

The nominally retired Emperor had violated the wife of one of his imperial kinsmen, driven the latter to rebellion and death, and taken the unhappy widow as his fifth consort. In the inner apartments of the palace the five consorts, the concubines, and attendants were terrorized by the insensate rages of Yü-wen Pin. Yang Chien's daughter was of a kind and gentle disposition and managed to maintain morale among the beleaguered women. Pin had threatened her with the extermination of her whole clan, and when she remained calm and unruffled in the face of his abuse, he went into a towering rage and ordered her to commit suicide. Her mother went to the palace and made an impassioned plea for her daughter's life, and after what must have been a stormy scene, the daughter was spared. Pin's next move was to order Yang Chien to appear in court and to give orders to the royal attendants that if Yang's demeanor changed in the least, he was to be killed on the spot. Yang Chien proved as steady under pressure as his daughter, and the assassination did not occur. But his friends at court told him of the plot, and he must have come to the conclusion that, under the governing if unspoken axiom of these situations, "Kill or be killed," he would have to move against the ruling house or face the certain extermination of himself and his family.

At this juncture Pin suffered a stroke and died shortly thereafter, but his death was kept secret, and two of Yang Chien's friends forged an imperial edict ordering him to take charge of all military affairs of the empire. With the military under his control, he moved quickly to assume full powers and to act as regent for the child emperor. This was an open challenge to the dynasty and its supporters, for a regency, though not in itself a usurpation, was an important step along one of the well-recognized routes to the establishment of a new dynasty. Yang Chien and his friends were in no doubt as to the stakes, and his wife counseled him that it was too late to turn back and she quoted the old proverb that when one is riding a tiger and there is no way to get off, the only thing to do is to spur him on!

Yang Chien began immediately to take further steps that would lead to the founding of a new dynasty. He sent intermediaries to sound out key people to persuade them to join his group. One of those recruited was Li Te-lin, a literatus needed for the skilled manipulation of the words and the symbolism that would disguise the forcible seizure of power and make it look like a legitimate succession. Another was Kao Chiung, a man of great intelligence and ability, a successful general and skillful political strategist. With control of the army and diversified talents in his immediate circle, Yang Chien could move with speed and effectiveness. Late in the fifth month he summoned the five senior princes of the Yü-wen clan to the capital, ostensibly to take part in the wedding ceremony of a daughter of one of them, who was to be married to the Turkish khan, but actually to remove them from the areas where they had local followings and might have organized resistance. In the sixth month the princes, one of them under duress, arrived at Ch'ang-an where they were kept under constant watch. When they attended the funeral of Yü-wen Pin the following month, they were "escorted" by six thousand cavalry commanded by a Yang kinsman. But the Yü-wen too were experienced in the murderous intrigues of the northern courts, and they fought back. During the sixth month one imperial prince was apprehended plotting against the regent and was immediately executed. Late in the next month, Yang Chien barely escaped assassination by two of the senior princes; the plot was discovered in time, and they were caught and put to death.

More serious by far was the open military opposition of those still loyal to the Yü-wen that showed itself in many parts of the empire. In the sixth month the old and respected warrior Wei-ch'ih Ch'iung climbed up to one of the gate towers on the north wall of the city of Yeh in Honan (once the Northern Ch'i capital) and addressed the assembled citizens:

> Yang Chien, who has taken advantage of his position as father of the empress, has intimidated our young lord in order to usurp his powers. Conduct inappropriate for a subject is there for all to see. I am a relative of the ruling house which has given me both military and civil responsibilities. Our late ruler placed me here with the intention that I should pacify disorder. Now I would like all of you to join righteousness with bravery so that we may rescue the rightful dynasty and protect the people. What do you say to this?

It is said that the people rallied *en masse* to Ch'iung. Ch'iung rose in the very heart of the North China Plain where he commanded formidable resources and a strong following among the powerful local clans. In the middle of the seventh month another group of loyalists joined the armed opposition, and later that month Ssu-ma Hsiao-nan, the father-in-law of the child emperor, proclaimed common cause with Wei-ch'ih Ch'iung and found a following in nine prefectures north of the middle Yangtze, where he had the backing of the "legitimate" if enfeebled southern dynasty of Ch'en. Early in the eighth month the governor of Szechwan also rose against Yang Chien. In the far northeast a former Ch'i official with Turkish allies made ready to join the others. Yang Chien was hard-pressed, but he had some substantial advantages. He had a secure and strategic base of power in the Kuan-chung Plain, and he had, for as long as he showed signs of succeeding, the loyalty of the powerful military machine inherited from the Northern Chou. He also had the advantage of a unified command against his scattered opponents with their local interests, conflicting private ambitions, and lack of a coordinated strategy.

There was, nonetheless, a period of great uncertainty in the late summer of 580 when men close to him wavered, important local and regional leaders remained uncommitted, and a vigorous move by one of Yang Chien's rivals might have brought disaster. But the adherence of the great Kao Chiung proved decisive. When Yang Chien's other supporters found excuses not to take the field, Kao Chiung led the northwestern armies eastward through the passes and into the heart of the North China Plain. There he moved to strike at the most formidable opponents of the Yang cause: Wei-ch'ih Ch'iung and his allies. Kao, using many of the ruses and tricks of traditional strategy, won some preliminary skirmishes and soon faced the main force of the enemy deployed outside the south wall of Yeh. That force was formidable indeed, made up of some one hundred and thirty thousand men, with Wei-ch'ih Ch'iung in charge of a special force of men from Kuan-chung loyal to him, and his two sons in command of other units. At first the attackers had no success. The battle had, however, attracted a huge crowd of spectators from the city. Kao Chiung or one of his subordinates had his archers suddenly shoot into the crowd, which then stampeded. The defending army, in the ensuing chaos, broke ranks, fled, and took refuge within the city walls of Yeh. The attackers surrounded the city, climbed over the walls, and soon had the city in their hands. The aged Wei-ch'ih Ch'iung fled to one of the gate towers, where he was soon cornered. Knowing himself beyond help, he threw his bow to the ground and, laying a last bitter curse on Yang Chien, killed himself. Historians usually place the blame for Wei-ch'ih Ch'iung's defeat on his incompetent chief of staff and on his use of former Ch'i officers. However that may be, Kao Chiung had destroyed the only significant rallying point for the opposition, and the lesser dissidents could not continue their resistance. Between Kao Chiung's victory at Yeh in the middle of the eighth month and the collapse of Wang Ch'ien's power in Szechwan three months later, all serious opposition crumbled. By the end of the year, all remaining resistance had been crushed. Yang Chien had been well served by Kao Chiung, his enemies had lacked both charisma and imagination, and his luck had held.

As the news of victories reached the capital, Yang Chien began to play out the scenario of virtuous succession, whose language, gestures, and symbolism echoed political transitions of the distant past.

In the histories the steps he takes are described in meticulous detail,
and separating these long accounts are laconic entries recording the
execution of one prince after another of the Northern Chou house. In
the ninth month of 580 there was issued in the name of the child emperor an edict praising Yang Chien in the most florid style; it was
written by none other than the literatus of Chien's inner circle, Li
Te-lin. Let us sample its rhetoric:

> Bearer of the gilded battle axe, legate with the emblems of
> command, Left Prime Minister, Commander-in-chief of all
> military in the capital and the provinces, Supreme Pillar of
> State, Grand State Minister, Chien, the Duke of Sui—re-
> sponsive to the mountains and rivers, answering to the ema-
> nations of the stars and planets, his moral force elevates both
> the refined and the vulgar, his virtue brings together what is
> hidden and what is manifest . . . harmonizes Heaven and
> Earth to produce the myriad things; obedient to the forces of
> yin and yang, he pacifies the barbarians of the four direc-
> tions . . . Wherefor he should be appointed Great Prime
> Minister, and the offices of Left and Right Prime Minister
> should be abolished. His other offices and honors are to be as
> before.

In the tenth month an edict conferred posthumous honors and
titles on Yang Chien's great-grandfather, grandfather, and father.
Then, in the twelfth month on a chia-tzu day, auspicious as the beginning of a sexagenary cycle, a further edict was issued enlarging
the Sui fief and exempting Yang Chien from certain rituals, giving
him access to the palace, and making him Prince of Sui with precedence over all other nobles. Chien of course formally declined all
these honors, "but the Emperor [then eight years old!] would not
permit him to do so." Early in 581 Yang Chien was granted the traditional nine symbols of authority: chariot and horses, robes of state,
musical instruments, bows and arrows, battle axes, and so forth.
Once again Li Te-lin wrote in mellifluous and high-flown prose the
edicts conferring these gifts. Shortly thereafter came the transfer of
the eight imperial seals from the Chou house to the Sui, then the
edict of abdication, again the work of Li Te-lin. In it he refers to the
ancient ideal kings, to the cosmic signs and signs in the natural world
indicating that a change of the heavenly mandate is at hand, to the
declining strength of the Chou house and the bright promise of the

Sui, to the manifestly potent virtue of Yang Chien. Yang Chien, following ancient custom, declined three times, but was finally "persuaded" to take the last awesome step and become Son of Heaven and supreme autocrat of the Chinese world.

Acts expected of a dynastic founder followed one after the other in a great burst of activity. Yang Chien put on the imperial robes, held his first dawn audience where he was thrice wished long life (*wan-sui*) by the assembled officials. He declared a general amnesty, proclaimed the dynasty of Sui, and selected as its first era-name the term K'ai-huang—a word used in Taoist contexts to name one of the cosmic ages. He ordered an altar prepared in the south suburb and sacrifices made there to inform Heaven of his succession. The same day he announced it to his ancestors in the imperial ancestral hall. With these and other solemn rituals of great antiquity, he let it be known that he now legitimately held the Mandate of Heaven. By the end of the following summer he had effectively insured against a counter coup by Chou loyalists. The eight-year-old emperor was at first granted a title, an income, and the exclusive right to maintain his carriage and clothing, his rituals, and his music in accord with the regulations of the defunct dynasty. But he had little time to enjoy his privileges, for he died in July of 581, "at the will of the Sui." In the same period his relatives, the other princes of the Chou house, were liquidated in a relentless bloodletting. The laconic entries in the standard history tell nothing of the toll of human suffering: "At the beginning of the Ta-ting period (580), the Duke, together with his five sons, was put to death by Sui Wen-ti." Or, "Chao, Prince of Chao-ts'an, [was accused of plotting rebellion] and this autumn (580) was executed together with his sons Yüan, Duke of Te-kuang; Kuan, Duke of Yung-k'ang; Ch'ien-hsien, Duke of Yüeh-hsi; and his younger brothers Ch'ien-ling and Ch'ien-chien. Their fiefs were all abolished." By the end of the terrible sequence, fifty-nine members, young and old, of the main branch of the Yü-wen family had been put to death. Although only one official—to the detriment of his career—protested this planned sequence of murders, they haunted Yang Chien the rest of his life.

But, by the middle of 581, Yang Chien's bid for power had apparently succeeded against heavy odds. Yet, if the Sui was to be anything more than another ephemeral northern dynasty, if it was, rather, to develop into a stable and effective government ruling over a consenting if not contented people, then there were large and intractable problems to be solved. It was to these problems that Yang

Chien devoted the rest of his life, and that is the subject of Chapter
Four. Here let us turn to the character of Yang Chien, to brief charac-
terizations of his closest advisors, and to the style of governing
which they developed.

Yang Chien was in many respects a product of his time and culture, a northern mixed-blood aristocrat of the second half of the
sixth century. To such a background we can attribute many of the
traits of character, the instinctive patterns of behavior that are manifested in his life first as grandee and then as emperor. Some of these
are fairly obvious, and we have talked of them generally in our chapter on sixth-century China. But they may be worth recalling here as
they are manifested in Yang Chien. The military arts, the hunt, falconry, the cult of fine horses—these were the focus of interest among
people he knew, and he was introduced to them (we may assume) in
his early teens at the latest. And, as seems inevitable with aristocra-
cies of all times and places, life on horseback, whether on campaign
or in the hunt, bred a robust anti-intellectualism, a disdain for book-
learning and those whose lives were devoted to it. Yang Chien's
contempt for book-learning, for scholars, for fine distinctions, and
fine rhetoric is manifested at every stage of his career and is expressed, for example, in his policies on Confucian education and on
official language. With Yang Chien's class, as with other aristocra-
cies, their combination of style and outlook was sustained by inherited wealth in land and peasants and by the presumption that
members of their class would inevitably have a monopoly of all positions of power in society. Yang Chien was born to wealth and
power and assumed both to be his birthright.

The family culture of the northern aristocrats was strongly influenced by the ways of the steppe peoples with whom they had in-
termarried for generations. Women, we have noted, were given
much training in the practical arts plus at least the rudiments of literacy, and they customarily took a far more active role in life than did
Chinese women of earlier or later times. There is abundant evidence
that northern women were strongly influential in the lives of their
sons and that jealousy and suspicion were common feelings between
fathers and sons—again very possibly a carry-over from Turko-
Mongol mores. The monogamous family was the rule, and the senior
women perpetuated its ethos and its ideology. The twin supports of
this social system were the endemic rather simplified Confucianism
expressed in the *Classic of Filial Submission* and Buddhism whose basic
tenets were articles of a fervent faith.

Much of Yang Chien's behavior is understandable against this background. He is reported to have been a model son, attending his mother uninterruptedly during the three years of her final illness. He was devoted to his wife, who was his most influential counselor, and gave way to her even when, late in life, her judgment was badly impaired. He apparently had little affection for his sons and, as they came of age, became pathologically suspicious of their every move lest it pose a threat to his power; one of the real causes of discord was the rejection, on the part of some of them, of the strict standard of monogamy set by their parents. Yang Chien's favorite handbook of public and private morality was the authoritarian *Classic of Filial Submission,* and he maintained a childlike faith in its efficacy. When one of his close associates had been indicted for the practice of black magic and for consigning his mother to a separate dwelling, Yang Chien was obviously reluctant to apply the appropriate sentence—reduction to the rank of commoner—and instead issued an order: "Let him be presented with a *Classic of Filial Submission* and ordered to read it earnestly, and further, let him bring his mother back to their common dwelling." One suspects that Yang Chien had been given the same book to memorize when he was a child; its harsh authoritarianism, its insistence on the absolute submission of inferior to superior in a hierarchized social order, its warning against the slightest deviations from orthodoxy in thought or deed were all echoed in the policy edicts, the homilies and exhortations of his years as emperor.

The other support of the social order into which Yang Chien was born was Buddhism, the faith of aristocratic families and—in other forms—of the peasant villages. By the sixth century the cults and practices of aristocratic Buddhism in the north were almost infinitely varied. But underlying them all was belief in karma, belief that the thoughts and deeds of past lives determined one's fate in this one and, further, that what one did in this life could augment one's positive karma or diminish it and thus affect one's level of incarnation in the next life. This is crude; it sounds like a merchant's device of keeping a running balance, from day to day, of net gain or loss; it implies the continuing existence through many lives of individuality, of a soul—a notion that was anathema to Indian Buddhist theologians. Nevertheless this was the fundamental belief of all Buddhists except for a few learned monks. Buddhist laymen and laywomen of families like the Yangs engaged in a wide variety of activities designed to increase their positive karma. For example, they could and did make religious donations of all kinds—gifts to the poor; gifts, often on a great scale, to monasteries for their charitable activities;

the building and endowment of monasteries or reliquaries; endowment of special masses to be said in perpetuity, often for the spiritual welfare of a deceased family member. The wealthy could also gain credit by such things as financing the copying of Buddhist scriptures, contributing to the casting or carving of a holy image, or the painting of a scriptural scene on temple walls, donating a slave or a group of them to work in a monastery, paying for a noted preacher to give a series of sermons to gatherings of clergy and laity. All these and many other activities were commonplace among aristocratic families. Yang Chien no doubt heard much about them in casual talk and, in sermons, he heard repeatedly about the law of karmic causation. All this merely reinforced the strong Buddhist influence of his childhood years. After he seized power, Buddhism was influential in a number of ways. First of all he was now able, as all-powerful emperor, to perform a grand sequence of acts of piety that might undo the negative karmic effects of the numerous murders he had committed in the course of his rise; these haunted him, and monks proposed remedial measures. He was hagridden not only by remorse but by hubris, the fear that comes from rising too high too fast and thus risking the jealousy of unseen forces in the universe. Here again prayers, incantations, appeals to the divine aid of Buddhas and Bodhisattvas were a natural recourse. As Yang Chien slowly became a highly successful emperor, certain Buddhist models of great antiquity and high prestige were suggested to him, and we observe him behaving not only as a Grand Benefactor (Mahā-dānapati) but as a semidivine Defender and Propagator of the Faith in the manner of the great Emperor Asoka of the Mauryas. We shall return to these grand imperial moves, but here it is sufficient to emphasize how deeply Yang Chien was enmeshed in the Buddhist beliefs of his class and time. They defined his moral universe, gave him his view of the afterlife, governed his calendar of religious observances, and to some extent assuaged his fears and his insecurity.

The mores of his class and the influence of prevailing beliefs explain much about the man. So does his particular life history, and so too does the frighteningly exalted role of emperor and Son of Heaven which he had suddenly to learn to play. These are the things that help us to understand some of his characteristic patterns of behavior as we find them recorded in the histories. Many of these patterns are to be understood in relation to the fears, the sense of insecurity that bedeviled him after he become emperor. The reasons for such fears are, when we first consider them, quite obvious. Yang Chien and his wife grew up in the midst of the violent and predatory politics of a divided North China, riven by internecine feuds and racial hatred. His father-in-law had been obliged to commit suicide, and he himself narrowly escaped his royal master's jealous violence. When he was obliged to eliminate, one by one, the Yü-wen princes—some of whom he had known and worked with—he came to fear their malevolent ghosts and the ghosts of those who had died in the Yü-wen cause, like Wei-ch'ih Ch'iung, cursing Yang Chien with his last breath. One source tells us that, after he moved to his newly built capital, he flooded the palaces of old Ch'ang-an so that the ghosts of the murdered Yü-wen would have no place to return to and would thus trouble him no more. Yet fear and insecurity stayed at the root of much of Yang Chien's behavior as emperor, and we might consider some of their manifestations.

The commonest is the syndrome of a real or imagined affront or official wrongdoing precipitating violent overreaction, followed by remorse and efforts to make amends. On one occasion when the Emperor, taking common gossip as evidence, was determined to summarily execute an official of the Board of Punishments, the vice-president of the High Court of Justice remonstrated, saying that under the law the man was not deserving of execution. The Emperor, in a rage, ordered his chief minister to seize the vice-president and have him put to death. The vice-president went to the audience hall, took off his robe, and waited calmly to be beheaded. The Emperor sent someone to get his last words, and when he said that he would hold to the law with his whole heart even at the cost of his life, the Emperor came running from elsewhere in the palace, stopped the proceedings, set him free, and the next day made him rich gifts. There are numerous passages describing the Emperor's beating officials to death in halls of the palace, usually with a bastinado but sometimes with a horse whip. This was the subject of at least one collective remonstrance by his senior advisors, who urged that it was unseemly for the Emperor to administer punishment himself and to turn the audience hall into an execution ground. One incident will serve to illustrate the syndrome we are interested in. The Emperor, in a towering rage, had killed a man in the audience hall. A vice-president of the Board of War strongly remonstrated with him, and the Emperor killed him too, but later was filled with remorse, sent condolences to the official's family, and was angry with his other officials for not remonstrating with him!

There were other, less violent, reactions which reflect the same insecurity, a hypersensitivity to what he imagined to be aspersions on his character or his rule. For example, in 590 he proposed summarily to abolish certain recently established local offices which his inspectors told him were being abused. One of his civil officials urged that more care and deliberation were needed in making changes in the law, otherwise public confusion would result. At this the Emperor sensed an indirect comparison between himself and the notorious usurper and timeless legislative tinkerer of the Han, Wang Mang, became angry, uttered a great curse, and said: "Would you make me out to be Wang Mang?" The other side of the same coin: Yang Chien's appetite for reassurances of all kinds was insatiable. Many of these he found in the ancient imperial rituals which, as he performed them following the instructions of his ritual specialists, must have reassured him that he was indeed Son of Heaven. Others he found in the daily Buddhist ceremonies of his household, in making great gifts to the Buddhist Church, and in the elaborately staged empire-wide Buddhist observances that he himself planned; these we shall discuss in later chapters.

One of his perennial sources of reassurance was the court historian Wang Shao, who was ever obliging and resourceful in meeting his imperial master's needs. At one time he produced an elaborate cabalistic reading of the alchemical-magical Taoist text known as the *Pao-p'u tzu* and of the meaning of the Emperor's name and surname (all interpreted as guaranteeing boundless felicity), rendered this potpourri into two hundred and eighty poems, and presented them to the throne. The Emperor is reported to have believed all this and to have rewarded Wang Shao with a thousand bolts of silk.

Being a usurper and a man who had risen to become "lord of men" in little more than two years, Yang Chien was anxious—far more anxious than rulers of established dynasties—about the degree of acceptance his new dynasty could elicit; many of his policies were designed to win public acceptance. Second, he was anxious about the approval or disapproval he might expect from posterity. One anecdote exemplifies the first of these concerns. When someone reported to him, probably slanderously, that his most valued minister Kao Chiung was plotting rebellion and should therefore be executed, Yang Chien apparently believed the reports. But he pointed out to his ministers that he had recently executed two ranking officials and went on to say: "If on top of them I put Kao Chiung to death, what will the world say of me?" On the judgment of history, we have noted that he was sensitive to any statement that suggested he should, in some respect, be classed with a negative figure of the Chinese past—no doubt reduced in his mind to bare behavioral stereotypes. At the same time he sensed the ultimate power of historians to pass judgment on him and on the Sui Dynasty. This is suggested in the following incident. After the death in disgrace of his third son, members of the prince's household petitioned to erect a commemorative stele. To this Yang Chien replied: "If one wants to seek fame, one roll of a history book will surely suffice. What need is there for a stele?" As to his own image in the histories, he was no doubt reassured by the character of the man whom he put in charge of the Sui history office—the office that compiled the day-to-day record of the dynasty as it unfolded. These duties were carried out for some twenty years by the sycophant Wang Shao who, as we have noted, produced the compendia of favorable portents and other works which reassured Yang Chien about the success of his reign and the continuity of his house.

Yet another characteristic attitude of Yang Chien as emperor was an insistence on uniform enforcement of the written law to the letter. The first unified empire had been welded together, seven hundred years earlier, by a body of draconian laws uniformly applied to high and low alike; it was only in this way, the statesmen of the first empire had reasoned, that the myriad local, regional, and generally centrifugal forces in the land could be prevented from tearing the empire apart. Whether Yang Chien perceived the analogy between that situation and his we do not know, but his insistence on uniform laws was unwavering. One of the tests of this is whether he would allow the law to take its course when it affected one of his own family. On this point one incident illustrates his attitude with particular clarity. Yang Chien's third son, just mentioned, had abused his high offices to build an elaborate palace ornamented with jade and precious stones. When his father the Emperor learned about it, the son was stripped of all offices and confined to his house in the capital. Various officials pleaded for clemency. To one he replied, "The law should not be broken." To another he replied at greater length: "I am the father of five sons. If I follow your advice, would I not be establishing special laws for the sons of the Son of Heaven? If one takes such a man as the Duke of Chou [an ancient statesman idealized by Confucius] as an exemplary man, still he punished his brothers Kuan and Ts'ai [in accordance with the law]. I certainly am far from being the equal of the Duke of Chou. How can someone like me curtail the working of the law?"

Despite a generally draconian enforcement of the law and at least one brief, ludicrous effort to employ extreme sanctions—when he imposed the death penalty for petty theft—Yang Chien occasionally bent the law to his feelings. For example, a valued friend and early supporter had been appointed governor of a certain prefecture which suffered a severe famine, and the price of grain soared. Though it was strictly forbidden to sell grain, the official did so anyway. He was arrested and tried. The penalty for such a crime was death, but perhaps because of his association with the Emperor he was given the lesser but still drastic sentence of removal of his name from the roll of officials and reduction to the status of commoner. Some time later he was in the Emperor's entourage on a progress to Loyang. Yang Chien, taking advantage of the informality of a stop on the journey, said to him: "Now that I am busied with the affairs of empire, I still feel for you some of the old affection. . . . When you occupied the position of governor, why did you not think of repaying my kindness? But now that it has come to this, I cannot bear to have you put to death. And what I am doing is simply twisting the law in deference to my private feelings." And the Emperor restored him to his old position.

We have described some of the traits of character manifested by Yang Chien after he became emperor, many of them linked to his fears and insecurity: his rages followed by remorse; his hypersensitivity to negative judgments, real or imagined, of those around him; his tireless search for favorable portents and his credulity toward all that were presented; his jealousy and suspicions of one and all who seemed to threaten his preeminence; his harsh authoritarianism expressed in many ways but particularly in the rigid application of legal sanctions, softened only by his loyalty to old comrades. Yet the question presents itself as to whether success did not in time temper some of these habitual ways of behaving. Chinese biography, like its Western counterparts until only recently, did not present a man as having his character subtly modified by the experiences he lived through; rather what is present at any one stage of a man's life is presented as "characteristic" of the man. In the case of Yang Chien, we fortunately have one bit of information that suggests a mellowing in later years as success in many fields brought the Sui a large measure of acceptance and respect. This is a description and a judgment of Wen-ti's conduct of the business of government. The reporter is Hsiao Yü, brother-in-law of the man who became Crown Prince in 600, later the Emperor Yang-ti. Hsiao Yü, because of his relationship to the imperial family, was first appointed to offices in the capital about 600, and he may well have been an eyewitness of what he describes. Hsiao Yü, in the passage that follows, was responding to the T'ang Emperor T'ai-tsung who, in 621, asked him: "What sort of ruler was Sui Wen-ti?":

> He got himself under control and returned to ritual proprieties. He labored diligently and concentrated on good government. Every time he held an audience, it could last until late afternoon. He would invite officials of the fifth rank and above to sit and discuss affairs of state, and he would allow the palace guards to eat their evening meal while on duty. Though by nature he was neither benevolent nor enlightened, he was nonetheless a hard-working and perspicacious ruler.

Whatever the truth of this picture, Yang Chien did not come to his own style of governing by himself, for he was under the strong and continuous influence of his close associates whom we should now consider. The closest and most influential of all of these was his Empress, who has already appeared briefly in our story. Yang Chien and his wife had many things in common: their class—the mixed blood aristocracy of North China; their background—the unstable, predatory, and brutal courts of the north; their religion—fervently Buddhist; their values, which came partly from the mores of the north, partly from Buddhism, and partly from an admixture of simplified Confucianism. More important than all these was their strong love for each other, strengthened by their common experience of deadly perils on the way to the summit of power. The Empress showed, in the early years of the Sui, great political acumen. For example, she declined to have purchased for her a fabulous pearl that had appeared in one of the Sino-Turkish trading posts along the frontier and said that the vast sum required to purchase it might better be used to give rewards to officers and men who won distinction in the wars against the barbarians. When the Emperor wished to grant clemency to one of her male relatives who had been condemned to death, she is reported to have declined the offer, saying: "In affairs of state, why should one take account of private concerns?"

But she was also soft-hearted and at times sentimental; whenever she heard that the High Court had sentenced someone to death, she wept. She had lost her parents at an early age, and whenever she met a courtier who had both his parents living, she would arrange to have gifts sent to them. The Emperor and his consort were inseparable and usually of one mind on problems facing the Sui. In the palace they were referred to as "the two sages." When the Emperor went to audience, she would ride in the palanquin with him. When he entered the audience chamber, she would wait outside but send a eunuch in to watch the Emperor and report to her. If she noted what she regarded as errors, she would send in a sharp remonstrance. After it was all over, they returned together to their private apartments. Her influence was thus considerable in all matters of state policy, and his trust in her was total. But this complete mutual trust was broken late in her life by an incident which had unbalancing effects on her subsequent conduct. The Emperor had taken a fancy to a young and beautiful woman of the palace, and the Empress took advantage of his holding audience to have her secretly killed. When he discovered this, the Emperor was furious, got on his horse, and galloped off into the mountains. He had gone some six miles across country when his close advisors Kao Chiung and Yang Su caught up with him, reined in his horse, and earnestly admonished him, no doubt stressing the risks he was taking; he sighed a great sigh and said, "I am honored as Son of Heaven but that doesn't get me any personal freedom." He was inconsolable, but was finally persuaded to return to the palace in the dead of night. The Empress was waiting, and in tears she asked his forgiveness. The two loyal ministers stepped in to reconcile the imperial couple; whereupon the Emperor ordered up food and wine and proceeded to get very merry. The *Sui History* says that from this time on, her disposition changed for the worse. We see in the sparse words of the history the signs of a deep neurosis. She overheard Kao Chiung say, in what she took to be a criticism of the Emperor's recent affair, that he himself was "a one-woman man." Though they had long been close friends, her antipathy became more virulent after his wife's death. At that time he announced that he had grown old and would devote himself thereafter to reading Buddhist scriptures. Shortly thereafter he got his concubine pregnant. The Empress began to slander Kao Chiung and thus to undermine the Emperor's deep trust in him. Whenever an imperial prince's or a courtier's concubine became pregnant, she would urge the Emperor to punish them. Her judgments, so long a positive force, became badly flawed. Yet the Emperor continued to consult her on every matter. As we shall see in a later chapter, it was the plotting of this very sick woman that brought about the deposition of the Crown Prince and the elevation of her favorite son, Yang Kuang, in his place. When, after her death, the Emperor had two consorts, he was suspicious of both of them, and when he fell ill, he said to his attendants: "If the Empress were still here, I would not have come to this."

Next to the Empress in influence and more important in shaping the policies and style of Yang Chien's reign was Kao Chiung. He had been born into a northeastern family which chose to leave that area and adhere to the Northern Chou, where they attached themselves as a client family to Tu-ku Hsin and were given his surname. When Tu-ku Hsin was forced to commit suicide, Kao Chiung's father became the foster father of the child who later became the first Sui empress. The fortunes of the Yangs, the Tu-ku's, and the Kao's were thus closely intertwined. Young Kao Chiung is said to have early shown a sharp intelligence, practical ability, a quick grasp of the ancient classics and the histories, plus a special aptitude for legal matters. He took his first post at the age of sixteen, as secretary to one of the Northern Chou princes. His rise thereafter was speedy. He served in the campaign that crushed the Northern Ch'i and was suitably rewarded. He was then attached to an imperial prince during a successful campaign against "barbarians" in the north. So it was quite natural for Yang Chien, when he had seized *de facto* power, to send an intermediary to ask Kao Chiung to join him. Given the family connections, Kao Chiung had little choice, for if Yang Chien's bid for power failed, all the Kao's would face certain death. So he came over to the Yang side and quickly gained Yang Chien's confidence. What cemented their relationship was Kao Chiung's stunning victory, in the summer of 580, against Wei-ch'ih Ch'iung—the strongest among those opposed to a Yang takeover.

After Yang Chien proclaimed the Sui and became its first emperor, Kao Chiung was appointed to the highest offices in the central government and, for nearly twenty years thereafter, was indisputably the most powerful minister at the Sui court. His mark is upon nearly all the bold measures to deal with the problems facing the Sui, measures we shall discuss in the next chapter. Here it is worth noticing some of his personal characteristics, especially those which either coincided with or complemented those of his imperial master. Perhaps because he was not the principal usurper, nor—over the bodies of the Yü-wen princes—Son of Heaven, he appears in the sources as more even-tempered, more commonsensical than his master. But he shared with him a certain decisiveness, a directness, and an impatience with cant and pretense. He, like Yang Chien, clearly believed in authoritarian government implemented by clear and strictly administered regulations. And, again like Yang Chien, he was a devout Buddhist; early in the Sui he donated his mansion to be made into a temple and shortly thereafter he became the patron of the monk Hsin-hsing, who preached a doctrine later found to be subversively heterodox. If we can believe the sources, he was far more fertile of ideas—strategic, administrative, fiscal—than his master, and it is clear that he had a genius for implementation, for making his subordinates carry through expeditiously and to the letter what had been decided at the highest levels.

For all his qualities and his record of achievement, Kao Chiung was periodically attacked, directly or indirectly, by groups of court officials who were jealous of his influence with the Emperor or wanted a share of his power. When Kao Chiung was leading the campaign against the Ch'en state in the south, some officials told the Emperor that he was plotting rebellion. Yang Chien had them put to death. On another occasion, two officials accused him of responsibility for weather unfavorable to the crops and asked that he be dismissed. (That the ruler and his high officials were responsible for the balance of natural forces was axiomatic for the Chinese.) Again Yang Chien rejected their advice and had them punished. But when, in the later years of her life, the Empress became somewhat unbalanced and pathologically jealous, she began to undermine Kao Chiung's position and to take every occasion to speak ill of him to the Emperor. And when he opposed the Empress's scheme to depose the Crown Prince and elevate their second son Kuang, Prince of Chin, in his stead, the plots and accusations came thick and fast. Finally it was secretly reported to the throne that Buddhist clerics, in their role of prognosticators, had spoken to Chiung of the imminent end of the first Sui reign. It was further reported that he had, in conversations with his son, drawn the parallel between himself and the actual founder of the Chin Dynasty (265–420), a man who had served as prime minister of the preceding dynasty and then engineered the accession of his grandson as first emperor of a new dynasty. The Emperor then had Kao Chiung's name stricken from the official rolls and ordered him reduced to the rank of commoner. As we noted in discussing Yang Chien's character, it was only his uneasiness about possible public reactions to a *third* execution of a high ranking minister that saved Chiung's life. He was to survive Yang Chien and to serve under the next emperor, at whose hands he finally met his

death. Kao Chiung was, in the years of establishing the dynasty, unquestionably the most able and imaginative of the inner circle of officials. Compared to his achievements in policy formulation and
implementation, the contributions of other members of the group
are markedly less significant. Yet these men too helped shape the
style and policies of the first reign.

The man who shared great power with Kao Chiung and survived
during Kao's disgrace in 599 was Yang Su, member of another Yang
family with the same native place as that of the Sui founder. Yang Su
was less sober, less judicious than Kao Chiung. A man with a striking air, a handsome beard, many talents, and boundless energy with
ambitions to match, he had no doubts about his own superiority.
Like Yang Chien, he began his career with service under the Northern Chou, and he achieved a striking victory against great odds in the
campaign of 579, which brought all of North China under Chou rule.
Unlike Yang Chien, he was quite learned and wrote elegantly with
virtuoso brush strokes; at one point in his career, when he had fallen
into disfavor with the Northern Chou ruler, his ability to compose
and write edicts is said to have pleased his master and saved him
from execution. He joined the Yang forces in 580 and in the summer
of that year won military laurels in a campaign against Chou loyalists; this was the first of countless victories won for the Sui house,
and it is worth looking for a moment at the military techniques that
made him the most famous field commander of his age. He was a resourceful strategist, quick and aggressive. He enforced a discipline
so ferocious that it reminds one of that used by the Mongols in their
bid for world dominion seven centuries later. Any soldier who de-
viated in the slightest degree from military orders was immediately
beheaded with no chance for clemency. Yang Su would order a
group of soldiers to move forward and break the enemy's line; if
they failed to do so and retreated, they were all beheaded and a second attack ordered before the bodies of the first group grew cold.
When army units engaged in plundering, he would seek out those
responsible and have them all executed. The historian remarks,
"With the blood of those executed gushing out before him, he would
laugh and joke as usual." It was the "do or die" spirit instilled by his
discipline that mainly accounted for his victories. But men chose to
follow Yang Su, despite his ferocity, because he was scrupulous
about recording all noteworthy feats on the battlefield and thus assured all his men of their proper rewards.

When Yang Chien ascended the throne in 581, he moved Yang

Su from a military role to a civil office, and he was appointed President of the Censorate (*Yü-shih ta-fu*), with overall control of the apparatus for policing officialdom. During the first years of the dynasty he was in the Emperor's confidence and frequently put forward strategies for the conquest of the south, a project that was much on Yang Chien's mind from the moment he seized power. But this intimate relationship was rudely disrupted in 584. Yang Su's wife was a notorious shrew, and at one point she goaded him to such fury that he exclaimed: "If I become Son of Heaven, you most certainly are not going to be my empress." She, quite in keeping with her character, reported her husband's remark in a memorial to the throne, and Yang Su was stripped of his offices.

It was not long before Yang Su was called back to government service; he was loaded with imperial gifts and made governor of the area of easternmost Szechwan where the Yangtze comes out of its gorges and broadens into the plain (then an aboriginal area and a "hardship post"). There he used his master's gifts as capital to build the naval force that was to play an important role in the conquest of the Ch'en. In that campaign he commanded this force and won great glory (see Chapter Four). He was richly rewarded with titles, perquisites, vast amounts of silk and gold; in addition he was given, for his household, the younger sister of the last Ch'en ruler and fourteen of his concubines. However, he had little time to enjoy the fruits of victory before he was sent south again to put down widespread rebellion; after much ferocious fighting, this was finally accomplished, and Yang Su returned to receive once more rich rewards from his grateful master, which this time included a house, a vast tract of land, two hundred horses, and two thousand sheep! His next assignment was to supervise the construction of the detached palace known as the Jen-shou Kung; in this project he drove his workmen with characteristic ruthlessness, and many of them died. Word reached the Emperor that the cries of their ghosts could be heard around the palace. When the negative reports were confirmed by inspection, Yang Su feared for his life. But he enlisted the help of the Empress, and after her intervention he was not only not punished but was once again showered with imperial gifts.

Against the Eastern Turks and their leader Tardu, Yang Su, typically, persuaded his troops to abandon the traditional Chinese strategy against cavalry charges—based on a defensive square of wagons and soldiers—and to form cavalry ranks. This proved successful, the Turkish army was scattered, and Yang Su and his sons were the recipients of more imperial largesse. Some three years later he led a second aggressive and successful campaign against the Turks and was again rewarded. Shortly thereafter he was put in charge of the layout and construction of the tomb of the Empress, who had died in 602. Once more his imperial master was pleased and rewarded him, his sons, and grandsons on a lavish scale. The *Sui History* remarks that at this point he and his family all were rich in titles, honors, and possessions. "The manservants of his household numbered several thousand. The silk-clad beauties of his Inner Court were numbered by the thousand. His mansions were extravagantly ornamented and their plan and scale resembled those of the imperial palace." He had retainers noted for prose composition and for calligraphy, and among his household slaves were members of the southern élite who had been captured along with the leader of their resistance to the Sui. "His relatives and his old servitors were ranked with the most illustrious. The scale of the honors received by Yang Su was unheard of in ancient or modern times."

It would have been out of character for the Emperor not gradually to have become suspicious and jealous of his flamboyant and high-living minister. In 603 and 604, Yang Su continued to be showered with favors but was gradually eased out of substantive policy making. In the year 600 Yang Su had been a party to the plot to depose the Crown Prince and elevate Yang Kuang in his stead. In 604 he may well have been in on the dark deeds at the Jen-shou Palace which prevented the Emperor from reinstating the former Crown Prince and perhaps hastened the Emperor's death. Yang Su was appointed to office by the new Emperor and, on his behalf, crushed the rebellion of his brother Liang, Prince of Han. But this was his last bloody exploit for the Sui house. Shortly thereafter, he fell ill, and his new master sent the imperial physician to attend him, with instructions not to let him recover. Yang Su had been a party to too many dark plots to have any doubt of the physician's intent. He took his medicine, and his final words, uttered in a last access of Buddhist faith, were, "Shall I not be reborn in a moment?"

Yang Su was the "hatchet man" of the Sui. His energy and resourcefulness were used again and again to supervise building projects, to drive off the Turks in the northwest, to crush the southerners who rose against the Sui, to scatter the substantial forces that had rallied around the Prince of Han. He is credited with few policy initiatives, but his was the kind of military genius that a new dynasty, with its great plans and far-flung problems, urgently needed. He was as authoritarian as the Sui founder and like him a Buddhist, if by no means as devout a one. And for all his ruthlessness, he had a softer side, a certain elegance, and a literary virtuosity that went far beyond the drafting of official documents. Let us leave him by quoting one of his poems, "Sitting alone in my mountain studio," which he wrote for the noted literary figure Hsüeh Tao-heng:

Dwelling in mountains, my view blocked on all sides,
Wind and clouds last all the way from dawn to dusk.
A deep creek ravine stretches across before ancient trees,
Bare cliffs where rest hidden stones.
The sun comes out and distant pinnacles brighten
Birds scatter and the deserted forests grown silent.
Yet in my orchid yard hidden airs stir,
And an empty whiteness appears in my bamboo cottage.
Falling blossoms fly into the doors,
Delicate grasses gather on the steps.
To no purpose does this cassia wine fill my cup,
For my old friend is not at the mat with me.
At sunset in the recesses of the mountain
I face the winds looking for the feathered immortals.

Yang Su, who was not a man to hide his feelings, had a high regard for Kao Chiung, respected the Confucian scholar Niu Hung, and had a literary friendship with Hsüeh Tao-heng. But for Su Wei, the last person in the inner circle to be considered, Yang Su had nothing but contempt, and he did nothing to hide it. Su Wei was the son of Su Ch'o, a statesman greatly honored by the Northern Chou rulers and remembered with awe and reverence by their successors, the Sui. Su Ch'o was an authoritarian Confucian (personally a Buddhist) who had been the chief ideologue and legislator for the Turko-Mongol founder of the Northern Chou. Su Ch'o prepared a series of enactments designed to demonstrate that the dynasty he served, despite its non-Chinese ruling house, represented a revival of the political order idealized by Confucius, that of the early Chou (c. 1050–900 B.C.). All the offices of government were renamed to accord with the *Rituals of Chou*, a work believed to reflect that ancient ideal order. He further drew up a set of six principles for civil government which all officials were obliged to memorize if they hoped to be appointed or to stay in office. These six principles are a blend of rather simplified Confucian ethical ideas with standards for public administration that were centralizing and Legalist tempered by common sense and Confucian ideals of humanity. Su Ch'o had also persuaded his masters, most of whom were scarcely literate in Chinese, that official documents of all kinds should avoid the effete literary styles of the southern dynasties and return to the austere—not to say crabbed and archaic—style of the ancient *Classic of History*. All these moves were meant to signal to the rest of China that the rulers in the far northwest, the Chou state whose military might was so greatly feared, were somehow the natural and legitimate reunifiers of the empire. When the task of reunification was preempted by the Sui, this part of the Northern Chou heritage and its formulator Su Ch'o were taken with great seriousness. This then is the main motive for the Sui founder's seeking out Su Ch'o's son Wei and appointing him to office, done despite the fact that Wei had retreated to the country during the actual seizure of power.

Su Wei had, no doubt, a Buddhist upbringing and began his official career in the long shadow of his father's reputation; he was soon honored by being given a daughter of the Chou ruler to wed. When the violence of the Sui coup d'état had passed, Su reemerged and was given honors and high office; when he tried to decline, the Emperor rejected his plea and said: "When ships are large they are given heavy loads; when horses are fleet they travel fast to distant places. Since you have the talent of two men, there will be no escaping a multitude of tasks." In the early years of the dynasty he used the influence for demilitarization, for frugality at court, for reduction of taxes and forced labor requirements, for an easing of the penal code. Although he was apparently maladroit in the formal argumentation of an imperial audience and often stubbornly insistent on minor points, his was an important humanizing influence, and he is to be credited with many of the measures that gradually gained for the Sui a measure of acceptance among the population. The more drastic measures of institutional reform were not his but Kao Chiung's. In a sense Su Wei's Confucian-inspired policies of conciliation complemented Kao Chiung's Legalist policies of radical centralization.

Su Wei's tendency to monopolize too many offices and to indulge in nepotism got him into periodic trouble, but his rather doctrinaire approach to political problems—always relying on arguments from Confucius and from his father—was more troublesome for the dynasty. When the south had been conquered, there were very large problems for the Sui in ameliorating the southerners' hatred and suspicion of their new rulers. Su Wei's contribution at this juncture was as characteristic as it was counterproductive. He developed a kind of catechism of public and private morality called "The Five Teachings" (Wu-chiao) and persuaded the newly appointed Sui officials in the south to require that everyone, regardless of age, be required to memorize it. Here, Su Wei was applying one of his father's methods of indoctrination by forcing it upon a social landscape of which he had scant knowledge. Resistance sparked by this requirement and by rumors that the Sui intended to transport the whole population of the old Ch'en Empire to the north broke out all over, and as the rebels disemboweled the Sui officials or cut them up for food, they would say: "This will make you better able to recite the Five Teachings!" It was then that Yang Su had to be called back into service and to fight a long war of attrition in the south before peace was restored.

In handling day-to-day work Su Wei was apparently very effective. In the latter years of Wen-ti's reign, however, he was frequently in disfavor. His tactlessness and his playing of favorites often had him in disgrace. At one point he was accused of manipulating the appointment of numerous unqualified people, many of them his relatives. This was investigated and found to be true. When Su Wei took off his official hat, bowed low to the Emperor, and showed signs of repenting, the Emperor remarked caustically, "Your apology is belated indeed!" Stripped of his offices and honors and put under house arrest, Su Wei nevertheless shortly returned to power and lived through more periods of favor and disgrace. He saw service under the second Emperor and survived until the early T'ang Dynasty, dying at the ripe age of eighty-two.

Many others had an influence, direct or indirect, on the policies and style of the first Sui reign. And, unquestionably, Yang Kuang, especially after his elevation to the position of Crown Prince in 601, exerted great influence. But the Empress and the three officials we have just considered, in large measure, made the first reign what it was. It is worth noting, finally, that whether by accident or design, the intimates of the first Emperor had first-hand knowledge of or kinship ties with the major regional élites that the Sui had first to win over and then understand, mollify, and manipulate if the dynasty was to survive. Yang Chien himself, though born halfway between Ch'ang-an and Loyang, was the descendant of men who had served for many generations on the western end of the northern frontier. He was thus well acquainted with (and no doubt related to) the powerful

families of this area. His Empress came from the northern part of the
Great Plain; she was descended on her father's side from several
non-Chinese families which had served the Northern Wei, and her
mother—as noted earlier—was a Ts'ui of Ch'ing-ho, one of the most
prestigious Chinese families of this rich and populous area. Kao
Chiung came from a town somewhat further to the north and east.
Yang Su had the same birthplace as the Emperor and may have had
deeper family roots in that central area. Su Wei was a native of the
area "within the passes" (Kuan-chung) and, because of his father's
renown, if for no other reason, must have had a wide acquaintance
among the northwestern aristocrats. Yang Kuang was betrothed and
then married to a southern girl of royal lineage; a convert to southern
culture and fluent in the dialect of the lower Yangtze, he was first his
father's effective viceroy of the south and, later, an advisor with deep
familiarity with the south, with southern families, and with southern
problems. Thus the first Emperor and his intimate advisors were
people of extraordinarily diverse talents and personalities and, at the
same time, they encompassed a wide knowledge of all the far-flung
areas which it was the achievement of the Sui to unite into a single
empire.

CHAPTER 4

Reunification

Nearly four centuries had passed since the end of the Han, the last dynasty to rule over the whole of the Chinese world. The Sui leaders were aware of the formidable problems they would have to overcome to achieve once again hegemony over a subcontinental area that the years of disunion had fragmented. They had to go beyond the time-honored rituals of legitimation and elicit general acquiescence first in the north, the Great Plain, and later in the south; they had to gain the active cooperation of substantial segments of the regional élites who, if they chose, might rally their people in resistance to the unifiers. They had to sweep away the institutional detritus of the centuries of disunion and build a new structure, new laws and institutions that would effectively centralize power in the new dynasty. Further, they were faced with the ramifying and subtle problems of reviving ancient cultural traditions, of blending these with elements from popular religions to provide a common set of values, a common culture, for a reunified empire. For no Chinese emperor was simply the head of the apparatus of state; he was at once cosmic pivot and moral law-giver, the guardian and interpreter of ancient cultural traditions from which the norms of proper behavior, public and private, were ultimately derived. In this chapter we shall see how the Sui leadership dealt with these problems during the reign of Wen-ti (581–604). As we consider them, one by one, we should remind ourselves that nearly all these problems were being dealt with simultaneously and that a formidable capacity for positive action was characteristic of Sui leadership—men who knew that time was critical, that nothing could wait if their great enterprise was to be crowned with success.

Very early in the new dynasty, the Sui founder and his intimate advisors began to discuss the building of a new capital. Yang Chien had seized power in the strategic area of Kuan-chung, "the land within the passes," a well-watered and fertile plain surrounded by mountains. Kuan-chung had long been the base from which expeditions set out to conquer other areas of China, and by Yang Chien's time it had been the site of royal or imperial capitals for fifteen hundred years. The tombs of ancient rulers were scattered through the hills and in the plain itself, and countless ruins testified as well to the labors of long dead dynasts and their toiling people. If one tries to visualize the distinctive features of the terrain and climate, one might view Kuan-chung as an oval bowl, elongated to the east and west and bounded on the south by the formidable Ch'in-ling shan, the watershed of China, the barrier between the humid rice lands of the south and the relatively arid lands of the north. Bisecting the plain is the shallow swift-flowing Wei River making its way from the western highlands to a junction with the Yellow River near its great bend. North of the bowl-like plain, the land rises more gently and is topped by layers of the fertile wind-driven dust known as loess. On the east are mountain barriers pierced by the few passes where many decisive battles for the control of China were fought. While Kuan-chung has an elevation of nearly thirteen hundred feet, the Yellow River Plain to the east and beyond the passes is relatively flat and low-lying. The mountains to the south of Kuan-chung are a barrier to the monsoon rains; the annual rainfall is only some twenty inches. Except for seasonal rain and frequent dust storms, the Kuan-chung Plain is bathed in sunshine, and annual temperatures average about sixty degrees.

The city where Yang Chien first proclaimed the advent of the Sui was irregular in shape and quite near the Wei River. It had been the capital of the last dynasty to control the whole of China, the great Han, which had endured from 206 B.C. to A.D. 220. But by Yang Chien's time the city had survived four centuries of adversity: the prolonged death agonies and the final collapse of the Han, sackings and burnings, innumerable massacres, murders, and executions. Yang Chien and his advisors found it cramped, depressing, and redolent of past failures. One counselor remarked that it was filled with the ghosts of murdered men; another pointed out that the city had now been lived in for eight hundred years and the water supply was brackish. Moreover, there were men around the new emperor who knew about the more spacious and more functional cities built elsewhere in recent times, notably the Wei capitals at Loyang and at Yeh in Honan.

In the Chinese world, the choice of a capital site was not determined solely by strategic and political considerations; it was a matter of ritual-symbolic, indeed religious, importance, for the capital was both the functional center of power and a sacred symbol. A site therefore had to be strategically located and easily supplied, and the capital designed to be a microcosm of the ordered universe over which the Son of Heaven presided. To do this meant taking into account ancient classical prescriptions for the building of capitals, historical precedents, and the various symbol systems by which the Chinese measured the disposition of Heaven and the unseen forces in the universe. Among the latter were the balance of the complementary forces yin and yang, to be reflected in the city's plan; the relation of the city to the points of the compass and particularly to the sun and the polestar; the relation between and among the numbers of streets, wards, etc.—for numbers were not simply notations of quantity but were also symbols of cosmic relationships.

In a long edict Yang Chien reported to his people the earnest attention he and his ministers had given to all these considerations. Divinations had been made by the use of the great tortoise shell— that is, the diviners had asked for and received supernatural guidance by "reading" the patterns of heat-induced cracks in a tortoise shell; astronomical calculations had been made; and the angle of the sun measured by means of a gnomon, a shadow-stick. He goes on to say that his ministers are now of one mind in recommending the construction of a new capital. "This being the case, it should be remembered that a capital city is the administrative seat of the myriad officials and the place to which all those within the four seas will turn. It is not the sole possession of Us the Emperor. If the project seems likely to be beneficial to all creatures, why should I oppose it?" Then, asking his people to take on the burden of the work, he says: "Planning the new and getting rid of the old is like a farmer looking forward to autumn; although for the time being the work may be arduous, he knows that at the end he will be peacefully at ease." Then, he speaks of the site that has been chosen, the Dragon's Head Rise: "The well-watered plain is luxuriant and beautiful, the growing plants rich and abundant. Having divined regarding the productivity of foodstuffs and the goodness of the land, We declare it to be entirely fitting that We establish a capital here. The foundations of our capital will last forever, and immeasurable will be the accomplishments made in it." Here the hyperbole ends, and the edict turns abruptly to practical matters: "As to official bureaus and private houses, their design and location, the expenses of construction and of materials, as may be appropriate We shall send up memorials item by item."

The Emperor then appointed his most trusted counselor Kao Chiung head of the commission in charge of the project, but the principal architect was Yü-wen K'ai, the most brilliant architect and engineer of the time. He was, ironically, a member of the clan of the previous ruling house—a clan which Yang Chien had slaughtered in large numbers in his rise to power. Yü-wen K'ai and those associated with him in building the new capital were northerners of mixed descent; nearly all came from the great plain to the east; some were descended from recent immigrants from Central Asia; one had a Zoroastrian personal name. All felt free to innovate, to borrow ideas from recently built cities and to take only some features of the ideal royal capital as laid out in the Chinese classical tradition without being bound by all its prescriptions.

The demolition of old Ch'ang-an proceeded apace, villages and graves were cleared away, and the building of the new city began on gently rolling land to the south and east of the Han city. Kao Chiung, in his role as supervisor of construction, sat under a large *huai* tree on the northern part of the site. There he no doubt gave orders and received reports from his subordinates in charge of various parts of the work. The labor force was made up in part of people from the Kuan-chung Plain serving their annual requirement of up to thirty days of work for the state; one source tells us that corvée laborers were also brought in from the areas to the east of Kuan-chung. As in the building of other capitals, there also must have been a drafting of artisans from near and far: tile makers, carpenters, builders, masters of painting and ornamentation. The most formidable task, requiring uncounted thousands of workers, was the building of the outer walls, which when completed measured 5.92 miles east and west, 5.27 miles north and south. The building material was the light brown earth, the loess-alluvium of the Kuan-chung Plain itself; possibly some of it was excavated to form a moat outside the walls, and much of it was dug out of the beds of ornamental lakes, planned as part of the parklike setting of the imperial palaces. To build the walls, the earth of the walls' base was first tamped down hard to make a foundation. Then earth was brought in baskets to the work site; there it was mixed with water and laid down in thin layers of mud which, when tamped down and dried in the sun, had a thickness of about nine centimeters. Layer followed layer until the wall reached its full height. The outer walls were from three to five meters thick at the base, wider where gates were to be located. The best estimate of their height is thirty-five feet. But these walls simply articulated the outer limits of the complex whole.

Inside its outer walls the city was divided into three zones. Backed up against the central portion of the north wall was the palace city, also walled, which contained the imperial residences, the main audience hall—called by the Sui Ta-hsing tien, "Palace of the Great Revival," and by the T'ang T'ai-chi tien, "Palace of the Cosmic Ultimate"—the courts and lesser audience halls, pavilions and gardens for imperial pleasures, quarters for guards and palace servants. The more important of the buildings in the palace complex were placed on pounded earth foundations, built up in the same manner as the walls. The buildings were then constructed in the traditional post-and-lintel manner, the wooden framework supporting a roof of colored tiles, and the walls themselves—"filler walls" of sun-dried brick—were plastered and white-washed, sometimes with color added. The great south gate of the palace city, called in Sui times "Gate of the Diffusion of the Yang Force," gave on a glacis some three hundred feet wide. It was from atop this gate that official proclamations were read out, and it was from the same position that the victorious Sui founder looked down on the captured royalty and nobles of the defeated Ch'en dynasty and berated them for their moral delinquency (see page 154). South of the glacis was a second walled enclosure, the administrative city (*huang-ch'eng*). Within it the government offices were to be located along seven north-south and five east-west streets, all of them a hundred paces wide and lined with trees. The administrative city was an innovation because previous capitals had their government buildings scattered through the whole city as in modern London and Paris. One source says flatly that this innovation should be credited to the Sui founder, but it seems more likely to have been developed by Yü-wen K'ai and his fellow planners. Beyond these two walled enclosures there were laid out in a U pattern 108 rectangular walled compounds ranged along eleven north-south and fourteen east-west streets. We should note the symbolism of the layout: 108 has its cosmic significance because it is the number of ordered time (twelve months) times the number of ordered space (the nine regions of China in legendary antiquity). The four wards ranged just south of the administrative city were said to symbolize the four seasons, while the four tiers of nine wards each stretching from the south of the imperial city to the outer walls were meant to reflect the highly schematic symbolism for capitals of the ancient ritual text known as the *Chou-li*. Of the 108 compounds, 106 were to be residential while two were to be markets where commerce would be centered under government supervision; eventually the east market became somewhat specialized in domestic products, while the west market had a high proportion of goods from Central and Western Asia. The market and residential wards were more lightly walled than the city or the palace compound and these walls were of pounded earth or sun-dried brick; a report of 755 tells us that after sixty successive days of rain (most abnormal for the area), the walls of the wards and markets almost completely disintegrated. Most of the wards were served by internal streets in the shape of a cross with gates centered in each of the four sides; under the T'ang and most likely under the Sui the gates were shut at sundown and opened at sunup, and residents were forbidden to leave their wards during this time. At the time of the building of the new city, residential wards were granted to anyone who would occupy them, and as the old city was demolished parts of the new were occupied. One ward had been the site of a Han Dynasty pleasure pavilion, and, we are told, "The people [who had been assigned the ward] divided the land, the timbers, and building materials among themselves."

The main axis of the city was the wide north-south Street of the Gate of the Vermilion Bird (Chu-ch'iao-men chieh), which led from the south-central gate of the administrative city (from which it took its name) to the five-portaled main gate in the center of the city's outer walls, the Gate of Brilliant Virtue (Ming-te men). The city itself and the principal palace were named Ta-hsing, after the fief given the Sui founder before he became emperor. But the term *ta-hsing* was also freighted with felicitous meaning, particularly happy for a dynasty that sought to restore the glorious universal rule of the long-vanished Han. It meant something like "great (*ta*) prosperous revival or restoration (*hsing*)." All the names given to wards, gates, and pal-

aces were carefully chosen for their explicit or subtle reference to
something in the value galaxy of the Chinese. The "vermilion bird"
used in the name of the main south gate of the palace-administrative
city complex was, as Edward Schafer puts it, "a primitive image, an
auspicious sign of divine blessings . . . the true firebird, infused
with the spark of divine solar energy." It also symbolized the *yang*
force, the power wielded *par excellence* by the emperor and his surrogates. The principal gate in the east wall was called the Gate of the
Brightness of Spring (Ch'un-ming men) because in that direction the
sun rose, brought warmth, a hint of spring, a return, after winter, of
the *yang* force. Many other names reflect the ancient moral values.
For example, the ward which would later house candidates for the
capital examinations was called the Ward of Exalting Goodness
(Ch'ung-jen fang), another the Ward of the Great Way and its Power
(Tao-te fang). All the nomenclature is shot through with words symbolizing the perennial desiderata of the Chinese: "tranquility" (*an*),
"peace" (*p'ing*), "prolonged" (*ch'ang*) used with other words meaning
life, suggesting longevity for the new dynasty and so forth. Despite
the influence of Buddhism, only one or two proper names in the
city—except the names of Buddhist establishments—had something
of a Buddhist flavor. A few names such as Sweet Spring Ward (Li-
ch'uan fang) were derived from natural features.

For all the hopeful and auspicious nomenclature, the city itself
had a very unfinished look when, after nine months of construction,
the Emperor mounted his horse and rode in to take up his residence
in the Palace City. This was on April 15, 583. Manual laborers were
still working, by the thousands, on the outer walls; builders, paint-
ers, and decorators must have been as omnipresent as the piles of
building materials they had yet to use. The huge city—which turned
out to be the largest in area of any Chinese walled capital in imperial
history—was mostly empty, and many wards were still devoted to
agriculture. Indeed the whole project must have seemed to many a
vain exercise in grandiosity on the part of a monarch not yet three
years in power.

Yang Chien was aware of its emptiness, and he took various
measures to attract population and encourage building. He ordered
his sons to build their mansions in the southwestern sector of the
city, in the hope that their retinues and their activities would stimu-
late other building. One of them, the Prince of Shu, was rich enough
from the income from his lands to build a mansion of some magnificence. The Emperor offered imperial name plaques, amounting to
charters, to anyone who would build a Buddhist temple. He led the

way by establishing the Ling-kan Ssu dedicated to the spiritual felicity of those whose graves had to be moved to make way for construction of the city. This temple, near the east wall, subsequently became the Ch'ing-lung Ssu, an establishment famous throughout Buddhist Asia. We cannot be certain, but Yang Chien may have installed in the original temple the peerless Kuan-yin figure first dedicated in 570 and probably moved early in the Sui dynasty from the old Ch'ang-an to the new capital.

Yang Chien and his empress proceeded to build and endow one temple after another. They built temples in memory of several of their forebears and other temples honoring their favorite monks, even one honoring the imperial physician. The Empress began to build a very large temple with an impressive wooden pagoda in the west city. In 603, after her death, the Emperor rededicated it in her honor, and the great architect Yü- wen K'ai built in one of its courtyards a wooden pagoda 330 feet high and 120 paces in circumference. This was perhaps built to house a most famous holy relic, a tooth of the Buddha originally brought back from India in the fifth century by the pilgrim Fa-hsien. The principal halls of the temple were decorated with paintings by famous artists of the time, and some descriptions survive. By the time it was completed, observers commented that it outshone in magnificence all other temples in the empire.

Imperial princes and princesses emulated their parents in similar acts of piety, some donating their own mansions to be converted into monasteries or nunneries. The great officials followed the fashion, and in some cases they donated building materials from their mansions in old Ch'ang-an to help build a new temple. This was the pattern of many pious donations, and in each case the Emperor would award an imperial name plaque for the new establishment. Palace women and at least one eunuch joined in the pious competition, as did several rich merchants. The most important of the official religious establishments were the head metropolitan temples for Buddhism and religious Taoism, built in two wards which faced each other across the great north-south thoroughfare. On the east was the Buddhist, and this was named, to reiterate the name of the city and the principal palace, Ta-hsing-shan Ssu. While the Buddhist headquarters occupied a whole ward, the Taoist, across the street, occupied far less than a ward. By the end of his reign the Sui founder could look out upon his capital and see a hundred and twenty Buddhist establishments, many of them embellished by the paintings of noted contemporary artists and many with Buddhist reliquary pagodas which enlivened the skyline. In addition there were ten Taoist temples within the city's walls.

For all this carefully fostered building activity and measures designed to attract population, much of the city remained unoccupied by the end of the first reign, indeed at the fall of the Sui. The archaeologists who have excavated the foundations of the city walls have found that the Sui walls sometimes show signs of hasty construction and were less solid than the rebuilt walls of T'ang times. The outer gates of the Sui city had no gate towers; these were to come in the T'ang era. Private dwellings of Sui times were built on a modest scale, and a great eighth-century statesman who acquired one complained that its rooms were small and constricted and that if one rode a tall horse, one couldn't get through the outer gate. The noted early T'ang minister and historian Wei Cheng lived in another of these houses, and his imperial master, as a kindness, provided the material and labor to add to it, for the first time, a reception hall! Yet there must have been impressive architectural survivals from Sui times, though we have only one bit of evidence. In the reign of the third T'ang emperor (r. 650–683), his daughter wished to demolish a pair of gate houses to make way for her own construction. The Emperor forbade her to do so, giving as his reason that they had been built by the great Yü-wen K'ai and had some remarkable features in their construction.

But it was not until long after the T'ang had succeeded the Sui and improved communications with their vast and relatively stable empire that the capital city grew to its full magnificence to become, in the eighth century, the glittering cosmopolis of eastern Asia and by far the world's greatest city. The Sui design of the city and the vast work of construction they undertook were acts of faith, expressing the confidence of the founder and his advisors that their dynasty would have a wider sway and a longer life than the regimes that preceded them. About the former, at least, their faith proved justified, for the T'ang made this city their capital and from it dominated China and all of eastern Asia for nearly three hundred years. The Sui founder and his planners would also have been pleased with the judgment of a noted authority who surveyed the whole history of Chinese capital planning and judged their plan to be the most usefully innovative and functional in a millennial tradition.

There were problems of appalling difficulty that had to be attacked with bold, sweeping, and effective measures if the new dynasty was to have a chance to survive and a chance to reunify the empire. First there was the structural reform of the central government and staffing the new offices with experienced and loyal men. Second there was the more complex problem of the drastic reform of local government throughout all the diverse regions of the empire and the devising of means to recruit new men of demonstrable competence to fill the offices in the new structure.

When the Sui founder usurped the power of the Northern Chou, he inherited a central government in which official titles and the names of government bureaus had been deliberately archaized (as part of the Chou's own planning for ultimately reuniting China) on the model of the ancient and venerated ritual canon, the *Chou-li*. But behind this façade of archaic nomenclature, real power was held by members of an oligarchy of northwestern military aristocrats, mostly of Turko-Mongol or mixed descent. The Northern Chou ruling house itself and 65 percent of its high officials were of non-Chinese descent. The Sui founder had grown up within this system, and his wife and intimate advisors came from this group. Yet he aspired to be sovereign emperor of all China, and if he was to succeed he needed to broaden the base of his support, reorganize the central government, and fill its high offices with men who were familiar with and could speak for the diverse groups and regions of the new empire. A measure of Sui success in this effort is that, for the whole of the Sui period, the proportion of Chinese to non-Chinese in high office was exactly the reverse of that of the Northern Chou. Further, if one excludes imperial family members, other geographical regions contributed more high officials than did the northwest. But these ultimate attainments were the results of years of far-reaching reforms, enacted and carried through with assiduity and political acumen.

In the second moon of the first year of his reign, Wen-ti abolished the Northern Chou official nomenclature and proclaimed his intention of following the precedents, in all such matters, of the last great Chinese empire, the Han, and its "legitimate" if short-lived successor dynasty, the Ts'ao-Wei (220–265). Though in fact he borrowed much from the highly Sinicized governments of sixth-century North China, reference to Han and Wei precedents was one among many signals that the Sui had ambitions to become something greater and more enduring than a regional successor state.

The central government, as it emerged during the early years of the dynasty, had many offices with Han Dynasty names, but the structure and the distribution of functions were new in many re-

spects, and in broad outline they prefigure the central government of
the T'ang. In imitation of the Han, the three top posts in the imperial
service were the Three Preceptors (*San Shih*) and the Three Dukes
(*San Kung*) who were supposed to be—as they were in the idealized
structure of the ancient Chou—supreme advisors of the emperor. In
fact, these were not functional offices, and they often went unfilled
for long periods; at other times the lofty title and generous stipend of
one or another of them would be granted to someone the emperor
wanted removed from actual power; occasionally they were conferred on imperial princes. The greatest concentration of real power
was at the next level, which encompassed the Three Principal Departments (*San-sheng*)—the Department of State Affairs (*Shang-shu
sheng*), the Imperial Chancellery (*Men-hsia sheng*), and the Imperial
Secretariat (*Nei-shih sheng*). By far the most important was the first of
these, the *San-sheng*, for under its jurisdiction were the six functional
ministries; the division of function was allegedly divided according
to a similar division in the old *Rituals of Chou*, but no archaic nomenclature obscured the Sui names for the ministries: Civil Office (*Li-pu*),
Finance (*Min-pu*, later *Hu-pu*), Rites (*Li-pu*), Army (*Ping-pu*), Punishments (*Hsing-pu*), and Public Works (*Kung-pu*). Outside the structure
of the three principal departments and the six ministries, the Sui established other offices: the Censorate (*Yü-shih t'ai*) whose members
were to remonstate with the ruler and supervise the corps of officials
at all levels; the Inspectorate General of Water Works (*Tu-shui t'ai*,
later *Tu-shui chien*); the Nine Courts (*Chiu-ssu*), among which were the
Court of Imperial Sacrifices, the Court of Imperial Banquets, the
Court of the Imperial Family, and so forth. Further, they set up a supervisory office for the State University (*Kuo-tzu ssu*, later *Kuo-tzu
chien*) and inspectorates-general for imperial works and for imperial
ateliers. All the principal officers of these bureaus had their titles and
their set number of subordinates at all levels. The regulations specified the official rank (*p'in*) which the incumbents of all these offices
were required to have, and salaries were apportioned according to
rank. There were nine ranks, each divided into an upper and a lower
grade, and salaries for capital officials ranged from nine hundred
bushels of grain *per annum* for the upper first rank down to fifty
bushels for the lower eighth. (Ninth-rank officials were not used in
capital service.)

This was an impressive and sophisticated bureaucratic structure,
but one office that had been the summit and pivot of the Han governmental apparatus was missing: the office of Chancellor (*Ch'eng-*

hsiang). (This was the office Yang Chien held under the Northern
Chou just prior to his usurpation of the throne.) Yang Chien chose
not to establish this exalted office and, as we shall see, dealt personally with the ranking officials of the three principal departments. He
thus served as his own chancellor, and while he deprived himself of
an all-powerful chief of government, he protected himself against a
potential usurper who might use that office as a springboard to supreme power. Officialdom, for its part, lost, by this arrangement, a
supreme arbiter and spokesman for bureaucratic interests as a
whole. The second emperor continued this practice and, if anything,
gathered even more power into his own hands than his father.

A symmetrical table of organization, with the names of offices
suitably redolent of Han and earlier traditions, and with much of it
familiar from the practices of the recently defunct Northern Ch'i,
was relatively easy to construct. The real problem lay in winning
over a new Sui Dynasty élite, some of whose members would share
in the major tasks facing the new dynasty and others who might be
recruited to fill, loyally and efficiently, the posts in the new official
hierarchy. In recruiting a new élite, the new regime had to take account of a great variety of factors. Regional interests and antipathies
were particularly strong after a long period of partition and war; and
these antipathies, as we have seen, expressed themselves in divergent and often discordant mores, habits, and life styles; to put it another way, it was difficult to get people who were long-accustomed
to referring to each other as "barbarians" to share power and authority in a single officialdom. Great entrenched families guarded
their perquisites with jealous pride, and they often both represented
their own interests and served as spokesmen for their regions. Further, the military had long held a disproportionate share of official
power in north and south alike; the question was how to reduce and
reorganize the military and how, simultaneously, to return civil
functions to a civil officialdom responsible to the capital. And underlying all these conflicting interests was the cleavage between the
Chinese and those of steppe ancestry. Admittedly this had been
ameliorated by long practice of intermarriage and by the Sinicization
of institutions, but it was still a latent tension that could erupt into
active hostility. Finally—and this was particularly true in the early
Sui—there was the question of old loyalties versus new. Men like Li
Te-lin had served the Northern Ch'i until its conquest by the Northern Chou; others had residual loyalties to the Chou and reservations

about the Sui which had usurped its power. After 589, southern loyalties had to be considered when an office was to be filled, particularly when that office carried with it local or regional authority. The question "How loyal is the candidate to the Sui?" was of obsessive concern to Wen-ti, and it remained a crucial question even when, with the passage of time, repeated successes in the military, civil, and cultural spheres had gained for the Sui the appearance of stability.

The core group that helped the Sui founder seize power or that rallied early to him took the leading part in the design of Sui policies and institutions and were the active agents for the recruitment of a broader governing élite. This group was made up of ranking officials of the three departments (including the close advisors discussed in Chapter Three); all were eligible to participate in imperial audiences and in the less formal meetings devoted to major affairs of state. If one eliminates temporary carry-overs from the Northern Chou and those who took office briefly in the turmoil at the end of the Sui, there remain eighteen men in this group. It will help us to understand Sui policy making if we consider briefly the make-up of the core group.

Of the eighteen, five were princes of the blood. Of those who had held office under a previous dynasty, eleven had been—like the founder himself—officials of the Northern Chou. The fathers of fourteen of them had served under the Northern Wei or one of its successor states, a very high proportion under the Northern Chou; the average level of their fathers' offices had been well below their sons'. Only one was a southerner, and he was appointed in 600 or 601, shortly after his younger sister became Crown Princess. As for geographic origins, fifteen came from a relatively narrow west-east band of territory running from T'ien-shui (in modern Kansu) in the west through the capital region and terminating at Loyang in the east. Five of the group came from Wen-ti's birthplace near the center of this west-east band. A total of eight out of the eighteen were related by blood or marriage to the ruling house.

In culture most of these men, like their master, were Chinese in name, but some came from families that had long intermarried with Turko-Mongol aristocratic clans and, in general, they were typical northerners of their time: tough, ruthless men of action, skilled in horsemanship and archery, resourceful military leaders, experienced in the politics of their time. As we have had occasion to note in Chapter Two, their Confucian learning was rudimentary and their knowledge of Chinese literature and philosophy thin; the overwhelming majority were Buddhists. Li Te-lin—a full-fledged literatus from the eastern plain, with a rich knowledge of Chinese learning and historical precedent—was isolated in their midst. The long dominance of steppe people in the north was reflected in their personal culture even though those from families with Chinese names outnumbered those with non-Chinese surnames by a ratio of eight to one. This was in contrast to the comparable Northern Chou power group in which non-Chinese families predominated in a ratio of two to one.

Given this core group, how were the rest of the central government officials selected? From the beginning of his reign Wen-ti had been determined on the centralization of power, and this is reflected in the machinery he set up. For appointment to offices of the fifth rank or above, two of the three highest organs of government, the Imperial Chancellery and the Imperial Secretariat, would investigate and send up a report to the Emperor who, if he approved, would send down an order making the appointment. Persons selected in this manner staffed the whole upper echelon of government: the three departments, the six ministries, the Censorate, the nine courts and so forth; lesser but still influential officials in these various bureaus were chosen by the Board of Civil Office. This ministry was the principal mechanism for the selection and appointment of officials of the sixth rank and below, and its president was always a man of great influence, and not simply during his own incumbency; his appointees, as they moved up in rank, determined the future character of the bureaucracy. In the early years Su Wei held the presidency among his many offices, but from 599 to 610 the president was Niu Hung—a man of impressive appearance, with a formidable beard, an equable disposition, and a serious speech defect. He was a northwestern aristocrat, but unlike others of his background, he was devoted to learning and deeply versed in many fields: ritual, law, music, history, and poetry, among others. During his tenure as president of the Board of Civil Office under both Wen-ti and his successor, Niu Hung won a reputation for probity and for the discernment he exercised in choosing candidates. His criteria of judgment tended to be more Confucian than Legalist—that is, he considered moral qualities more important than technical or literary competence. He and his devoted associates obviously did much to maintain general confidence in the Sui's Board of Civil Office.

Wen-ti was almost obsessively concerned with official appointment and with performance. In 588, for example, he is said to have personally examined all the high officials, and when he held a levée of court officials he would order them to give impromptu accounts of their own meritorious actions. His policy was to screen candidates carefully, appoint those who appeared most deserving and competent, monitor their performance in office (annually at first, later every three years), demote or punish severely all doubtful performances, and reward lavishly those who had done exceptionally well. The *Sui History* says that "although he was naturally parsimonious, there was no stinginess in giving rewards to the meritorious officials." For example, in 595 the governors of all the prefectures were examined at court, and one was chosen the best in the empire; he was given a reward of three hundred pieces of cloth and his merit proclaimed in an edict to the empire. After the conquest of Ch'en, the governors of the whole empire were again rated, and one Yang Ta was chosen as the top performer and rewarded with a double promotion to the presidency of a ministry. Here one feels a twinge of skepticism; Yang Ta was a Yang of Hua-yin, the Emperor's native place!

Given the Emperor's tireless concern with the character of his bureaucracy and the apparently vigorous operation of the Board of Civil Office, what profile can we draw of the bureaucracy? The clearest view we have is of the top central government officialdom, that is the presidents of the six ministries. Here we find that of the forty-six presidents who served during the Sui, 65.2 percent were from Chinese families and 23.2 percent from non-Chinese families (balance uncertain). Forty-two of these men were sons or grandsons of officials who had served the Northern Wei (13) or the Northern Chou (29). Only three had Northern Ch'i backgrounds, and all of these were in the Ministry of Finance, which was in charge of taxation and land allotment for the empire. The highest proportion of non-Chinese was in the Ministry of Works, where 45.5 percent of the presidents were non-Chinese; this is usually explained by the strong traditions of innovation in engineering and building techniques in certain of these families. The next highest proportion was in the Ministry of War, where the military traditions of the non-Chinese peoples accounts for their strength. In the Board of Civil Office which, as we have suggested, was the most important of the ministries, only 12.5 percent of the presidents were non-Chinese. The geographic origins of the presidents are similar to those of the highest government officials; thirty of the forty-six came from the same narrow west-east band stretching from T'ien-shui to Loyang; the next highest concentration was Shansi with seven, and the places of origin of the balance were scattered across the North China Plain.

The Sui government at its two highest levels obviously was not representative of the various regions and populations of North China, much less of the south. While its composition reversed the proportion of non-Chinese to Chinese that had prevailed under the preceding dynasty, it strongly favored people and families of the same region and class as the two emperors. There is a relatively high concentration of the Yangs of Hua-yin in the upper stratum of government, but neither the first nor the second emperor gave high office to his empresses' family members—thus consciously avoiding the abuses that historically stem from this practice; since the Yangs were related by marriage to the house they forcibly replaced, they were on their guard.

Given the character of the capital bureaucracy, we must look elsewhere to find evidence of the Sui's efforts to build a more broadly based, empire-wide official élite that would be necessary in the long process of reunification. For this, we must examine the sweeping reform of local government and the new system of appointment to local office.

When the Sui came to power, it fell heir to institutions of local government evolved over the centuries by various dynasties but by now—everywhere in the land—in various stages of advanced decay, seedbeds of inefficiency, corruption, and oppression. To understand some dimensions of this institutional shambles, we must look for a moment at its root causes. According to some scholars, one of these causes appears as early as 106 B.C. In that year the Han Dynasty modified the highly centralized system of local government it had inherited from the Ch'in. That system had provided for two levels of local government, the commanderies (*chün*) and under them the counties (*hsien*). The chief officers at both these levels were appointed by and responsible to the capital. The Han now introduced another level, the office of *Tz'u-shih*, often translated "Inspector." The inspectors were charged with the supervision of a group of commanderies. This institution itself might not have led to serious difficulties if the governments of the Later Han (A.D. 25–220) and its successor states had retained a strong central government. But weakness at the center led, as it did many times in China's imperial history, to the devolution of power upon regions and localities. The assertion of power at the local level then led to the establishment of permanent seats of the *Tz'u-shih* known as *chou*, usually translated "prefectures." Thus a large formal administrative unit was interposed between the imperial capital and the old commanderies, each comprising several counties.

Under the conditions of almost incessant war that prevailed from the third century onward, the *Tz'u-shih* of a prefecture (now functionally a governor rather than an inspector) acquired military as well as civil responsibilities in the area of their jurisdiction, and in addition to the civil staff for the prefecture, an increasingly elaborate *fu* or headquarters staff evolved. At the beginning of the Sui, the governor of a prefecture of the highest grade was entitled to a total of 323 officials, both civil and military. In the course of the evolution of the system of dual staffs, the power of civil officials was gradually taken over by the military. The main reason for this was that, in this period of constant warfare, the governor's principal interests were in maintaining order within his prefecture and in keeping his troops in battle-readiness; consequently his military and logistic staff became more and more important, and the power of the civil officials gradually atrophied. The governors assumed wide *de facto* powers of appointment. For example, they would appoint officials of the commanderies and counties under them with a *pro forma* request to the court for approval. Many of their military staff held concurrent posts as prefects or magistrates, and the bulk of the governors' staffs were friends, clients, or relatives. In sum, the prefectures had become virtual satrapies, and governors retained most of the tax funds to be used for their own benefit, and used their troops at their own discretion—or whim. Thus the Sui inherited an expensive, corrupt, and redundant system of local government, a system that perpetuated the diffusion of military and civil power and thus fostered endemic weakness in the central government.

A further abuse had developed along parallel lines in the north and the south. This was the continuous creation, without regard for local needs or administrative rationality, of local government units to which officials were appointed with stipends, lands, and perquisites, most of which had to be exacted from the local population. In 556 the Northern Ch'i emperor, trying to institute some reforms, described how the proliferation of local units had occurred. He noted that powerful families and great clans had abused their positions in the central government to set up new prefectures and commanderies for their own benefit; imperial princesses and palace women would take bribes to ensure the establishment of a prefecture or a commandery. As a result, the edict says that a hamlet of a hundred houses was proclaimed a prefecture and the people of three households would idly boast of being a commandery!

In the south a different sequence of events had produced similar abuses. The Chinese who fled from North China to the semicolonial areas of the Yangtze Valley from A.D. 312 onward transplanted—as immigrants will—many of the place names from their original homeland. An example was the prefecture of Shuo-chou, with five commanderies subordinate to it, transplanted in the south in an area of less than eight hundred square miles! It has been calculated that the number of prefectures in the whole Chinese culture area had increased twenty-two-fold from the end of the Han to the beginning of the Sui, while the number of commanderies had increased six-and-a-half-fold! Under the southern dynasties even more than in the north, this fragmentation brought with it military decentralization to the extent that emperors often could not make a move without first getting assurances of support from the military governor of this or that key prefecture.

These chaotic conditions were enough to daunt all but the most intrepid would-be reunifier, but the Sui leadership was both decisive and courageous. In 583 Yang Shang-hsi, in a cogent memorial, analyzed the administrative chaos which the new emperor had inherited in assuming power over North China: the multiplication of local government units, the proliferation of officials, the staggering expense of their salaries, the pitiful tax yield of these units, the oppression of the peasants, and so forth. Yang remarked that the number of officials appointed in relation to population was like using nine shepherds for ten sheep. Wen-ti was pleased and impressed with this analysis and promptly issued an initial reform decree. In this he ordered the abolition of all commanderies—more than five hundred—in the area he then controlled. He thus took an essential step toward the restoration of a two-level system of local administration that had had its origins with the founding dynasty of the Chinese empire, the Ch'in. After his conquest of the south in 589, the same reform was decreed in that area. In the reign of his successor, the number of prefectures (now called *chün*) in the reunited empire was reduced to 190. The counties subordinate to them numbered 1,255, or an average of more than six counties per prefecture. The territorial jurisdiction of the average prefecture and of the average county was thus much extended, with resulting reduction of administrative expenses and greatly increased net tax yield.

The initial reform decree of 583 had also ordered the appointment of officials of suitable rank by the Board of Civil Office in the capital. Prefectures and counties were ranked into nine grades in each category, and the grading was according to the population of the local unit. Each grade had a fixed salary in bushels of grain to be paid to the appointed officials twice yearly; the officials also had carefully defined rights to the income from official fields for public and private expenses connected with their offices. Finally, the first reform decree consolidated under the governor the long-separate civil and military staffs at the top level of local government; the military *fu* was eliminated, and all its functionaries were now integrated into the governor's civil administrative staff. The names of the staff offices retained their military nomenclature, but their functions under Sui regulations were purely civil. A second reform decree of 595 ordered the abolition of a host of nominally civil local offices which had anachronistically continued while their functions were being performed by officials in the newly instituted governor's staff system.

These were the steps by which the Sui sought to rationalize the system of local administration, reduce the number of officials, and subject them to the strict control of the central government. Yet much of this reform would have proved abortive if the Sui had not at the same time centralized the military power, so long diffused among the governors. The measures taken to this end are discussed below in the section on military reform.

The reform of local government structures was in itself a major achievement, but its ultimate success depended—as did the success of reunification itself—upon the people appointed to the new offices; and the quality of the appointees depended on the criteria and methods of official appointment. Here again the Sui fell heir to an antiquated and corrupt system. The system of provincial and sub-provincial Recommending Legates (*Chung-cheng*) had its origin in the chaos of the end of the Han, when both the educational system and the system of official selection had broken down. These legates were then appointed—usually while holding other offices—to recommend and rank candidates from a given area for posts in the imperial bureaucracy on the basis of their local reputation, family status, intelligence, moral worth, and social conformity. Within a few years, the posts of Recommending Legates were virtually monopolized by the great aristocratic clans. The basis of their recommendations tended to become first of all the genealogy (as validated by official genealogical records) and power connections of the candidates, and second the personal likes and dislikes of the legates. Both south and north were saddled with this system, though in the north it did not come into full and general use until the Sinicization measures of the

Northern Wei in the late fifth century. There survives an interchange between two sixth-century officials in the north, both wanting to be named Grand Recommending Legate of the prefecture of Yen. Contestant A, boasting of his lineage, says, "My family for successive generations have been governors (*Tz'u-shih*) of this prefecture. Yours for generations have been old servitors of my house." Contestant B replies, "From the time your ancestor Pi Kuei was executed [in the third century A.D.] your family has been inactive and has produced no notable personalities. In recent times, the governorship of this prefecture has been awarded on the basis of military feats. Then and now, what have you to boast about? How can you match our Han Dynasty Metropolitan Prefect, our Chin Dynasty Grand Preceptor of the Heir Apparent, our moral and scholarly achievements spreading excellence for one hundred generations." This interchange illustrates the overriding influence of genealogy on appointments that derived, in part, from the operation of the system of Recommending Legates.

The Sui abolished this system in 583, eliminating the positions of the various Recommending Legates and, we may assume, the staff positions that had grown up under them. They substituted for it central appointment by the Board of Civil Office, with the added safeguards of annual reviews by a special bureau of the Board of Civil Office (or, at his pleasure, by the emperor himself). The *T'ung-tien* (an eighth-century encyclopedia) sums up the changes with, perhaps, some degree of hyperbole: "From this time on, all within the four seas was under a single rule; thereby . . . the prefectures and counties did not again have corrupt officials." As usual, our sources take action decreed for action completed and give us few details on implementation. Six years after the reform decree, Li Te-lin, arguing against a proposal to create a new echelon of local officials, says: "Furthermore, at present, people chosen at large by the Board of Civil Office cannot staff more than a few hundred counties out of the whole empire. If, out of a population of six or seven million families it is only possible to select a few hundred county magistrates—and still without being able to say much about their abilities—then . . . etc." This gives us a glimpse of recruitment difficulties which probably took a decade or more to overcome.

The return to a two-level system of local administration could become a working reality only when two further steps were taken: centralization of the power of appointment and the recruitment of new men to fill the offices. The first step was taken, as we have noted, at the very beginning, and the Sui emperor summarily abolished the

Recommending Legates, who for centuries had monopolized the recruitment of officials, and he also abolished the rights of appointment that had been gradually taken over by governors and other
local officials. All such powers he vested in the Board of Civil Office in the capital. Hereditary privilege had been for so long a part of
the social landscape that the Sui had need for countervailing principles and procedures. They were more fortunate than Charlemagne
in finding these ready to hand in the legacy of the Han Empire. Most
of the new measures and the arguments in support of them have
their prototypes in the Han bureaucratic system and in its ideology
which, for lack of a better term, we call imperial Confucianism. A
basic principle of that ideology had been restated only a generation
before by the famous and revered statesman Su Ch'o, advisor to the
Sui's predecessors. In the midst of a savage attack on existing practices, he asserted that "the selection and promotion of officials
should not be constrained by hereditary privilege but should consist
simply in getting good men." And it was only by proceeding on this
principle that the Sui could get a pool of talent relatively free of old
ties, malleable to new standards, and able to adjust to the institutions
of centralized government.

For this purpose, the Sui devised a system of selection that had
been prefigured in the Han but that became the precursor of the
elaborate civil service examination system used for the recruitment
of officials until 1905. Details on the Sui system are unfortunately
few, but its broad outlines can be sketched. Early in 582 the Emperor
ordered the nomination of "the worthy and the good" for possible
appointment to office, and late in the same year he made generous
gifts to all those students in the state-supported school in the capital
who had mastered a Confucian classic. In 587 he ordered that all the
prefectures in the empire should send three worthy men annually to
the capital for possible appointment (merchants and artisans were
disqualified). When they arrived at the capital, they were examined
in interviews by high officials who were to put them into two categories according to their personal qualities. Some were immediately
appointed; others after a period of further training or probation, we
do not know which, were ranked and given appointments by the
Board of Civil Office. If this procedure was regularly followed it
would mean that, after the full reunification of the empire, nine hundred candidates would arrive in the capital each year. The personal
qualities and educational backgrounds of these candidates undoubtedly varied greatly, and this was probably what led the Sui to insti-

tute written examinations to test their competence. The first mention of one of these is an order of 595 for the examination of candidates for the *Hsiu-ts'ai* degree. Details are missing, but from one biography we get a glimpse of how the examination was conducted. "Tu Cheng-hsüan was nominated for the *Hsiu-ts'ai* degree. The president of the Board of Civil Office administered the examination, and the questions concerned the modes of action suited to certain situations (*fang-lüeh*). Cheng-hsüan's responses were quick as an echo. He no sooner put his brush to paper than his essay was complete." Later in the dynasty two other examinations were established: the *ming-ching*, which tested a candidate's mastery of a single classic, and the *chin-shih*, which tested for general literary ability. Other examinations were decreed at irregular intervals and conducted in the prefectural capitals. Initial appointments based on examination results may have been made, as they were later in T'ang times, on a descending scale within the lowest two of the nine government ranks. We do not know what proportion of new Sui officials were appointed from the prefectural nominees and what from those who took one or another examination. There is much we do not know about the Sui system, but we do know that both emperors took a strong personal interest in its functioning, tried to appoint men of discernment and probity to the Board of Civil Office, and repeatedly insisted in imperial edicts on the strict application of the merit standard to appointments and promotions. This then, in broad outline, was the way the Sui recruited its new officials. To see to it that officials, once appointed, carried out their duties with honesty and effectiveness, many regulatory measures were taken. We might describe a few of these.

One was the "rule of avoidance," which meant that prefectural and county officials could not serve in their place of origin, where the pressures from kinsmen and friends might tempt them to favoritism. Subordinate officials were forbidden to occupy any post in local government which they had previously held, lest they become enmeshed in a network of local interests. For the same reasons, the terms of service were deliberately kept short: three years (later four) for principal local officials, four years for subordinate officials. A decree of 594 prescribed that officials assigned to a local post could not have their parents or sons fifteen and over accompany them. This was of course to prevent such relatives from becoming "conductors" of undue influence from the wealthy and powerful in the area.

Wen-ti revived yet another Han institution designed as a regular check on local conditions and the performance of local officials. He ordered that each prefecture should send a delegate to the capital for the grand New Year audience. These were the *Ch'ao-chi shih,* literally "delegates to the court assembly." The Emperor would receive reports on conditions in the various parts of the country, and he would comment, praise, or condemn an official in front of the entire company. Here is one of his speeches, this in praise of a county magistrate whose performance had won approval:

> Fang Kung-i's purpose is at one with the dynasty's, and he loves and nurtures my people. These are things which High Heaven and the spirits of our ancestral temple cherish. If We disregard this and fail to reward him, High Heaven and the spirits of our ancestral temple will most certainly punish me. All of you should take him as your model.

And the Emperor immediately promoted him to be governor of a prefecture. These annual assemblies were also used to impress upon the local officials the power and grandeur of the dynasty. We know few details of the functioning of the delegate system in the Sui, but in the T'ang it was continued; the governors usually attended and brought with them the quota of candidates to be presented for examination and also tribute for the Emperor which they presented at the New Year's audience. (In T'ang times reports, rewards, etc. were taken care of a month in advance by the Ministry of Finance.) It was sufficiently regular and important enough so that the T'ang built a special lodge in the capital for the convenience of the annual delegations.

This annual assembly was only the most formal of the means the Emperor used for checking on the local officials. He himself was often on the move and personally questioned local residents about the performance of their officials and would promote or demote the incumbent in the light of what he found out. On one of his visits to his native place to pay homage at its shrine, the local elders showed that they had not understood the meaning of an imperial edict, which it was the duty of local officials to make clear. "The Emperor, in a fury, cashiered the magistrate and left." To see that field observation was carried on regularly he appointed itinerant inspectors who were to serve as "the emperor's eyes and ears in distant places." On the basis of their reports, those who served in "distant places" would be rewarded or punished.

In addition to such inspectors, there were the regular censors who sometimes traveled and returned to the capital with a bill of impeachment against one or more officials. For the most part, the censors' duty was to keep the high officials in the capital under surveillance. The sources agree that Sui censors "made their investigations and recommendations without fear or favor, their bills of impeachment without bending or flinching." Once when the Emperor was on holiday, he left Su Wei in charge at the capital. He returned to find a censor's indictment of Su for laziness and neglect of duty. The Emperor was angry and sternly rebuked Su, despite his position as a member of the imperial inner circle. At one New Year's reception there were irregularities in the dress and arms of the military officials present. The Emperor noticed these and also noted that the censor present had failed in his duty to report these deficiencies. "You are a censor," he said to this unfortunate man. "What is this laxity, this permissiveness?" and ordered him executed along with another official who had intervened on his behalf. So constant and remorseless were the censors' activities that at certain festive banquets, when some degree of relaxation was desired, the Emperor would have to order them to suspend their impeachments for the occasion.

The elaborate system of surveillance just described was no doubt seen as necessary when the new dynasty was breaking with many traditions and appointing newly selected, often inexperienced, officials to posts where there were many temptations to accommodate to local interests rather than to act at all times as the Emperor's surrogates. (It was also consistent with the coercive Legalist strain in Sui policy making.) The system of recruitment, examination, appointment, and surveillance was far from perfect in its functioning, but it represents a bold and thoroughly ruthless effort to neutralize entrenched local privilege and to discipline local officials to be responsible only to the central government. Like many other Sui variations on earlier policy themes, these features of the centralized system reappeared in the institutions of later dynasties.

Given the reformed structure of recruitment and appointment and the use of an elaborate system of surveillance, how did an average official carry out his duties at the local level? Some, we are told, were harsh and followed all laws and ordinances to the letter, imposing harsh sentences on their own kinsmen and neighbors, on rich and poor alike, according to their crimes. These officials governed by coercion and are so categorized in the *Sui History*. Another group— and one favored by the Confucian chroniclers—governed by educa-

tion, example, and persuasion, the classic Confucian alternatives to
the use of law and repression. Let us look at one such official and see
how he went about his tasks. As we do so, let us remember the *Sui
History*'s tendency to stereotype and to indulge in moral didacticism.

Liang Yen-kuang had a background typical of Sui local officials.
His father and grandfather had served earlier dynasties as local officials in the area of modern Kansu. As a child he was of outstanding
character, and his father was led to remark, "This boy has unusual
qualities; he is bound to bring prosperity to our line." About 560 he
attended the Northern Wei élite school known as the T'ai Hsüeh,
where he quickly mastered the classics and the histories. He was,
typically, taken from the school and given his first post at the age of
seventeen. He served the Northern Chou in various offices and rose
to the rank of prefectural governor.

When the Sui seized power, Liang was made governor of Ch'i-
chou, a prefecture not far west of the capital and not far from his ancestral seat. Since he knew the population well, he was able to govern effectively and without expending much effort; thus he became
known as one of the greatest governors in the empire. His next post
was far different; it was to be governor of Hsiang-chou, the area in
the eastern plain that included the old Northern Ch'i capital of Yeh,
where the Sui had decisively defeated its eastern opponents and
where the people were traditionally hostile to anyone from the
northwest. There he tried his accustomed mild measures, and the
local population proved incorrigible. He wrote a song to the effect
that they could not be reformed. The Emperor heard of this, dismissed and punished him, and little over a year later offered him another, less demanding governorship. Whereupon he addressed his
sovereign: "Your servant formerly deserved punishment for his performance in Hsiang-chou. There the common people jeered at him
as a hatted sugar lump. Your servant resigned on his own initiative,
without the expectation of ever resuming official status. . . . I beg
to return to the governorship of Hsiang-chou, to change my strategy
and alter my tactics [literally my strings and my tune], by which I
may hope to reform their evil ways and thus adequately respond to
your majesty's bounty."

This speech persuaded the Emperor, and Liang once more
moved east to Hsiang-chou. "When the local strongmen heard that
Yen-kuang was returning at his own request, there were none who
did not guffaw with contempt. No sooner had Yen-kuang got out of
his carriage than he began exposing villainy. It was as if he had su-

pernatural discernment. Whereupon, among the scoundrelly riff-raff, there were none who didn't go into hiding, and the whole area was astonished."

The *Sui History*—in an excursus into Confucian sociology—explains that when, a few years before, the Ch'i had been conquered and annexed by the Chou, the officials and the educated people had for the most part moved west to the Chou capital, leaving only tricksters, merchants, and déclassé families to move into the city. Whereupon, our chroniclers tell us, human sentiments became depraved, and evil customs proliferated, so that the judicial officials were overwhelmed with work.

Yen-kuang was determined to remedy these ills. By offering suitable emoluments he attracted some great Confucian scholars and set up a school in every hamlet, for, he reasoned, "without the writings that contain sagely wisdom one would never succeed in bringing about moral reform." Usually in the last month of each season he would summon the students to an assembly and would personally take part in examining them. He gave recognition to the outstanding achievers in front of all the rest. When he recommended a candidate for the *Hsiu-ts'ai* examination, he gave a public farewell feast in the suburban temple to Heaven and helped with the expenses of his journey to the capital. In consequence, the atmosphere of the prefecture completely changed; officialdom and people were happy and contented, and there were no more litigants.

CHAPTER 5

The Restoration of Cultural Hegemony

Throughout the history of imperial China it was axiomatic that successful political domination could survive only if sustained by universal cultural norms that all would obey and rejoice in. To be a true Lord of Men and Son of Heaven, a monarch was obliged to give to his people universal weights and measures, coinage acceptable everywhere, a standard orthography for written communication, standard-sized modules for all construction, as well as a standard musical scale, a calendar that specified the seasons and days appropriate for all human activity, and many other norms for the practical business of life. Beyond all this and in his role of Son of Heaven, it was his solemn obligation to assure harmony in the cosmos as a whole and to provide his people with the moral norms, the values, and ritual standards by which they could live their lives in harmony with nature and with each other. In fulfilling this obligation he was thus supreme ritualist and moral law-giver, guardian and propagator of all the best that had come down from the golden age of the ancient sages. But it was beyond possibility that a human emperor, who had come to his exalted position by military prowess or by inheritance, could unaided fulfill all these functions and thus gain such total cultural hegemony, without which his political dominion would collapse. Just as there were technicians to assist him in laying down practical standards, there were men of learning to assist in the formulation of policy, and particularly of moral, legal, and ritual norms. At the beginning of the Sui these men were few and important; they were, for the most part, members of families that had preserved throughout the centuries of disorder and disunion one or more strands of Han imperial traditions, mastery of one or more Confucian classic containing the wisdom of the ancient sages.

This heritage had been, in its origins, the orthodoxy of the great Han Empire; it had been a strange and rather forced amalgam of elements from many schools of thought from the pre-imperial period. Its central figure was Confucius—not the simple teacher he had been in life, but the apotheosized "sage of ten thousand generations." It incorporated the many symbol systems by which the early schools had sought to analyze time, space, and phenomena into some sort of order. It contained a great residue of ancient cults and practices; some—the worship of tutelary divinities, for example—went back to the dawn of time. Its "classics" were heterogeneous as to age and provenance, but they became the classics by Han fiat and thus the basis of education and the ultimate source of ethical standards and behavioral norms. This patchwork of beliefs and practices had not survived intact during the centuries of disunion, and a Confucian historian of the Sui describes it thus: "Since New Year's days ceased being the same [i.e., there was no central authority to promulgate a universal almanac/calendar], nearly three hundred years have passed; the interpretations of the various masters have become confused and entangled, and there is no way of choosing what is correct." Thus, the scholarly specialists of the beginning of the Sui were obliged not only to draw on parts of this heritage for specific purposes but also to restore it to some semblance of its ancient symmetry and completeness.

In examining the process of restoring cultural hegemony, it is the work of such specialists, as reflected in imperial edicts and regulations, that we shall first consider. Several questions must be dealt with by way of prelude. In ideal circumstances, a historian would have available full accounts of the discussions that led to formal acts of government, detailed records of how the enactments were made known to people in all parts of the huge empire, and, finally, reliable data on how people in different communities and at different social levels reacted to them. In the Sui case, we have the texts of various imperial pronunciamentos and believable accounts of ritual performances that were meant to dramatize a particular part of the cosmic or moral role of the emperor. But we have virtually no direct evidence of any kind on how these things were received by the capital population and by the different communities and social classes in the rest of the empire. Rituals were performed in and around the capital city, where the spectators were probably limited to the imperial family and officialdom. Edicts and pronouncements were sometimes read out from the top of the great south gate of the palace city to what was probably a carefully screened audience on the paved open space below. We know from the surviving T'ang ritual code that imperial communications were often ordered "distributed to all the prefectures," and that they would be carried by official couriers along the post roads to the prefectures of the empire, there to be read out by the prefect, according to prescribed procedures, in the courtyard of his official headquarters to a representative audience of local residents. Since the Sui and T'ang codes are known to be very similar, we may infer that some of these procedures were used by the Sui in communicating imperial pronouncements to the people. We know that local officials were always under orders to exhort the local populace to virtue and to use various devices as incentives for approved behavior; these will be discussed below. But we do not know how various segments of the population reacted.

The first task of the Sui's scholarly specialists was to design and carry through the ritual steps that would legitimate a dynasty that had come to power by a coup d'état, steps that would cloak in rituals of ancient sanctity the sordid sequence of intrigue, betrayal, and murder that had in fact brought the house of Yang to rule over "all under Heaven." Since many successions in the past had come about in similar ways and had required just such ritual cover and moral justification, there was a rich store for the scholars to draw upon. The literatus Li Te-lin, whose character and role were described in Chapter Three, was the principal designer of the Sui procedures, and he drafted most of the needed documents. The steps were many and complex, the documents many and prolix. A summary must here serve to suggest the whole elaborate process.

The first step was, of course, the forging of a deathbed edict from the Northern Chou ex-emperor (who, we might recall, was Yang Chien's son-in-law—and who still held *de facto* power) ordering Yang Chien to take command of the armed forces and assist the child emperor in carrying on the government. This edict was full of historical resonance: it referred to the child emperor as "young and weak," terms that the educated knew had been used to refer to King Ch'eng of the Chou (r. 1115–1079 B.C.) in his youth when the revered culture hero, the Duke of Chou, selflessly served as regent. To "assist" the child emperor was also not neutrally descriptive, for it had been used of the notorious usurper Wang Mang (r. A.D. 9–23) in the years before his formal usurpation of Han power.

There ensued a long series of edicts and rituals that were intended to simulate the mode of succession allegedly followed by the sage rulers of misty antiquity, a procedure termed *shan-jang*, or abdication by one ruler and his yielding the throne not to a relative but to someone who had been searched out and found worthy to rule. This had been expounded by the ancient philosopher Mencius (who may indeed have invented it), and the steps were greatly elaborated first by Wang Mang and then by the Ts'ao family, which dethroned and replaced the last Han emperor. They had been used again and again in the Period of Disunion as one short-lived dynasty was replaced by another. In the course of the Sui reenactment, Yang Chien was first made prime minister, and in this and all subsequent edicts of the child emperor (written by Li Te-lin), Yang Chien is praised for his virtue, for the consonance of all his acts with earthly and cosmic forces, for his ability to bring harmony to the realms of heaven and earth and life to the myriad creatures. A later edict allows him to ennoble his ancestors, still another raises his rank from Duke to Prince and exempts him from certain formalities when he appears in court; he is forewarned to prepare to receive the "nine gifts," symbolic prelude to assuming the throne.

On January 24, 581, an elaborate edict was issued. Part One—a kind of prologue—heaps hyperbolic praise on Yang Chien and ends with these words: "Now We are about to confer upon you the powers and ceremonial obligations of kingship. May you listen reverently to this Our decree." This verbal formula is identical to the Han edict of 213, preparing the dictator Ts'ao Ts'ao to receive the nine gifts symbolic of the transfer of power. Part Two is a detailed chronological review of the meritorious deeds of Yang Chien: his loyal service to the Northern Chou house, his victorious campaigns against the forces of evil (actually, Northern Chou loyalists), his high moral qualities and marvelous virtue that have brought order out of chaos, etc. Then the child emperor is made to speak of his own inadequacy and urges Yang Chien, in archaic terms, "to leave his fief and come to the capital to carry out the great responsibilities of chief of all the ministers." Part Three of the edict describes the conferment of the nine gifts. The formula of conferment again is identical to that used by the last emperor of the Han in bestowing the gifts upon Ts'ao Ts'ao; the number of gifts—the nine perhaps symbolizing the nine primordial divisions of the Chinese world—was also the same. The gifts themselves in many cases refer back to precedents in the pre-imperial age; to explain the provenance of all would require a small volume. But, in one way or another, each is a mark of high honor and great power in the world of men:

1. Two different kinds of carriages with two teams of four black horses
2. A princely hat and a robe with a red sash
3. Musical instruments and six rows of dancers for use in ancestral rites
4. Red doors for his house
5. A covered staircase for his residence
6. A bodyguard of three hundred stalwart men
7. Two kinds of axes of authority
8. One red bow and a hundred red arrows plus ten black bows and a thousand black arrows
9. One flagon of herb-flavored millet liquor and a jade ceremonial vessel to serve it in

After a further conferment of symbolic gifts on February 24, Yang Chien, after the three required refusals, finally accepted them all.

The child emperor's edict of abdication, coming a few days later, is, by contrast, relatively simple. Li Te-lin has the child point to the signs in nature and the cosmos that favor a new order. He goes on to say that the virtue of his house is almost exhausted, that division of the empire would be undesirable. He praises Yang Chien extravagantly, saying "All twenty meritorious deeds of the sage emperors Yao and Shun do not equal his." He ends the edict: "Now I respectfully submit to Heaven's command, withdraw to a separate palace and abdicate the throne in favor of the Sui. In all this I have followed the precedents of the sage emperors T'ang and Yü, the dynasties of Han and Wei." Yang Chien formally declines three times, more messages go back and forth. Finally a noble messenger arrives to present the imperial seals and ribbons; now Yang Chien, no doubt mindful of the Han founder's receiving in 207 B.C. the seals from the last ruler of the Ch'in, accepts. The *Tzu-chih t'ung-chien* describes what followed on March 4, 581:

He accepted the patent and the seal and changed his clothing to a gauze cap and a yellow robe. He made an imperial entrance into the Lin-kuang Palace, donned the imperial robes, and held a levée similar to the New Year's audience.

Thus was the Sui inaugurated: the first emperor would be known by the name of Wen-ti. But further ceremonies legitimizing the new dynasty continued to be carried out under the ritualists' guidance for another year or more. We shall sample a few of these. The new emperor erected a platform in the south suburb and sent a messenger to make known to Heaven, by means of burnt offerings, his accession. "On the same day he informed his ancestors in the imperial ancestral hall of his accession and ordered a grand amnesty and changed the era name." "Informing the ancestors" was part of the state cults of the ancient Chou period, whereas the declaration of a grand amnesty to mark an auspicious occasion began with the first empire. The era name chosen to denote the dynasty's initial span of years (which lasted until A.D. 600) was K'ai-huang. This term may be the first era name in Chinese history to be drawn from the sacred texts of the developed religious Taoism of the sixth century. It is the name of one of the five great world-ages (*kalpas* in Buddhism) and designates the first of these, the age of creation. Thus here the Sui scholarly specialists are reaching beyond the words and symbols of imperial Confucianism into a tradition that by 581 had probably accumulated a considerable body of believers throughout the empire.

Time-honored changes in nomenclature and titles were made, but the next important ceremony occurred on March 15, when Yang Chien performed as emperor the ceremonial spring plowing of the imperial field. This ceremony was then of great antiquity, and its details had been elaborated in the ritual books of Han times. It was carried out with great pomp and circumstance, and it symbolized the Son of Heaven's role as mediator between natural forces and the fields and crops of his subjects. This solemn role, in which he was cast as first farmer of the empire, of course added a further aura of legitimacy to his new regime and to his house. On March 19 the new emperor took formal steps to deal with the defunct house of Chou. Some kind of ceremonial recognition of an overthrown house by the victors goes back at least to the years following the fall of the Shang, traditionally 1122 B.C. It is based on a profound belief in the power of intervention in the affairs of men—for good or evil—possessed by the spirits of the once-great dead.

Next, the Sui emperor granted the former ruler the title of Duke of Chieh and a substantial fief; he was given a special dispensation to continue using the banners, carriages, and clothing of the defunct dynasty, and to have its ritual and music performed at his ducal court. But, the *Chou History* tells us, the ex-emperor had all this on paper only; it was never put in effect. It records that he died, age eight, on July 10, 581, at the hands of the Sui. Perhaps the Sui monarch, with his deep Buddhist faith, did not believe in the efficacy of these ceremonial gestures for quieting the ancestral spirits of the defunct house; we do not know. But the Sui had not replaced an ancient and once-glorious house but an alien-dominated military regime that had lasted less than fifty years—this in a time of rapid, violent, and frequent transfers of power.

This sampling does not end the sequence of measures of legitimation; they go on throughout Wen-ti's reign, partly to consolidate the dynasty's legitimacy and partly to slake Wen-ti's unquenchable thirst for personal reassurance. One example must serve to illustrate this later sequence. Wang Shao was for some twenty years in charge of the Sui history office, but he served his imperial master in other roles: as soothsayer, interpreter of arcane lore, and so forth. On one occasion he argued in court that the Emperor, particularly in the eye structure of the face, had the natural contours characteristic of a Son of Heaven, and he expounded this in detail to the ministers; this gave the Emperor great pleasure and won Wang Shao a promotion. But his *chef-d'oeuvre* in this line was more elaborate. He was always sending up memorials to the effect that the signs favoring His Majesty's receipt of the heavenly mandate were very numerous. He finally collected snatches of popular songs from among the people, drew on the books of divination and the apocrypha to the classics, excerpted passages from the Buddhist scriptures, interpreted the esoteric meaning of the characters in the imperial names, and compiled the *Record of Auspicious Signs Favoring the Imperial Sui*, in thirty chapters. "The Emperor ordered that it be proclaimed throughout the empire. Wang Shao, when the representatives of the prefectures of the empire were assembled at their annual meeting, had them wash their hands, burn incense, and close their eyes while he read it to them. He inflected his voice as if he were intoning a Buddhist scripture. This went on [intermittently, one supposes] for ten days before he completed the text and ceased."

As claims of legitimacy continued to be asserted or implied by imperial actions, a variety of other measures were enacted—measures that over the centuries had been used again and again in each reassertion of cultural hegemony. Among the most important were codifications, compiled by imperial order and—when completed— promulgated throughout the empire. Of these codifications, that of the laws has familiar analogues in Western history, though the spirit and content of the law codes are sharply different. The second type of Chinese codification, that of the *Li*, is not paralleled in Western civilization. *Li* is difficult to translate, and only if pressed would I render it as "ritual norms and official protocol." It is easier and more accurate to describe what was subsumed under *Li*. The codified *Li* included detailed prescriptions for imperial performances: seasonal sacrifices, imperial visits, the coming-of-age and marriage cere- monies for imperial princes, prescriptions for imperial funerals, mourning rituals, entombment rites, and much else. All such pre- scriptions included provisions covering dress and headgear, the ap- propriate carriages, the ritual impediments, the music, the order of precedence among the participants, etc. Beyond these high solem- nities the *Li* also included what we would call rules of protocol: for example, prescriptions for the reception of envoys from tributary states (which we touched on in Chapter Four), procedures to be fol- lowed by a prefect in receiving an imperial courier bearing an impe- rial edict. These multifarious rules applied to the imperial family and to ranked officials, with variations according to rank specified to the last detail. There is an often cited axiom from an ancient ritual clas- sic: "The ritual norms (*li*) do not reach down to apply to the common people; the punishments [prescribed in the law codes] do not reach up to apply to the dignitaries of the empire." This surely applies to the codified *Li* that the Sui and its successors promulgated, and if one speaks on a somewhat metaphysical plane, then it is obvious that the Son of Heaven, his relatives, and his ranked surrogates were to behave with unvarying punctilio; thus the forces in the universe might work together without disruption by the slightest unseemly or unseasonable action on the part of any of those working for and with the Son of Heaven to ensure harmony in the cosmos and in the world of men.

The Sui, as we have seen, made great use of its ritual specialists in the early years of the dynasty, and in general the policy was to follow Han and Ch'in precedents; but codification was long delayed. The commission on ritual, headed by the redoubtable Niu Hung, was not formally established until 602; it drew on the ritual codes of the "legitimate" Liang state (502–556) and those of the Northern Ch'i and produced a code in one hundred chapters divided into five topical categories. We should note that here, as in so many other cases, the codification drew together traditions that had long prevailed in the south and in the north, thus aiming at general acceptability in all parts of the reunited empire. The Sui code was adopted by the succeeding T'ang, and later T'ang recodifications drew heavily on the Sui model.

But the ritual norms did not apply to the people at large. The laws and ordinances did, and in Sui practice, flavored as it was by the philosophy of Legalism, these were often applied to the upper classes as well. Early in the first year of the dynasty, a commission of ranking officials, jurists, and ritualists was appointed to revise existing laws and fix a new code. In the tenth month of that year the New Code (Hsin-lü) was duly promulgated. The New Code tempered many of the most severe punishments of earlier codes: exposure of the severed head of the criminal, dismemberment of the body, use of the whip, and so forth. The imperial edict of promulgation closed on a lofty and hopeful note: "The unusually severe penalties established on the basis of the 'Miscellaneous Regulations' are to be eliminated entirely. Preliminary to publishing laws and ordinances, it is Our wish that men should have no disposition to trespass and that, the state having regular punishments, they be administered in accordance with the lofty principle of no animus. Perhaps the time is not far distant when, though they have been promulgated, they will not be used. Let the ten thousand regions and the myriad princes know these Our intentions."

Two years later the Emperor ordered that the code be drastically simplified, and members of the same commission reduced the laws to five hundred articles. This codification, which took its name from that of the new era-name, was known as the K'ai-huang Code. The most learned and influential figure on the commission was P'ei Cheng, who had served in judicial offices under the Liang in the south, and after his capture in the sack of Chiang-ling (554), under the Northern Chou. In the view of the most eminent scholar of medieval Chinese law, P'ei's broad knowledge and experience had a decisive influence in making the K'ai-huang Code a workable synthesis of northern and southern legal traditions: basic structure from the Northern Ch'i code, and elements from the codes of the Ts'ao-Wei and the Chin, the Southern Ch'i and, most importantly, the Liang. Thus, it was, in its new and simplified form and in its derivations from many northern and southern legal traditions, well-suited to become the law code for a reunified China.

The code retained four main types of punishment: (1) the death penalty; (2) deportation, usually with a term of forced labor, sometimes specified as military service on the frontier; (3) a term of forced labor without deportation; and (4) beatings with the bastinado, the number of blows varying from one hundred down to ten according to the seriousness of the crime. For all officials, the code provided a scale of commutation of these penalties into fines calculated formally in pounds of copper. Officials could have their salaries used to pay the fine or the sentence could be commuted into an official demotion. The most drastic penalty for an official—short of death—was to have his name struck from the roles of officials and his status reduced to that of a commoner, subject to normal taxes and forced labor levies. The code thus preserved the ancient distinction—going back at least to the *Ritual of Chou* (systematized in Han times)—in legal treatment of officialdom and plebs.

Emperor Wen, characteristically, was not satisfied with merely promulgating the new code. In 586 he summoned ranking provincial officials to the capital, where they were examined on whether they understood the provisions of the new code or not. Throughout China's imperial history local administrators exercised judicial as well as executive powers in their areas, and routine trial and punishment was, in the Sui as in other dynasties, part of their regular duties. But their autonomy in legal matters did not extend to certain categories of serious crime specified in the code. These fell under the jurisdiction of the Tribunal of Censors (*Yü-shih t'ai*) whose chief was charged not only with the investigation and prosecution of very serious crimes but also with the general supervision of all officials in the empire. The High Court of Justice (*Ta-li ssu*), located in the capital and composed of both high officials and legal specialists, considered the written evidence regarding a serious crime, determined the legal character of the crime, and recommended the final sentence, which was pronounced by the Emperor. It is probable that the High Court was primarily a court of appeal or referral while the Board of Punishments of the Department of State Affairs gave judgments in the many cases where the law was clear.

For all the speed of compilation, the comprehensive coverage of the new code and the efforts made to instruct officials on how to apply its provisions, many bureaucrats remained attached to their old and frequently corrupt ways. Emperor Wen tried many remedies. At one point, in a rage at official malfeasance, he abolished all the posts of legal specialists at the provincial and capital levels. Again and again he tried exhortation, publicized rewards and pun-

ishments, procedural legislation. He ordered officials executed for
minor derelictions, other officials for failing to denounce a crime,
still others for accepting minor gifts. Characteristically, he personally
reviewed the status of all prisoners each quarter and before the autumn equinox (the time for executions) reviewed all provincial reports on pending criminal cases. We saw in Chapter Three the
Emperor's insistence that the punishments prescribed by law be applied to his own son. This might be interpreted as a public act meant
to emphasize the uniform application of the law regardless of persons or circumstances. Yet this principle found little favor among
bureaucrats who operated under the residual Confucian imperative
always to take account of the special human variables (jen-ch'ing) and
under the pressure for special treatment from their influential
constituents.

The K'ai-huang Code, despite its obvious merits, failed to com-
pel the automatic compliance of officialdom. Still less could it con-
strain the vagaries of the supreme autocrat who was constitutionally
above the law. Indeed the power of the autocrat—to some extent
shared with his close associates—continually corrupted the working
of the legal process. The Sui History, speaking of two sycophantic officials of the High Court of Justice, says: "If the Emperor was displeased with someone, they manipulated the procedure so that he
was severely condemned." They also knew how to please Yang Su,
the éminence grise of the Sui court. One of these officials, each time he
met Yang Su in the street, "announced to him the names of those
who had been given light or heavy punishments according to Yang
Su's wishes. Among those who were approaching their end and
being taken to the market for execution, there was none who did not
cry out against injustice and, weeping, call upon Heaven as his
witness."

Of equal importance for the governance of the realm was the
body of codified statutes(ling). The first corpus of these was promulgated in the seventh month of 582, and periodically they were aug-
mented and amended. The statutes included provisions relating to
officialdom, bureaucratic procedure, land regulation, taxation, and
many other subjects of concern in day-to-day administration. Although the K'ai-huang statutes have disappeared, substantial quotations survive in other works. Here again, in scope, length, and topical
divisions, this compilation appears to be ancestral to the first set of
T'ang codified statutes issued in 624.

Although Emperor Yang ordered the compilation of a law code

and a compendium of statutes for his reign, which were duly promulgated in 607, these seemed to have followed closely the K'ai-huang
models, and indeed the principal compiler had also been prominent
in the earlier work of codification. Emperor Yang is credited
with a general reduction of penalties in two hundred out of the five
hundred articles in the code. But this amelioration of sanctions was,
we are told, reversed as the dynasty faced internal crises consequent
on its successive invasions and defeats in the northwest.

It had long been universally recognized among Chinese thinkers
and statesmen that neither the ritual punctiliousness of the upper
class nor the sanctions of punitive law nor the most detailed regulations for the conduct of government could ensure social harmony.
For that the ordinary people must be so molded in their character
and behavior that they would of their own accord be orderly, indus-
trious, and submissive to their lot in life and to the orders of their su-
periors. However attenuated the Confucian tradition became, it was
usually the Confucians who insisted on this principle and proposed
the devices for its realization. Early in his reign, Yang Chien realized
that long years of bitter civil war had left in their wake a demoralized
peasantry and an élite that was more familiar with sword and battle
ax than with the techniques of civil control of the populace. Inevitably, an early supporter, a Confucian, came to the new emperor not
only with a diagnosis of social conditions but with a prescription.
Succinctly stated this was "Promote learning and foster the practice
of the proper norms of behavior." The argument begins in traditional style: "Your servant has heard that when emperors and kings
receive the mandate to rule, they establish schools and regulate the
norms of behavior. Therefore they are able to change the ethos of
the preceding period and effect a complete reform of popular customs." He closes with a peroration arguing that if the Emperor will
foster the proper norms and promote learning, society will be transformed, families will abide by the norms, individuals will follow the
ways of righteousness, and all will be well. The Emperor was apparently impressed by these arguments, and echoes many of them in
an edict ordering that the recommended steps be taken. The edict
closes with this passage: "The pattern of study among the ancients
was to alternate farming and self-cultivation. Now, when the able-
bodied males among the people have days free of labor service, and
in the time remaining from agricultural work, if they are urged to
undertake studies and instruction in following the canonical norms

of proper behavior, they will spontaneously in their families reverence the great Way of the sages and in their persons aspire to ultimate virtue. Is it not so that if they simply know the rules of proper
conduct and are aware of uprightness and modesty, the father will be
compassionate and the son filial, the elder brother respectful and the
younger obedient? Beginning with the capital and proceeding to the
prefectures and commanderies, it is appropriate to accord with my
ideas and encourage study and practice of the proper norms." By
this edict, the *Sui History* tells us, there were scholars appointed to all
the prefectures and counties to provide instruction, especially in the
behavioral norms.

Such, at any rate, were the Emperor's expressed hopes and plans
for the education and indoctrination of the populace as a whole. For
the education of potential officials, he set up centers of advanced
study in the capital, and these were all placed under control of an
Inspectorate of Education known as the Kuo-tzu chien and headed
by a fairly high-ranking official. Under the inspectorate were three
residential colleges for instruction in the classics (open mainly to
upper-class sons) and less prestigious schools of calligraphy, ac-
countancy, and law (the last-named attached to the High Court of
Justice). In the early years of the dynasty the Emperor took pains
to staff the principal colleges with Confucian scholars of repute; he
visited the colleges from time to time and made imperial gifts to
worthy students. On one occasion he feasted the examination
candidates, and on another he personally visited one of the colleges
and took part in the sacrifices offered to honored teachers of the past.
He then ordered the scholar in charge to lecture on his favorite classic, the *Classic of Filial Submission*. The scholar performed with such
éclat that the Emperor expressed himself as delighted and rewarded
him with one hundred feet of silk cloth and a robe.

As to what versions and what interpretations of the classics
should be taught, this was a subject of much disputation during the
Sui. As we noted, differing traditions of interpreting the ancient
books had developed in the southern courts, in the northeastern
plain, and in the northwest. The disorganized condition of Confucianism in the early Sui, the rather haphazard modes of training and
selecting scholars for public service, the variety of expertise expected
of them, and the extreme vulnerability of Confucian scholars to the
vagaries of chance, intrigue, and the capricious exercise of political
power are all illustrated in the life of one scholar of some distinction,
and we venture to offer it here for just this reason.

Liu Cho was the son of a minor official in the northern part of the Great Plain. He was, it is said, precociously intelligent, physically weak, and not fond of games. He swore an oath of eternal friendship with another youth of the same surname, Liu Hsüan, and they went to receive instruction in the *Classic of Poetry* from a master in Hsüan's home area. Later, with a master in another town, they moved on to study the Tso commentary to the ancient chronicle, attributed to Confucius, known as the *Spring and Autumn Annals*. When they had finished these studies they moved on to the study of the ritual classics with still another master. After this they were attracted to a household renowned for its large library; the two young men presented themselves and settled down for ten years to study, specializing in classical texts, quite unconcerned about their tattered clothing and shortage of food. Finally, Liu Cho had such a reputation that he was made a prefectural scholar, perhaps one of those appointed under Wen-ti's edict for local education already discussed. The local governor took him in his service and nominated him for the *Hsiu-ts'ai* degree. He passed the examination with the highest marks and was assigned to the history compilation bureau in the capital and concurrently as a consultant in the making of the imperial calendar. At the same time he served as a policy advisor in the imperial chancellery. Somewhat later he was assigned to serve, with other Confucian scholars, in the imperial library, where he edited and corrected official documents. On a holiday visit to his native place, he was drafted into the service of the county magistrate there, but he shortly returned to the capital. There he became engaged in formal disputations at the imperial college with a galaxy of scholarly notables on debatable interpretations of the classics and on points which his scholarly predecessors had not comprehended. It is said that every time he went up to the speaker's place, his arguments were irrefutable, and all the learned scholars were humbled. In 586, after they moved the ancient classics graven on stone steles from Loyang to the capital, many of the characters had been worn away and were no longer legible. Liu Cho received an order to collaborate with his old sworn brother Liu Hsüan to correct the damaged texts. The two Lius' success in scholarly disputations finally excited the envy of certain of their rivals; they were slandered in an anonymous canard and as a result their names were ordered removed from the official rolls and they were reduced to commoners. Whereupon they wandered about from village to village, giving instruction and continuing their writing. Liu Cho wrote treatises on mathematics, on calendrical science,

and commentaries to the Five Classics. Later Yang Yung, deposed as
Crown Prince in 600, summoned Liu Cho into his service. But before
Cho could respond, he was ordered to join the staff of the Emperor's
fourth son, the Prince of Shu. Liu was dubious about this appointment and delayed proceeding to his post in distant Szechwan. The
Prince was furious and sent men to get him, and he was taken off,
accompanied by a military escort. There he was in charge of collating books in the Prince's library. When the Prince was accused of
practicing black magic and reduced to the rank of commoner, Liu
Cho took the long road back to the capital, where he was made part
of the prestigious commission engaged in codifying the rituals promulgated in 602.

At the accession of the Emperor Yang he was made a principal
scholar at the imperial academy, but resigned the post because of illness. He was shortly called back into service as a policy consultant at
court. There he presented to the throne what appears to have been a
masterly treatise on calendar computation. But this was objected to
by the head of the astronomical bureau, whose own calendar had
long been officially in use. Liu Cho died soon after, aged sixty-seven.
His life-long friend Liu Hsüan petitioned the Emperor for the conferment of a posthumous title as a mark of recognition, but the court
refused the request.

There is one further measure of Wen-ti's which concerns Confucian books and the Chinese literary heritage generally. It was traditionally one part of the reassertion of cultural hegemony to
sponsor an empire-wide collection of books and manuscripts and
then put official scholars to work classifying, collating, and annotat-
ing with a number of official clerks to make fair copies of what had
been collected and processed. The first such undertaking occurred in
the second century B.C., when princes of the Han ruling house undertook to reassemble the ancient literature scattered in the violent
and prolonged upheavals that accompanied the ending of the old
order, the founding of a united empire by the Ch'in, and the bitter
civil war that followed its collapse. Yang Chien was reminded of the
Han precedent in a long and eloquent memorial by Niu Hung presented in 582, at a time when the Sui had barely secured its hold on
power. Niu reviewed the initiatives taken by rulers from remote antiquity onward to collect and preserve writings. He also reviewed the
five disasters in which books and documents had been destroyed in
the repeated civil upheavals from the end of the Former Han down
to the rise of the Sui. Then he proceeded to his argument:

In your servant's view, it is now nearly a thousand years since classical writings began with Confucius. They have suffered five destructive disasters, after which periods of vigorous re-collection have restored the sagely heritage. In my humble opinion, now that Your Majesty has received Heaven's clear mandate and rules over the universe . . . your territory is larger than that ruled by the three kings [of the Hsia, Shang, and Chou dynasties] and your population is greater than that ruled by the two Han dynasties. As regards human factors and timeliness, the moment to act is now. You should undertake to disseminate widely the cultural heritage so as to improve customs and assure peace. And if there are items missing among the books of the empire, you should regard this as out of keeping with the sagely character of your rule and with your obligations to transmit the moral teachings of the sages without limitations. . . . We know that state management and government are to be found in documents and statutes; they are the very root of the state, and nothing is as important as they are.

He then goes on to say that it is intolerable for private houses to possess books that are lacking in the royal offices, that it is necessary to encourage owners to come forward out of awe of the power of heavenly government or to attract them with a hope of profit.

As this proposal was carried out, the government's representatives offered one roll of silk for each roll (chapter) of writing. And when the imperial librarians had collated and copied a book, it was returned to its owner. Inevitably, spurious texts were concocted to get the reward, and indeed the sworn brother of the hapless scholar Liu Cho was indicted and convicted on a charge of forging one hundred rolls for the imperial collectors; he escaped execution because of an amnesty but was degraded to the rank of a commoner. Nevertheless, the first imperial effort to reassemble the literary heritage, augmented by other measures later in the dynasty—notably after the conquest of the south—was a success. For the reassertion of cultural hegemony, it had great symbolic importance; for posterity, it preserved materials on a vital if disordered period of China's history.

Yet for the first Sui emperor, there were two further steps to complete the assertion of imperial control over the written word. One was to proscribe books thought to be morally corrupting or likely to be used for subversive purposes. Thus one order of 593

forbade the private possession of the apocrypha and prognostic texts
that had often been used to inspire rebellion; another forbade the
unofficial compilation of history and the practice of character reading (which had subversive potential). As early as 583, Wen-ti felt
obliged to execute an old friend and supporter who was alleged to
harbor imperial ambitions based on the prognostic texts and on the
predictions of a physiognomist. Later Wen-ti was to proscribe certain Buddhist and Taoist works as subversive. His whole reign was
marked by suspicious and unrelenting vigilance over the written
word.

The last of the imperial interventions in this sphere was in regard
to literary style. In the Chinese tradition, literary style had long been
regarded as a symptom of the health of the social and political order.
Wen-ti may well have been influenced by his close advisor Su Wei,
who laid great stress on this connection, but the Emperor's views are
quite consistent with what we know of his character generally. He
had a deep dislike for flowery language, which he regarded as pretentious and associated with dynastic decadence. Early in his reign
he ordered that in all public and private documents a matter-of-fact
style should be used; about this time, an unfortunate official submitted a memorial in florid style and was committed for punishment.
And in order that officials throughout the empire would get the full
import of the order to use simple language, the Emperor had circu-
lated everywhere the text of a memorial that argued the point with
reference to recent history. Its text reads in part:

> The three rulers of the Wei state [which replaced the Han]
> exalted literary style and neglected the great way of the ideal
> prince. They loved the minor tricks of literary orna-
> ment. . . . With the Ch'i and Liang dynasties, this abomina-
> tion became still worse. They strove for clever tricks with a
> single rhyme and struggled for a cute effect with a single
> character. The ability to do such tricks became the way to
> wealth and preferment. . . . Therefore their literary compo-
> sitions daily proliferated while their government day by day
> fell into disorder. They discarded the immemorial models of
> the great sages and tried to make what was useless serve a
> useful purpose.

For the first eighteen or twenty years of the dynasty, Wen-ti
made full use of all the traditions, the arts and techniques, the cults

and symbolism associated with Confucianism. He himself in 594 made preparations to worship Heaven on the summit of Mount T'ai and made a progress through the most populous part of his realm to perform the solemn imperial sacrifices that, in the eyes of many Confucian literati, constituted the Emperor's decisive report to Heaven on the achievements of his new dynasty. Wen-ti's observance fell short of the full ritual performance, either out of fear of the consequences of presumption or out of concern that the famine conditions in the country he had just passed through cast a shadow on his own stewardship of the realm. But by his dramatic playing out of the role of sage king, by his patronage of learning and of scholars, and by his restoration of literature during these years he seemed to many (as he intended) to be an imperial patron of Confucian tradition. Indeed, an essay by a younger contemporary celebrates the revival of Confucianism in these years: the growing numbers of students, the respect shown Confucian masters, the availability of schools in the capital and the provinces. And he goes on to say, ". . . the sound of intoning the classics was unceasing in the streets, and the flourishing condition of the Confucian arts was unequaled in the period since the Han and Wei dynasties."

The same author notes the disenchantment with Confucianism that characterized Wen-ti's later years, accompanied, he says, by a disposition to favor Legalist dogmas over the Confucian arts, not surprising since Wen-ti was in many respects harshly Legalistic from the opening of his reign. It is the edict of 601 that expresses his dissatisfactions with Confucianism and decrees drastic measures. Some passages will illustrate its tone and content:

> The principles of Confucianism are for the training and instruction of the people, making them aware of the righteousness that should inform the relation of father and son, prince and minister, of the proper gradations of honorable and mean, of age and youth. . . . We, in peacefully governing the world, have given thought to spreading the virtuous teachings; we have gathered together students and have carefully established village schools. We have opened the way for official advancement and have waited for men of outstanding worth. The ranking scholars of the national academies now number almost a thousand, and the students in the prefectural and county schools are by no means few. Yet they merely have their names on the rolls while they idly waste

their years, without possessing the virtue to be models for
the age nor the capacity to be used in state service. It seems
that the policies for establishing schools stressed numbers
without attention to suitable refinement. Now it is appropriate to reduce numbers and clearly add some incentives to
industry.

The *Sui History* goes on to say that two out of the three colleges in the
capital were abolished, and only seventy students were kept in the
one that remained, while all the local schools in the empire were
abolished. Then it adds, "It was on this day [the emperor's birthday]
that they distributed holy Buddhist relics to all the prefectures of the
empire."

This brings us to the problem of Buddhism, the dominant faith
of the new dynasty's subjects, the religion of the imperial house and
many of its intimate counselors. We have described in Chapter Two
something of Buddhism's domestication in China and its spread
throughout the Chinese culture. As it grew in importance, it not only
deeply affected all aspects of ordinary life, but also presented rulers
of China with unprecedented problems, both of principle and practical policy. In the classic definition of emperorship by the Ch'in and
Han dynasties, the principle was established that the emperor was
supreme in all matters, moral and religious. In practical policy this
meant that the emperor issued edicts and regulations governing the
li, which, as we have described them above, governed the norms of
behavior and ritual observances of the élite. He further ruled on
moral matters, taking steps to inculcate acceptable values and discourage what was undesirable by, for example, indoctrination in the
schools, or the singling out of moral exemplars. And among the varied cults and religious observances practiced in the towns and
countless villages of the empire, the policy was to have local officials—as surrogates of the emperor—keep a sharp watch for any cult
that might seem potentially subversive of good morals or of the political order. Any such cult would be declared heterodox, its leaders
and adherents would be disciplined, usually harshly, and its practices strictly forbidden.

Buddhist teachings presented a view of the universe vastly expanded in time and space, a universe that a mortal Son of Heaven
could not conceivably control, and doctrines of eternal validity,
transcending all enactments of mere secular power. It thus directly

challenged the principle of the Son of Heaven's supremacy in matters of faith and morals. In terms of public policy, it presented a host of unprecedented problems. For example, it extolled a celibate life apart from society, whereas Chinese emperors had always designed their social policies around the family as the unit of agricultural productivity and a continuing source of useful manpower. Again, as Buddhism's celibate adherents grew in number and its pious believers built and endowed monasteries and nunneries, the emperors continually lost subjects who would normally have been liable to tax levies and to labor and military service, while monastic estates—being tax-exempt—reduced the amount of registered taxable lands in the empire. Further, in the countryside generally, people proclaimed themselves priests, wore the Buddhist habit, and carried simplified doctrines—new magical potencies, new ways of foretelling the future, spells for exorcising illness, and much else—into the villages, where they replaced the local shaman or shamaness who had long ministered to such needs. These self-consecrated priests claimed exemption from taxes and labor service and, worse still, they often preached certain Buddhist teachings that were profoundly subversive—for example that the end of the world was at hand and that all normal social obligations were irrelevant. And some among them claimed to be reincarnations of a Buddhist divinity—usually the Buddha of the Future Age, Maitreya—and ended by leading their followers in rebellion against the state.

The intractable problems created by Buddhism had been met and dealt with by the many ephemeral dynasties of the Period of Disunion. Distinctive styles of dealing with Buddhism had developed in the alien-dominated north and in the southern empires. So Wen-ti had numerous and varied historical precedents to draw on in formulating his own policies toward Buddhism. In his own case, the complicating factors were many and should be borne in mind as we discuss his Buddhism and his policies toward the monks and laity of his vast empire. First of all, his upbringing had instilled in him a deep Buddhist faith, and this was reinforced by the relentless piety of his empress and by the ambience of the palace, with its puritanical strictness, the daily intoning of scriptures in incense-filled halls, the sermons and religious lessons of noted monks. Second, he found in Buddhism formulas to assuage his own feelings of guilt and insecurity, formulas that provided, in addition, dramatic gestures to legitimate his dynasty—gestures that the mass of his believing subjects could see and understand. At the same time he was jealous of the prerogatives of a Son of Heaven and neither he nor his officials wanted to cede an iota of secular power to the Buddhist clergy. Further, the Legalist and physiocratic thinking of the Emperor and his advisors made them sensitive to the dangers inherent in an empire-wide Buddhist establishment that could command enough manpower and wealth to become a threat to the dynasty. Thus, measures of control were taken and, despite his personal piety, Wen-ti included Buddhism firmly within the sphere over which the Sui asserted cultural hegemony.

One of Yang Chien's first acts following his seizure of *de facto* power from the Northern Chou was to take steps, in the summer of 580, to rescind the Chou proscription of Buddhism and Taoism—a measure that had decreed the laicization of monks and nuns, the destruction of temples (or their conversion to other uses), and the confiscation of temple lands. The feelings of the Yang family toward the proscription are reflected in the fact that their household served as a refuge for the Buddhist nun who had been Yang Chien's childhood mentor. The first step, taken in the sixth month of 580, was to proclaim (in an edict issued in the name of the Northern Chou emperor) that clerics of notably high resolution should resume their religious lives. A month later, a second edict ordered a noted monk to collaborate with a high-ranking noble to examine candidates and ordain 120 monks who were to reside in temples in Ch'ang-an and Loyang. To each of the newly ordained monks, Yang Chien presented a religious habit.

These were a cautious beginning, but we may surmise that they were not only consonant with Yang Chien's own feelings but well-calculated to win for his cause the support of the Buddhist faithful. More dramatic measures followed rapidly after his accession. In the intercalary third month of his first year on the throne, he issued a decree that touches on many of the themes that would recur throughout his Buddhist enactments: unity, harmony, the cultivation of goodness, peace:

> The Buddhist teaching knows no difference between esoteric and exoteric. A myriad good deeds have the same point of reference. Though different teachings may be shallow or deep, all paths converge on a common destination. We make humble obeisance before the transforming power of the Way and cherish in our thoughts the ideal of pure tranquility. It is fitting that at the base of each of the five sacred mountains,

there be established a Buddhist monastery (and that farm land be set aside to support it).

The five sacred mountains are the primordial holy places of the Chinese world, tutelary divinities of the four directions and of the center, the home of numerous gods and potencies, their peaks the awesome places where mediation takes place between the world of man below and Heaven above. To order Buddhist monks to serve the cults of these holy places was a dramatic indication of the new dynasty's religious preference. More than that, it showed what tremendous inroads a once-foreign religion had made into the Chinese realm of things sacred.

The building, endowment, and embellishment of Buddhist temples is a constant theme in the history of the Sui, and we should note, in the various measures taken, some of the motives that lie behind this ceaseless activity. Demonstrating the piety of the imperial house is an obvious motive; similarly, the piety of the rich and the powerful whose piety as expressed in temple building would bring its own rewards and also the approval—sometimes the favor—of the emperor and empress. Then, more subtly, there were motives of commemoration, of filial regard for the souls of one's ancestors, of concern for those who had died in battle, or—like the Chou emperor who proscribed Buddhism—those in particular need of places and services of atonement. Then there was the dynasty's interest, seen in a series of edicts, to rehabilitate temples destroyed by the Northern Chou and thus appear as fervent patrons of the faith. And most important of all was the Sui's interest in establishing splendid temples in the capital and a network of imperially supported temples in the main cities and prefectural capitals—temples that would be tangible evidence of the power of the Sui, secular and religious, and would serve as places for the performance of masses and observances decreed for the whole empire.

In the seventh month of 581, the Emperor ordered the establishment of national commemorative temples at places that had been important in his father's military life, and the next month he founded a monastery on the battlefield of Hsiang-chou, where his forces had fought the decisive battle against the principal enemy of the Sui's rise to power, Wei-ch'ih Ch'iung. In an edict of 583 he ordered regular services performed daily from the eighth to the fifteenth days of the first, fifth, and ninth months in all officially established temples in the capital and prefectural towns; during the periods of these observances, the killing of any living thing was strictly prohibited, and the people were exhorted at the same time to follow the religious prescriptions for the months of Buddhist abstinence. It is not quite clear what temples were included in this sweeping order, but they probably included the local temples of North China that the Chou had destroyed or closed down and that the Sui or local initiatives had rehabilitated. The order no doubt very soon covered the official temples in the forty-five prefectures that Yang Chien had traveled through before his accession; all of these were named Ta-hsing-kuo Ssu. The first two characters were the same as the name of the Sui capital, which in turn was named for the fief Yang Chien had held before coming to power. They also had, as we noted in discussing the new capital, a felicitous meaning with the suggestion, when used in a temple name, of a dynasty that greatly propagated (*ta-hsing*) the Buddhist faith after its cruel suppression under the Northern Chou.

Local temples were by no means limited to those established by official initiative. There are hundreds of stele inscriptions of Sui date, often with a list of donors on the back, that testify to intense building activity at the subprefectural level. One that is dated September 15, 585, commemorates a building project at Ting-hsien in the modern province of Hopei:

> The former supervisor of monks for Ting Prefecture and head monk of the former Monastery of the Seven Wei Emperors, Hui-yü, the master of images Hsüan-ning and others, in honor of their late preceptor Seng-yün who had died in the sixteenth year of T'ai-ho [492] made a gilded image of Maitreya [the Buddha of the future] which was 38 feet high. In the sixth year of the Chien-te Era of the Later Chou [577], the government destroyed the great image, and the monks and nuns were returned to lay life. In the sixth month of the seventh year [578] the Chou Emperor Yü-wen Yung, because he had extinguished the Three Treasures [the Buddha, his teaching, and the Buddhist order], was afflicted with a fatal case of jaundice, the power was passed, and the succeeding emperor changed the era-name to Hsüan-cheng. In his second year, because his father had greatly damaged the teaching and destroyed the holy orders, he vowed [in expiation] to make a great Buddha-image, and he changed the era to Ta-hsiang [meaning "great image"]. But since the Chou was

about to be extinguished, he was unable to carry out his vow ere he passed the emperorship to Yang Chien, Emperor of the Great Dynasty of Sui who changed the era to K'ai-huang. From the time this sage prince assumed control of the world, customs and morale improved, the state grew in size, the people were at peace, and the peripheral peoples of all regions were obedient to his rule. He protected and defended the Three Treasures. He revived and restored all that had been ruined [in the proscription]. First and last in his edicts and his orders, the Buddhist teachings were given the highest position.

Hui-yü together with his disciples, Hsüan-ning, and others took a vow to restore their old temple and to reinstall the former image. What there was at the old site and other charitable sources were insufficient. . . . So the Great Patron, the former administrator of Ting Prefecture, etc., Ts'ui Tzu-shih of Po-ling, the former official of Sa-fu, the merchant Ho Yung-k'ang, combined to redeem the temple compound of the Temple of the Seven Wei Emperors. . . . Beginning in the first year of K'ai-huang, they fabricated the head and arms of the image and cast a great bell. By the fifth year they had set up the torso and the legs and reconstructed the precious hall that was to house it. . . . The image had used 17,500 pounds of cloth, eleven hogsheads of lacquer, and 87,000 grains of gold. The image and the hall built to house it had together cost 5,700 strings of copper cash.

Suddenly the local people received an imperial order that the larger counties were each allowed to build two Buddhist convents, one for monks and one for nuns. The magistrate of An-hsi, P'ei Shih-yüan and his administrative aides Wang and Liu, inasmuch as the Temple of the Seven Emperors and its image hall had both been restored, requested the prefectural office to petition the ministry in the capital that they be allowed to establish this as an official county temple.

The petition was granted, a further broadly supported project was undertaken to enlarge and embellish the temple, and it became a thriving local center of Buddhism during the Sui and so continued at least into the middle of the eighth century. The names of those who participated in the 585 work of restoration are partially preserved in the inscription, and the list—like those on other Buddhist steles—testifies to the egalitarian spirit of these community projects. The inscription states that men and women, Chinese and non-Chinese, participated; it gives the names of ten prominent monks representative of the thirteen hundred monks who participated; it also lists the officially appointed supervisors of monks, numerous laymen, the names of the sculptors of the image, of those who worked with the lacquer, of the carpenters who restored the Buddha-hall, the name of the man who composed the inscription, of the calligrapher and of the craftsmen who cut the characters into the stone, and finally the names of the on-site supervisors. One must imagine such projects as this being initiated all over the empire, and monasteries, nunneries, and pagodas to house holy relics becoming the focal points of the Buddhist life of the country. Yet the center of Buddhism—the center of pious observances, of doctrinal developments, and of official control—was the capital. The capital set the tone as well as the policies for the Buddhism of the empire.

The scale of religious building in the new capital has been described in Chapter Four; here we might reiterate that by the end of the first reign no less than one hundred and twenty Buddhist establishments had been built and imperially chartered. In the year the city was first occupied, Wen-ti wished to encourage Buddhist temple building, and aside from his own and his empress's examples, he went so far as to put out in a palace courtyard one hundred temple name plaques (which constituted imperial charters) and issue an order that anyone with the means and inclination to build a temple might take one of the plaques. There is a story of a humble commoner who summoned up his courage, went and got one of the plaques, and put it over the gate of his very modest house. Later other donors provided more land and buildings so that a functioning nunnery was duly established. The donors, like those who participated in the provincial and local projects, represent most of the social groups in the capital. In addition to the commoner just mentioned, there were palace women, some princesses of the now defunct Chou Dynasty, rich merchants, laymen who became monks and converted their residences into monasteries, at least one palace eunuch, high-ranking officials and their wives, even a Turkish khan who had submitted to the Sui.

The most prestigious among all these establishments was the Ta-hsing-shan Ssu. Wen-ti had planned it and carefully chosen a site even before his new capital was finished. He began the great new complex with the re-erection of a late Northern Chou temple moved from the old capital. The name echoed the name given the new capital, as would the names soon to be given the official temples erected in prefectural cities. The Ta-hsing-shan Ssu was allotted a whole ward on the eastern side of the great avenue that led from the palace and official cities south to the main gate of the city. Its precincts and its buildings were continuously embellished; priceless relics and holy icons were installed in it; some of its walls were ornamented with paintings by the great muralists of the day; its halls of worship were graced by priceless sculptures. It was the site of the Sui's first project to translate Buddhist scriptures in which the central figure was the North Indian monk Narendrayaśas, assisted by thirty-odd Chinese monks, a pious activity that continued after the death of Narendrayaśas. The temple was also the center of a project to compile a bibliography of the vast corpus of Buddhist scriptures whose translation had by now been going on in various centers of the fragmented empire for more than three hundred years; it was the home-temple for nearly all the noted monks of the Sui period. It was the metropolitan temple for the whole reunited empire. It shared the authority over Buddhism with a government bureau that was entirely staffed with monks. But while the government office had management, fiscal, and supervisory duties, the abbot and monks of the Ta-hsing-shan Ssu had authority in matters of doctrine and religious observances, of setting the standards for entrance into the clergy, and much more. Wen-ti's remark of 584 to Lin-tsang, the first abbot of the Ta-hsing-shan Ssu, expresses his view of the division of power: "Your disciple [i.e., the Emperor] is Son of Heaven for the laity. You, O Master of the Discipline, are a Son of Heaven for the clergy." In using monks with official and semi-official status to be responsible for Buddhist clergy throughout the empire, the Sui perpetuated methods originally devised by the Northern Wei Dynasty at the end of the fourth century.

If the Ta-hsing-shan Ssu was the physical center of imperial Buddhism, what determined the doctrines that were to be propagated and those that were not? The Sui favored the many-faceted Mahayana Buddhism with its emphasis on multiple paths to salvation and its Bodhisattvas—as numerous as human needs—to help the faithful along the road to eternal bliss. To help spread desirable doctrines and scriptural interpretations, Wen-ti set up in 592 a "community of twenty-five" eminent monks. This was loosely structured but had its own titles, such as community head, deputy community head, craftsman of the Mahayana, chief of instruction in scripture reading, etc. Some monks were established specialists on an important Mahayana scripture, others on the books of monastic discipline, still others on techniques of preaching, scriptural exegesis, and the like. All of them received official stipends, most of them had periods of residence at the Ta-hsing-shan Ssu and periods of teaching and preaching and visiting monasteries throughout the realm. Though the evidence is fragmentary, it is apparent that this was an élite corps of monks appointed to set the standards of orthodox Buddhism for the empire. To head the Ta-hsing-shan Ssu, Wen-ti favored (from Lin-tsang onward) monks with special expertise in the field of monastic discipline, for it was to the advantage of religion and of the state to maintain rigorous standards of austerity among the Buddhist clerical communities—thus hoping to keep the clergy above reproach and discourage all but the most dedicated from entering the religious life.

There is an immense further range of pious activities—the giving of vegetarian feasts to the monks, the administering of lay vows to the imperial princes (and in one case to all officials of the fifth rank and above), measures taken for the copying and distribution of the Buddhist scriptures, the official proclamation of periods of Buddhist abstinence, the patronage of noted monks, the expression of the Buddhist virtue of charity (dana) in massive distributions of food to the poor. All these testified to the Buddhist faith of the ruling house and of their subjects. But perhaps the ultimate Buddhist enactment by Wen-ti came twelve years after his conquest of the south (see Chapter Six) and near the end of his reign, and it followed a year after his own completion of a sixty-year cycle of life—traditionally a solemn occasion to be marked by appropriate ceremonies. On this day, July 21, 601, the Emperor issued two edicts. One ordered the drastic limitation of support for Confucian education. The other was an edict ordering the distribution of holy Buddhist relics throughout the empire. It opened with high solemnity:

> We contemplate with awe the perfect wisdom, the great mercy, the great compassion of the Buddha that would save and protect all creatures, that would carry across to blessed deliverance all living beings. We give our adherence to the Three Treasures and have brought to new prosperity the holy teachings. It is our thought and concern that all people within the four seas may, without exception, develop transcendent wisdom and together cultivate fortunate karma,

thus bringing it to pass that present existences will lead to happy future lives, that the sustained creation of good causation will carry us one and all up to wondrous enlightenment.

The edict then gave instructions for the dispatch of commissions headed by eminent monks, who were to be both able preachers and expert in the interpretation of supernatural portents, to proceed to thirty prefectural capitals throughout the empire. En route they were to be accompanied by a secular official, by two servants and five horses, and they were each to carry one hundred twenty pounds of frankincense. They were to take with them holy relics and upon arrival select a suitable and important site and there build a reliquary pagoda. Noon of the fifteenth day of the tenth month was set for the simultaneous enshrining of the relics in the thirty pagodas; all the monks and nuns of the empire were to adhere to strict abstinence, and all offices of government in the capital and the country save the military were to suspend operations for seven days while their members engaged in religious services in honor of the relics.

Preparatory to the dispatch of the thirty missions, the relics were placed by the Emperor himself, with great solemnity, in costly double jars and stamped with the imperial seal. In the course of this ceremony, the Emperor burned incense and worshipped. He took the discipline's vows always to hold to the true teaching, to protect and maintain the Three Treasures, and to seek the salvation of all living creatures. At the time set for the simultaneous enshrinements throughout the country, there was a scene of great pomp and ceremony in the capital:

. . . the Emperor stood in the main hall of the Ta-hsing palace. Facing west, he stood holding the jade sceptre of his exalted rank and welcomed the Buddha images and three hundred sixty-seven monks. With pennons, umbrellas, incense and flowers, with songs of praise and instrumental music, they proceeded from the Ta-shing shan-ssu and took their places in the great hall of the palace. The Emperor burned incense and worshipped. Descending, he proceeded to the eastern verandah of the palace and personally led the various civil and military officials to partake of a vegetarian meal.

The reliquary installation of 601 was followed by a second and similar operation in 602 which included fifty-three more places throughout the country, and a third, in 604, added another thirty places. The three sets of ceremonies were dramatizations for all to see of the Sui commitment to Buddhism, a reminder that its ruler had indeed brought peace and unity, and that he should be reverenced as a great Son of Heaven and Defender of the Faith. Surviving inscriptions from the reliquary sites stress the common vow that all beings from the imperial ancestors and the Emperor and Empress down to the humblest creature might one and all attain the blessed fruit of enlightenment. The aging Emperor expected that the enshrinements would be the occasion of auspicious wonders, and such were duly reported through official channels. Among the pronouncements and in the official reports there are many references to the achievement of the great and pious Buddhist emperor of India, Asoka of the Mauryas who, by ordering the sun to stand still, completed the building of 84,000 reliquaries in a single day and ruled, in Buddhist legend at least, as a Sage King and a Turner of the Wheel of the Doctrine, a ruler who had once been given to violence but who ended his life in unifying his empire around the Buddhist faith. This was assuredly the model Wen-ti was following so many centuries later, and all these actions not only established the Chinese empire as a Buddhist empire, but added for Wen-ti new layers of legitimation to those derived from indigenous traditions.

Taoism as a religion had evolved slowly in the centuries preceding the rise of the Sui. The basic scripture of all the sects of religious Taoism was the *Tao-te ching*, and the principal deity was the apotheosized author of that work, Lao-tzu. But sets of revelations from the world of the perfected immortals, books of formulas for alchemy and immortality, and collections of magic spells and incantations gradually created an immense and heterogeneous Taoist canon. The earliest Taoist religion had perhaps been that of the Yellow Turbans, who rose in massive rebellion in the second century A.D. By the Sui, elements of that early religion were intertwined with the later strands, and such things as celibate orders of clergy, an immense pantheon of divinities, and much else had been borrowed from Buddhism to create a complex religion with appeals for people of all social levels and strong links with various traditional arts such as geomancy, chronomancy (and its scientific counterpart, calendar making), astrology (and astronomy), numerology (and mathematics), and others.

Early Sui policies toward religious Taoism, like their Buddhist policies, are to be explained in part by the aftermath of the Northern

Chou proscription which had encompassed the clergy and establishments of both. In the first year of the new dynasty, Wen-ti lifted the ban, and he granted the Taoists their own metropolitan temple known as the T'ung-tao-kuan. This occupied only part of a ward across the avenue from the far grander Ta-hsing shan-ssu. And the number of Taoist establishments in the capital was, at the end of the first reign, only sixteen as contrasted with one hundred twenty Buddhist. This reflects the ambivalence of the Sui leadership toward religious Taoism as well as the vastly greater popularity of Buddhism among the population as a whole. The Sui founder, as we have noted, had an insatiable thirst for reassurance, and Taoist interpretations of favorable portents were welcomed; he also had need of the Taoists' special calendrical skills and made use of them. But the esoteric aspects of Taoism, its never-forgotten link to the Yellow Turban uprising, the apocalyptic (and thus potentially subversive) character of some of its doctrines—all combined to keep imperial patronage to a minimum. Wen-ti repaired the shrine at Lao-tzu's alleged birthplace and in 586 ordered the greatest literary figure of his time to compose an elegant commemorative piece that was engraved on stone set up at the site. It is worth noting, however, that more than half the text is devoted to elegant praise of the advent of Sui rule. Taoist sacred writings were included in the widespread effort to reassemble the literary heritage; it is said that the abbot of the Taoist metropolitan temple worked at editing and collating some 8,030 rolls of Taoist writings and published a catalogue in seven rolls. One can compare the number of clergy of the two faiths who were officially ordained in the first reign of the Sui (not forgetting that unauthorized self-proclaimed practitioners were common to both). For the Taoists, the number is two thousand, for the Buddhists, 230,000. And if one turns from such capital-centered activities to the empire as a whole, the contrast between the innumerable Buddhist stone inscriptions of Sui date and the paucity of the Taoist, one is driven to conclude that religious Taoism had not yet developed the influence among the common people that it was to attain in later centuries.

In assuming power, the Sui founder claimed as a matter of right control over the doctrines and practices of the three traditions we have just discussed. At the same time, he sought from each of them elements that would strengthen and legitimize his rule, elements that would help create a contented and malleable populace and at the same time help to break down the parochialisms and regional chauvinisms that he inherited from the Period of Disunion. For the establishment of the credibility of the Sui house, for the promotion of a common code of morality, and for the training of men suitable for public employment, he turned to Confucianism. This tradition, in its broad and in its narrower technical aspects, was the inescapable carrier of the statecraft, the symbolism of the Chinese imperial system. Anyone wanting to restore the glories of the once great Han had of necessity to turn to this tradition. But, as we have seen, his personal faith was always in Buddhism, and in the great enactments of his later years he went a long way toward making Buddhism the religion of the Sui state and its people—no doubt partly in the belief that all his efforts toward this end would redound to his own spiritual benefit and thus bring him to a more fortunate place in the cycle of rebirths than the brutalities of his earlier career would have earned him. He drew little on Taoism, save for its proto-scientific branches and its omen lore. He is said to have detested Taoist adepts, and since, as we have suggested, religious Taoism was not a widespread faith among his subjects, he felt no need to give it more than minimum patronage.

Yet the public pronouncements show that the early Sui leadership drew on all three traditions to enunciate a political ideology that would gain support for their dynasty and its policies. The themes of harmony, unity, and acquiescence in one's lot are expressed in the metaphors of all three traditions. The theme of filial submission, respect for one's betters, and obedience is mainly from Confucianism; while the themes of compassion, charity, and concern for one's whole community are largely Buddhist in origin. It is clear that this amalgam of themes made Sui ideology a useful adjunct to the military and political power that brought about the reunification of empire. The amalgam also reflects, by what it uses and what it does not, the reassertion of cultural hegemony in the field of values, morals, and faith.

CHAPTER 6

Conquest of the South

Chapter Two described the steady deterioration of the southern dynasties and the enfeebled state of the last of the Nanking dynasties, the Ch'en. The Sui founder inherited the greatly expanded territories of the Northern Chou, so that the Ch'en, internally weakened, outflanked by the loss of the vast area of Szechwan, and stripped of all its territory north of the Yangtze, could hope for little more than a postponement of its inevitable fate. For six or seven years Sui Wen-ti was preoccupied, as we have seen, by threats from the Eastern Turks and by his sweeping program of reorganization and reform. During that period, military skirmishes and diplomatic exchanges continued between the Ch'en and the Sui; formal missions came and went, no doubt collecting intelligence for both parties. A military attack on the Ch'en in 582 was stopped on the advice of Kao Chiung, who pointed out that the Ch'en emperor had just died, and cited a classical injunction that "one does not attack a state that is in mourning." Both he and his master were, however, thinking of more than ritual punctilio, for they were just beginning to plan a massive campaign that would assure a speedy and decisive victory. Indeed, Wen-ti had been on the throne barely a month when he appointed two of his most successful and most feared generals to governorships along the lower Yangtze frontier with the Ch'en; there they had ample time to prepare for their parts in the eventual campaign. In 584 the first link in the Sui water-communication network was ordered, and a second link with its terminus at Yang-chou completed in 587. An empire-wide granary system was designed and began to operate, thus contributing to the logistical support of an eventual campaign. In 585, Wen-ti appointed the fierce warrior Yang Su, who had recently been in disgrace, to become governor of Hsin-chou, a key strategic prefecture on the north bank of the Yangtze in the easternmost part of Szechwan province, not far from where the great river comes out of its gorges and into the plain. Yang Su was loaded with treasure which, as soon as he arrived, he used to finance the building of the formidable fleet that three years later would be used against the Ch'en. Thus, in the first phase of preparation, diplomatic feints and thrusts continued along with the methodical buildup of the essential granaries, canals, and roads. Active military preparations were going forward at the two ends of the Yangtze frontier, but a thousand miles of river lay between those two points. To prepare a concerted attack, forces had to be strategically deployed along that great expanse and a means of getting them across the broad river devised. The Sui began with the center section.

The small state of Later Liang, with its capital at the old city of Chiang-ling, lay to the north of the central Yangtze, and its rulers—descendants of the defunct Liang ruling house—had paid allegiance to the Northern Chou. When the Sui overthrew the Chou, they transferred their allegiance to the Sui. In the eighth month of 587, Wen-ti summoned the Liang ruler to pay court at the Sui capital. The delegation, consisting of the ruler and some two hundred of his officials, duly arrived at the capital, but Wen-ti had used the time to send a strong force south to a point near Chiang-ling. Those left in charge of the city feared an imminent attack and sought to place themselves under the protection of the Ch'en prince who was governor in a nearby area. He arrived with troops and escorted them—those in charge and some hundred thousand others—to Ch'en territory. Upon receiving news of this, Wen-ti abolished the state of Liang, sent his chief advisor Kao Chiung to reassure the people who remained in Chiang-ling, and established Sui military garrisons along the more than two hundred miles of the Yangtze formerly controlled by the Liang.

Further to the east was the strategic Han River, flowing from the northwest to the southeast and entering the great river, as it still does, at Han-k'ou, "the Han's mouth." In the strategic city of Hsiang-yang, on the river in north-central Hupei, Wen-ti in 586 had set up a strong regional headquarters with his third son, Chün, the Prince of Ch'in, in command. The Prince, who had previously asked his father to let him become a Buddhist monk, now found himself, at the age of fifteen or sixteen, with authority over thirty prefectural commands in the area and commanding officer of a naval force of, eventually, a hundred thousand men. (Naturally, experienced officers were assigned to his staff.) Some two years later, Wen-ti established a similar regional headquarters at Shou-hsien, in the center of Anhwei province, with a level land route leading east-southeast to the Yangtze opposite Nanking. Here Yang Kuang, then only twenty years old, Prince of Chin, was placed in command, aided by the faithful and resourceful Kao Chiung. This was the strategic headquarters for the whole campaign, and though the Prince of Chin was nominally supreme commander, Kao Chiung's role was obviously decisive. Finally, some two hundred miles to the northwest, a formidable flotilla was being built which was later to sail down the coast and play a major part in the subjugation of the south. Thus, preparations of many kinds were proceeding along a zig-zag line from the Yangtze gorges to the eastern seaboard.

Wen-ti did not neglect the moral and psychological strategies that would, he believed, help assure victory. In the third month of 588 he issued a long edict, in thunderous rhetoric, laying out the perfidy and incompetence of the Ch'en ruler whom he scornfully referred to by his ordinary name, Ch'en Shu-pao. The edict appeals to classic Confucian moral-political standards. The Ch'en ruler is guilty of bad faith, wastefulness in the building of palaces and plaisances, indulging in licentious conduct with many concubines while neglecting his proper duties, oppression of the people, interference with agriculture, the execution of upright remonstrators, the extermination of blameless families, disregard for Heaven, and contumely toward the Five Forces that make for an orderly universe. The appearance of malevolent ghosts and the repeated occurrence of natural disasters, the edict concludes, are sure signs of the withdrawal of Heaven's mandate. He dispatched an imperially sealed letter to the Ch'en ruler, listing the twenty heinous crimes of a tyrannical ruler that made it no crime but a duty imposed by Heaven for Wen-ti to relieve him of his throne. And, resorting to what we have come to call psychological warfare, he had his edict of denunciation copied three hundred thousand times and distributed widely throughout the area south of the Yangtze. In the ninth month of 588 he gave an imperial feast for the generals who would command the southern expeditionary forces and made them appropriate gifts. A month later a formal diplomatic mission from the Ch'en was forcibly detained. On a *chia-tzu* day of the tenth moon, the auspicious beginning of a sexagenary cycle, the Emperor, having solemnly notified his forebears in the Imperial Ancestral Hall, ordered the attack on the Ch'en begun.

Meanwhile, the Ch'en ruler, according to our sources, continued to act like a silly and unregenerate playboy. Some degree of caricature must be suspected, for anyone destined to be a last ruler—in terms of the moral dynamics of Confucian historiography—had to be depicted as utterly incompetent and corrupt. Yet the circumstantial detail provided by several sources presents an undeniable picture of a foolish, pleasure-loving incompetent. As late as the autumn of 588 he was praising the Yangtze as an impregnable defense against northern invaders, citing the Northern Ch'i's three attempts to cross, and the Northern Chou's two, all ending in failure. How, he asks, will the Sui succeed? A sycophantic courtier embroiders his sentiments with boasts and jokes, and the Emperor laughs in agreement. Hence, the *Tzu-chih t'ung-chien* tells us, "He made no preparations in depth, but played music, gave himself up to wine, and wrote poetry unceasingly." In the eyes of later critics he was a truly accomplished poet, but in this moment of crisis, when other talents were needed, he was, beyond doubt, a total failure.

Chinese military historians term the amphibious attack on the Ch'en the "eight-pronged" assault. The total number of men in all eight forces is said to have been 518,000, and consisted of infantry, fast cavalry, armored cavalry, plus the sailors and marines aboard the three flotillas—on the sea, on the Han River, and in the upper Yangtze. The phasing in of each of the eight forces was carefully planned in advance. In describing the course of action, we shall identify each force by its commander's name and its base. From east to west they were as follows: (1) General Yen commanded the flotilla that was now in readiness on the northwest coast near the modern Hai-chou. (2) The formidable General Ho-jo had long been preparing his forces at Kuang-ling, just north of the Yangtze, opposite a point on the south bank approximately fifty miles east of the Ch'en capital, Chien-k'ang. (3) The army of General Han was south and considerably east of Ho-jo's headquarters. Han's camp was in the neighborhood of the modern Ho-fei in central Anhwei province, and his troops had a relatively easy march south and east to the north bank of the Yangtze opposite a point near the modern city of Wu-hu. Next to the east but some sixty miles north was the general head-quarters of the campaign, that of (4) Yang Kuang, the Prince of Chin. (5) General Wang's army was based at Ch'i-ch'un, in modern Hupeh, just north of the Yangtze, some hundred miles down river from the next and more important point in the Sui deployment, Han-k'ou, where the Han River enters the Yangtze. The Han was navigable well beyond Hsiang-yang, and there—at a historically strategic point—(6) Chün, the young Prince of Ch'in, was in com-mand of a major regional headquarters, where his forces rose to number over one hundred thousand men and a large fleet. Early in the campaign he moved his forces down the Han River and en-camped at Han-k'ou, where he was placed in charge of all com-mands on the upper reaches of the Yangtze. Further up river, (7) General Liu, governor of Ching prefecture, had his headquarters at the ancient city and former capital of the Later Liang, Chiang-ling. Furthest west of the eight commands was that of (8) Yang Su, who had been in charge of building the Sui fleet at Yung-an, on the north bank of the river east of the first three of its famous gorges. In the campaign, he shared overall command with the two imperial princes, the Prince of Chin at the general headquarters in Anhwei and the Prince of Ch'in at Hsiang-yang, later in the Han-k'ou area. The de-ployment of all these forces had been planned with great care to take advantage of terrain, of established land and water routes and of areas that could provide manpower and logistical support. A large supply, perhaps as many as a hundred thousand fresh horses, had been secured by an imperial commissioner sent, in 587, to get them from all the stud farms of the north and northwest. All the com-manders save the imperial princes were seasoned field commanders, veterans of campaigns against the Turks and of the civil war that led to the founding of the Sui. All were about to move into well-mapped but unfamiliar terrain and against a population that had been long-accustomed to fear and despise the barbarians from the northern plains. None had had previous experience in the naval warfare that had, in the past, often determined the outcome of wars among con-tending powers in the Yangtze basin.

The prime theater of action was the area of Chien-k'ang for the obvious reason that it was the Ch'en capital and command center and for the less obvious but still important reason that the city had been the symbolic center of the self-styled legitimate Chinese dynasties since 317, when the Chin Dynasty, having lost the whole of North China to alien invaders, established their capital there. From crude beginnings, its low-lying terrain was gradually freed of Yangtze flooding, many of the symbolic features of an imperial capital were introduced, and palaces and plaisances for the emperor and his court dominated the two walled inner precincts of the city. Still, save for its northern and western boundaries, protected by the Yangtze, the city was not well-suited for defense.

General Ho-jo had long been bartering old horses for boats and then hiding the boats. At the same time he gathered together in a place highly visible from the southern bank fifty or sixty derelict hulks, so that the Ch'en guards mistakenly believed the northerners had no usable boats. Then at each changing of his own river guards, he had these report to his headquarters where they put up tents in the fields and ran up battle flags, so that it looked as if the Sui army had arrived in force. The Ch'en were alarmed and began to prepare their defenses. Then word was "leaked" to them that what they believed to be the Sui army were only the river guards, and they then ceased being on the alert. As the moment for crossing approached, the general sent soldiers out disguised as seasonal hunters of the region; horses and huntsmen raised such a hubbub that the Sui forces crossed the Yangtze in their long-hidden boats without being detected. Ho-jo seized an important town not far east of Chien-k'ang and took the occasion to demonstrate the iron discipline he imposed on his own forces by executing one of his own men for a misdemeanor and, on the other hand, freeing six thousand prisoners incarcerated by the recent Ch'en governor, and providing them with food and passports to return to their homes. The Ch'en ruler received a report on Ho-jo's crossing but was too drunk to notice it, and it was later found, unopened, under his bed! Meanwhile General Han had crossed the Yangtze by night with five hundred men, found the guards on duty drunk, and seized a strong point. He too used magnanimity toward his captives to establish a reputation that won over whole families to his side. By this time, a few weeks after the first crossing, both generals were poised for a march on Chien-k'ang, Ho-jo eastward along the northern road and Han from the south.

As these two forces advanced, the Ch'en ruler ordered his top commanders to encamp their troops in various parts of the walled palace city, in the imperial parks and temples outside the walls, and outside the ceremonial main gate of the outer city. Although the Ch'en ruler had more than a hundred thousand troops for the de-

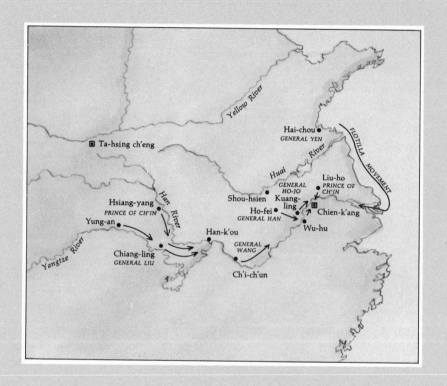

fense of his capital, he was both cowardly and vacillating, used a favorite to transmit all his orders, and even lost the loyalty of his commander-in-chief by having sexual relations with the man's wife.
Worse still, he vetoed all proposals by his commanders to go out and
give battle to the Sui armies, which were moving closer and in ever-
greater numbers to the city. Finally he agreed to a belated foray
northeast of the city by several units under his commander-in-chief.
But the units were ill-organized and could be seen by General Ho-jo
from a hill near his camp to stretch out over a distance of some six or
seven miles. Ho-jo quickly descended and assembled a force of eight
thousand armored men to attack the Ch'en troops. They met fierce
resistance from one of the Ch'en units and withdrew, leaving more
than 270 dead. While the Sui forces regrouped behind a smoke
screen, the Ch'en soldiers rushed to get the heads of the fallen Sui
warriors so as to collect their promised rewards. Ho-jo, watching this
and sensing overconfidence in the enemy, attacked one of the Ch'en
units, which broke and fled; the rest of the Ch'en force, both infantry
and cavalry, then broke ranks and fled in confusion, and the commander-in-chief was captured.

General Han had meanwhile been moving inexorably on the city
from the south. He encamped at Hsin-lin, only some twenty miles
away, and there received reinforcements sent by the Prince of Chin.
The general in command of the defense of the main gate of the city
came, with numerous cavalry, to surrender to Han. The same general
then led Han's forces to the gate. When the Ch'en soldiers guarding
the gate showed signs of putting up a fight, the defecting general
said, "I, your commander, have already submitted. What can you
soldiers in the ranks do?" So they dispersed and General Han's
forces entered the outer city walls.

Within the city, the demoralized officials, both civil and military,
mostly went into hiding. A few stayed in their offices as usual. The
Empress calmly remained with her attendants in her usual quarters
and the Crown Prince, aged fifteen, behaved with aplomb, bordering
on effrontery, when the Sui troops entered his rooms. The Emperor
was urged to follow the example of the aged Liang ruler Wu-ti, who
in 549, after the fall of Chien-k'ang, had worn his imperial robes and
received with dignity the rebel Hou Ching in the principal hall of audience. But the Ch'en ruler seemed bent on bathos and even fought
off the palace attendants in order to throw himself into a well in a
back courtyard. General Han's soldiers shortly broke in. They called
down the well and, getting no reply, were about to throw stones into

it when they heard a cry. They let down ropes and began to haul on them. They noticed the load was unusually heavy, and sure enough, when the bedraggled Ch'en Son of Heaven emerged, he had a dripping concubine hanging to him on each side. He was now a captive of the Sui. In the meantime, the nobles of the Ch'en house in Chien-k'ang, some hundred in number, had received an order to come to the palace and assemble under guard in the audience chamber. This was meant to prevent the defection of a potential puppet emperor to the Sui. But, on their way to the palace, the leader of the group got wind of the way things were going, and the nobles escaped from their escort and submitted *en masse* to the Sui.

Meanwhile, the Ch'en forces encamped in the imperial pleasure park north of the city fought bitterly against General Ho-jo's advancing forces, and the casualties were heavy. When the two armies disengaged at sundown, the Ch'en commander faced the palace and made obeisances. Then he tearfully said to his soldiers, "I personally am not capable of saving our dynasty. Deep is the shame I feel." His men were moved to tears and lamentations, and the whole force then allowed themselves to be captured.

Ho-jo's way was now clear to the city gates. Finding them deserted by their guards, he burned the main north gate of the palace city and entered and, learning with some chagrin that his colleague General Han had already seized the Ch'en ruler, asked that the ruler be brought before him. The ruler arrived in a fright, and made humble obeisances. The fierce soldier reassured him with a statement: "When the prince of a small state faces a grandee-minister of a great state, obeisances are then the protocol." This, to us, rather opaque utterance contains a historical allusion which the Ch'en ruler undoubtedly understood, namely that he would not be executed but would probably receive a fief as a form of pension from the Sui. Meantime he was placed, under guard, in one of his own palace buildings.

Yang Kuang, Prince of Chin, accompanied by Kao Chiung, had led his soldiers into Chien-k'ang after its fall. As the Prince was commander-in-chief, he promptly took charge of the city and its population, surrendered soldiers, officials, and ordinary people alike. He singled out four notoriously corrupt and oppressive Ch'en officials, beginning with Ch'en Shu-pao's hated favorite, and had them promptly executed. He sent Kao Chiung and a junior officer to gather up official documents and books and to seal the public treasury before any valuables could be taken. These acts are said to have won him considerable popular esteem. Because General Ho-jo had violated orders and crossed the Yangtze ahead of the appointed time, the Prince felt it necessary to place him in confinement and report the matter to the Emperor. An edict was quickly issued saying, with some justice, that conquering the area beyond the Yangtze was greatly to the credit of Generals Ho-jo and Han. The Emperor rewarded them generously and sent each an edict congratulating him on his prowess. One incident reveals the tension between the young commander-in-chief and his seasoned second-in-command, Kao Chiung. The latter had preceded the Prince into the city, and the Prince sent his personal secretary (who happened to be Kao Chiung's son) to Kao's headquarters with an order that he keep for the Prince's gratification the favorite concubine of the Ch'en ruler. Chiung cited the precedent of the righteous Chou conqueror putting to death the favorite woman of the last corrupt Shang king (c. 1122 B.C.) and had the concubine executed. When this was reported to the Prince, he conceived a deep hatred for Kao Chiung—a development that was to have serious consequences in later years. The Prince of Chin shortly ordered the captive Ch'en Shu-pao to write with his own brush an order to his commanders up river to surrender to the Sui. The order was entrusted to two high-ranking emissaries who were to deliver it to the key Ch'en commanders.

But defeat was not yet total; substantial Ch'en naval forces controlled the central Yangtze, and fierce engagements were being fought for the upper reaches of the great river. Late in 588 Yang Su readied the fleet that he had been building for four years at Yung-an, a port deep in the Yangtze gorges. The flotilla consisted of huge warships of the "five-toothed" class; these had a superstructure of five decks towering to a height of more than a hundred feet; right and left, fore and aft, were installed six fifty-foot booms that could be manipulated to batter an enemy ship to pieces, while crossbow men raked the decks from firing ports along the five decks. These ships had a capacity of eight hundred fighting men. Among those of lesser size and draft were ships of the "Yellow Dragon" class that carried one hundred marines each. The fleet sailed eastward and soon entered the famous Witches Gorge. A twentieth-century description may help to visualize the setting of the naval battles that were shortly to begin:

> The Witches Gorge . . . is the longest, most spectacular and impressive of all the great gorges. For twenty-five miles the

river turns and twists through scenery of unparalleled beauty and grandeur. The mountains rise sheer up a thousand feet from the water's edge, their heights just showing above fleecy clouds. Through the narrow side-glens and gorges that cut the barrier of hills, here and there glimpses may be caught of mountains rising higher and still higher.

The Ch'en, with a fleet of more than one hundred large ships of the "Azure Dragon" class and a supporting land force of several thousand men, decided to challenge the Sui fleet at Wolf's Tail Rapids. The surrounding terrain was so rocky and forbidding that the Sui men, accustomed to cavalry battles on the plains of the north, were frightened. Yang Su, concerned that his force was no match for the enemy if the fight took place in the rapids, decided on a deceptive maneuver and took his forces down river by night in dead silence. He then ordered a force of his infantry to attack the enemy's base camp and heavy cavalry to come up the north bank of the river and attack the Ch'en from there. The maneuver was successful: the Ch'en's stockaded camp fell, the admiral fled, and captives were taken on a huge scale. Then, as the *T'ung-chien* says, "Yang Su sailed his naval force down river, and warships covered the whole Yangtze, while the pennons flying and the armor made a glittering display. Su was seated, stern of aspect, on a warship. The Ch'en people, seeing him from afar, were filled with awe and exclaimed, 'The Duke of Ch'ing-ho [Yang Su] is indeed the God of the Yangtze.' "

There was still resistance to overcome. Further down river, a Ch'en commander brought up a substantial land force and, cutting a hollow in the rocks of the north bank, moored three strands of chains there, stringing them across the river in order to block the descent of the Sui warships. Yang Su and General Liu (who had moved up from his base at Chiang-ling) first attacked the Ch'en stockaded camp, and "the defending army scattered in the night." Yang Su cut the chains, and the fleet moved on down the river. The Ch'en commander made a final stand further east. This time Yang Su used his deadliest weapon: he sent four of the formidable "Five-Toothed" ships manned by a thousand aboriginal boat people from Szechwan. They broke out their fifty-foot battering booms and smashed ten of the Ch'en warships. There followed a major assault, in which enemy forces were defeated and more than two thousand armored soldiers taken prisoner. The Ch'en ruler had earlier sent two more officials to lead resistance, but they fled without a fight; his walled towns along the upper and central Yangtze were rapidly abandoned. Ch'en forces reassembled to move down river for the relief of Chien-k'ang, but were stopped by the Prince of Ch'in's forces based at Han-k'ou. The emissaries carrying the letter from the Ch'en ruler reached the commanders in the central Yangtze, and, after three days of grieving together, the Ch'en leaders disbanded their troops and went to make their submission to the Prince of Ch'in. The Sui General Wang set out from his headquarters down river from Han-k'ou and took the surrender of many Ch'en civil officials in the areas south of the Yangtze, while others crossed to Han-k'ou to surrender to the Prince of Ch'in. The whole of the Yangtze Valley was now in Sui hands, and Wen-ti sent emissaries to reassure the populations in the former Ch'en administrative units south of the river.

Ch'en loyalists rallied around the governor of Wu-chou in the area between the fallen capital and the sea. General Yü-wen led Sui forces to attack by land, while General Yen's flotilla, in readiness at the mouth of the Yangtze, took his ships and men into Lake T'ai-hu to support the land forces. The Sui troops fought fiercely, and their units struck with lightning speed. The commander who had been left behind to defend Wu-chou fled the city disguised as a Taoist priest, and the city fell to General Yü-wen's troops. The governor and leader of the resistance took what forces remained and dug in for a final stand on an island in Lake T'ai-hu. But Sui soldiers (or Sui hirelings dressed like native islanders) set upon his force and captured him. As the center of resistance crumbled, the officials in the coastal area surrendered, and their areas came under Sui control. Thus the main land area of the Ch'en, with its cities and its populations, were ready for incorporation into the Sui empire.

There remained the vast southern hinterland, stretching through thinly populated and mountainous landscape to the outpost of Canton, then beginning its growth into a major port. The scattered inhabitants of this immense area were largely aborigines of varied racial types and equally varied ways of life. In the fertile valleys and along the coast were walled towns and scattered settlements of Chinese colonists who would over the centuries bring the land and most but not all of the aboriginal peoples into the Chinese cultural sphere. Sui forces, moving into the far south, had limited objectives at this time. First, they wished to restore that measure of stability among the native tribes which formal submission to the Chinese dynasties at Nanking had brought. This meant persuading and winning over important chiefs who often dominated, through their own chiefs, a number of lesser tribes. Such important chieftains were the instruments of Chinese "indirect rule" in the southern hinterlands, and they had to be won over if the route to Canton was to be opened, the Chinese occupied towns protected, and the conditions for further colonization assured. Sui dealings with a noted chieftainess in the area of Canton and its hinterland show some of the strategies used to obtain their objectives.

Lady Ch'iao-kuo, to use her ultimate noble title conferred by the Sui, was by any standards a formidable and gifted woman. She was born into a family that for generations had dominated a large number of lesser tribes. She was precociously intelligent and early became well-versed in devising strategies and also in leading troops in the field. She encouraged her own kinsmen gradually to give up their ancient habits of making predatory raids on weaker neighbors, and her family came to control much of the southernmost part of China. About 540, the Liang Dynasty's prefect of Lo-chou, in the Canton area, heard of the young woman's qualities and sought her as a wife for his son, also a Liang official, and he did so partly because Chinese officials were losing their authority over the tribes nominally subject to their jurisdiction. Lady Ch'iao-kuo agreed, then negotiated a compact with her own tribesmen that they would abandon their ancestral ways and follow Chinese norms. The *Sui History* tells us: "Every time she and her husband sat in judgment on a case, even when it was a tribal chief who had violated the law, and even when the chief was her own kinsman, there were no exceptions made." It is said that orderly government was gradually restored, and no one dared violate the law.

During the Hou Ching Rebellion that ended the Liang Dynasty, she shrewdly advised her husband to withhold his loyalty from self-appointed saviors of the dynasty who were actually bent on usurpation. Finally she urged him to join forces with General Ch'en Pa-hsien, who shortly founded the Ch'en Dynasty. After her husband's death she assured order and maintained her loyalty to the Ch'en, and her son further enhanced the power and distinction of the family. They put down rebellions in the south, and both mother and son received lavish gifts, ranks, and noble titles from the Ch'en. Her son died just before the fall of the Ch'en. The dynasty's end left Chinese officials in the far south in a powerless limbo. The chiefs of several districts joined in elevating Lady Ch'iao-kuo, calling her "Sagely

Mother." She is said to have defended the frontiers, no doubt against tribal raids and marauding freebooters, and quieted the people.

After the fall of the Ch'en, a Sui force moved into the south, but at a certain point stopped for fear of serious resistance. Diplomacy was brought into play. The Prince of Chin had the captive Ch'en ruler write a letter of the type he had written to commanders in the Yangtze basin, informing Lady Ch'iao-kuo of the dynasty's fall and ordering her to submit to the Sui. Along with this letter the Prince sent an insignia of military rank and a rhinoceros horn staff. When she saw the latter, she knew the Ch'en had fallen; she had sent the same staff as a tributary gift to the Ch'en emperor. She then gathered several thousand tribal chiefs and they mourned together for a whole day the fall of the Ch'en. Then she sent her grandson to escort the Sui commander to Canton and welcome him there. She thus had used her prestige and influence with her own people to help establish Sui power in the south. When a revolt soon broke out, she sent her grandsons to the rescue of the beleaguered Sui commander. Shortly afterward, she herself, wearing armor, riding an armored horse, and carrying a brocade umbrella as a symbol of rank, commanded the detachments of mounted archers who served as escort for the imperial emissary P'ei Chü as he made his rounds of the population centers seeking the main leaders' submission to the Sui. It is said that when the leaders who had submitted to P'ei Chü reported back to their tribes, Sui rule in the south was finally established. The Emperor was appropriately grateful for Lady Ch'iao-kuo's assistance and granted governorships to her two grandsons and a posthumous governorship to her late husband, whom he also enfeoffed as Duke of Ch'iao-kuo. A special patent was issued making her "Lady of Ch'iao-kuo," and she was given munificent imperial presents including hair ornaments and a banqueting robe from the Empress. Thereafter she was given exceptional privileges, such as her own guard and official staff, and considerable latitude in dealing with southern problems. When she reported to the Emperor on the misbehavior of a local governor who had grossly abused one of the tribes nominally under her protection, the Emperor removed the governor, confiscated his ill-gotten wealth, and brought him to trial. When he sent her an edict ordering restitution to the maltreated tribesmen, she herself took the edict through more than ten districts and read it out (no doubt in the tribesmen's own dialect) and thus made known the beneficence of the distant emperor. For this she was once again rewarded.

She kept the imperial gifts of the three dynasties she had served in one treasure house and each year, probably at New Year's, she held a great reception when they were all displayed in her great hall. The *Sui History* tells us that she showed them to her sons and grand-sons and said, "All of you should give all of your loyal hearts to the Son of Heaven. I have served the rulers of three dynasties, ever with complete good will. These gifts that you now see have all been pre-served and they are the rewards of loyalty and filial submission. It is my solemn wish that you all thoughtfully reflect on this." It is ap-parent that the Sui had found in this woman a formidable instru-ment for their indirect rule; they used her well and wisely, and the transition from Ch'en to Sui suzerainty in the far south was rela-tively rapid and, as things went in those days, peaceful.

At the close of those far-flung campaigns, the Sui had taken complete control of the Ch'en domain: a total of thirty prefectures, one hundred commanderies, and four hundred counties—the whole of southern and eastern China from the Yangtze to the South China Sea. This was, given the technological level of the time, a veritable *Blitzkrieg;* it ensured the Sui of military dominance, but all the prob-lems of peaceful consolidation remained before them. Shortly after the end of the campaigns, an edict ordered the destruction of the en-tire city of Chien-k'ang, the capital and cultural center of the "legiti-mate" dynasties of China for 282 years; its walls, palaces, temples, and houses were to be razed and the land returned to agricultural use. Thus by a stroke of the brush the geographical rallying point of southern and legitimist sentiments, the command post for repeated attempts to conquer the north, the repository of records, literature, ancient traditions, and common memories was destroyed. The Sui was even then planning a new city without Chien-k'ang's hostile and separatist associations that was to become in time a new center of southern culture.

A problem that admitted of no such straightforward solution was what to do with the Ch'en ruler, his nobles, and his high officials—those who, in Confucian terms, had been morally responsible for the decline and fall of the dynasty. It was decided that all those notables should take the long journey west and north to the Sui capital where they would be forever separated from any dissident following that might rally around one or another of them. It was a long column of travelers, on foot and on horseback and in sedan chairs and carts that made its way toward the Sui capital—though not perhaps stretching, as one source tells us, 170 miles without a break. In the Sui capital, people were busy with preparations to receive the noble visitors. The Emperor made grants so that private houses could be replaced and repainted to accommodate the new arrivals, who were to be billeted among the townspeople of all classes. As the procession neared the capital, an imperial messenger went out to welcome them. As the *Tzu-chih t'ung-chien* tells us, "For the Ch'en people it was like a home-coming." Some among the party indeed could claim descent from aristocrats who had been driven from the northern capitals by foreign invaders nearly three centuries before. Nevertheless, both tradition and power realities required formal actions which would establish the Sui ruler as the one unchallenged Son of Heaven. In the steps he took, Wen-ti was undoubtedly guided by his Confucian advisors and ritualists, for the underlying basis of his reign is the moral-political theory of imperial Confucianism, and the acts are redolent of its symbolism. First the Ch'en ruler, his ennobled kinsmen, ranking generals, and ministers, together with their astronomical charts and imperial impedimenta, were presented as prizes of war to the Sui ancestors in the Sui ancestral hall. The two imperial princes who held high commands in the campaigns also took part in this solemn ceremony. The next day the Ch'en ruler, accompanied by twenty-eight princes of the blood and more than two hundred high officials, was led to the open plaza before the great south gate of the Palace City. Wen-ti, facing south, looked down on them from the gate tower above. First he had a palace official read out an edict of imperial commiseration on the sufferings they had undergone. Then a second official read out another edict blaming the ruler and his ministers who, unable to help one another, had brought their state to ruin. "Ch'en Shu-pao and his ministers all held their breath and prostrated themselves on the ground; filled with shame, they were unable to reply." Following this the Sui emperor in his role as supreme moral arbiter of the whole realm graciously granted them forgiveness. Two days later, at the same site, he gave a grand feast for his victorious troops. Piles of cloth lined the great avenue stretching three miles or more to the south gate of the city. To each soldier according to his rank a reward of cloth was made. No less than thirty million lengths are said to have been distributed on this day. After all these celebrations were over, Wen-ti issued an edict designating five families as guardians of each of the tombs of previous Ch'en rulers. Wen-ti, ever cautious, did not want all the surviving Ch'en princes concentrated in the Sui capital, so he had them installed in various prefectures and counties and each year sent them an imperial gift of a suit of clothes. As for Ch'en Shu-pao, Wen-ti was frankly fascinated by the debauched poet who had once been his enemy. Though both men were devout Buddhists, they shared no other taste or character trait. Yet Wen-ti invited Shu-pao to banquets and was apologetic about not having the musicians to play the Wu (southern) music for him. He asked Shu-pao's guardian about his likes and dislikes and learned that he had a fondness for donkey meat. When he asked how much liquor his household consumed, he was amazed to hear that Shu-pao and his sons and brothers drank a gallon every day. On one imperial progress, Shu-pao accompanied Wen-ti in ascending a mountain near Loyang; there, drinking with the Emperor, Shu-pao dashed off a poem of high praise for Sui rule, and later petitioned the Emperor, urging him to make the solemn sacrifices at Mount T'ai, symbol of universal rule. After more than a decade of comfortable wine-bibbing and poetizing, Ch'en Shu-pao died in Loyang in 604, the year before Wen-ti's death. He was given the incredible posthumous rank of "Generalissimo" and enfeoffed as Duke of Ch'ang-an County.

The treatment of Ch'en officials was similarly lenient. A few were given substantive office in the central government; many more were given nominal rank and a stipend. The Ch'en system of local administration in the south was at first simply taken over by the Sui, and Sui appointees replaced Ch'en officials. In the most thorough survey of the subject, I could find no case of a former Ch'en prefect being reappointed by the Sui. The number of prefectures in the Ch'en domain had been forty-two. Among the thirty cases of the renaming or establishment of prefectures by the Sui in the years 589 and 590, where anything is known about the prefects, they were all northerners. A generous conciliatory gesture was an imperial edict suspending all tax collection in the south for ten years. Yet no conciliatory measures could wipe out the hatred and distrust of northerners that the men of the south had built up over nearly three centuries. Certainly the prompt order to destroy the Ch'en capital, aside from the symbolic effect we have noted, meant the loss of the family homes of thousands and the dispossession of the Buddhist clergy of an estimated three hundred temples within the walls built under royal and aristocratic patronage. Former local officials were jobless and resentful. More than this, the Sui was determined to bring to an end the lack of respect for law, the unchecked exploitation of the rest of the populace by the great hereditary clans, and what northerners regarded as the moral slackness of the southern population. Here they tried to do too much too precipitately. Su Wei, who, we may recall, was a great Sui official and the son of a noted Confucian ideologue, wrote a kind of catechism of Confucian morality entitled "The Five Teachings" (*Wu-chiao*) expounding the basic attitudes that should inform human relations. The southerners, young and old alike, were required to commit this to memory. This elicited widespread resentment. Then a rumor—always efficacious in semiliterate societies—began circulating that the Sui planned the mass deportation of all the people of the south to northwest China. Panic spread and was followed by revolts which broke out all over the south. The rebels seized the newly appointed local officials and, sometimes, as they disemboweled them, said: "This will make you better able to recite the Five Teachings!"

Yang Su was immediately summoned to go back into action and suppress the rebellion. The fighting was ferocious, hundreds of desperate engagements were fought, no quarter was given by either side, but the Ch'en rebels were relentlessly pursued, even to their last refuges on the islands off the coast, and their leaders executed. A last flare-up of resistance endangered the Sui hold on the Canton area, but with the help of Lady Ch'iao-kuo this too ended in the restoration of Sui supremacy.

The Sui had conquered; the lands and peoples of the Ch'en state had been incorporated in the Sui empire, and rebellion had been ferociously but effectively put down. The tasks now facing the Sui were formidable: to break down southern hatred and fear of their new masters, to promote—widely and selectively—the spread of Sui culture, laws, and administrative practices throughout the south—in other words, to complete by patient and subtle means the integration of the south into the new unified empire. Toward the end of 590, Wen-ti appointed his gifted second son Yang Kuang, Prince of Chin (and, eventually, his successor), governor of Yang-chou, with his headquarters in the city that the Sui called Chiang-tu, the "Yangtze capital" (the modern Yangchow). Here he stayed for nearly ten years, virtually viceroy of the south, and the tasks of conciliation and integration fell to him. What he accomplished and what effects the southern assignment had on him may best be considered in the context of his biography and personality, the subject of the next chapter.

CHAPTER 7

The Second Emperor

Yang Kuang, known to history as Yang-ti (the Emperor Yang), was born in 569, the second son of Yang Chien and his non-Chinese wife. The first twelve years of the young man's life were, we may suppose, devoted to the pursuits common to his class and time: the rudiments of Chinese, regular Buddhist observances (he and his brothers had Buddhist childhood names, and one of them aspired to become a monk), training in horsemanship, and the arts of warfare and the chase. His biography says that he was studious and gifted in literary composition. It also tells us that he was deeply serious and of dignified bearing. His father's usurpation altered completely the life of Yang Kuang and his four brothers. From their comfortable but perhaps humdrum childhood as sons of a ranking official, they were catapulted into the life of a sixth-century court. They became imperial princes and were given fiefs and high-sounding titles. They also became pawns in the insidious intrigues around the center of power, where officials, palace favorites, soothsayers, monks, and charlatans jockeyed for advantage. As we have seen in Chapter Three, Yang Kuang's parents were uneasy and fearful in their sudden eminence—attained, as they knew, by usurpation, violent warfare, and wholesale murder. Their suspicions were easily aroused and played upon. The Empress was puritanical and insanely jealous, and she

meddled constantly in the lives of her sons, censuring the slightest
deviation from her strict standards. The Emperor had an obsessive
fear that one of his sons, as they grew to manhood, would emerge as
the center of a clique or cabal bent on replacing him. Of the five
sons, Yang Kuang was the only one who consistently escaped the
hostility of both parents. This was not wholly accidental.

Yang Kuang's first official post was as nominal head of a newly
established inspectorate in the north of the North China Plain. He
was then only thirteen. The Emperor sent seasoned civil and military
chiefs of staff to assist him—men who also had (and used) the authority to discipline their young charge. About the same time the
Emperor, perhaps as a stratagem in his unification plans, sought a
bride for his second son in the Sui satellite kingdom of Later Liang
on the central Yangtze. Oracles were taken, and they pointed to a
daughter of the former ruling house, a girl descended from the emperors of the older Liang Dynasty at Nanking. The young lady had
been well brought up; she was fond of study, highly intelligent, and
had literary abilities. Yang Kuang loved and respected her. She was
his consort and confidante throughout his life. It may well be that
she introduced him to southern ways and encouraged his fondness
for the south that grew to be almost obsessive.

Yang Kuang, nominally commander-in-chief of the expeditionary force against the Ch'en in 589, was richly rewarded for his part in
the conquest, returned briefly to a northern post and then proceeded
to Chiang-tu, where he became an effective viceroy. Except for
yearly trips to the capital to report to his father, and one brief period
in 600 as commander of an army sent against the Turks, he reigned
in Chiang-tu for nearly ten years.

His tasks in the south were many and complex: to reduce southern hatred and suspicion, to introduce rational administration in the
wake of military occupation, to break down the many political and
cultural barriers that prevented southerners from becoming loyal
subjects of the Sui. The measures he took to these ends complemented the general orders concerning the conquered south emanat-
ing from the imperial capital. For example, there was the order of
589 remitting all taxes in the former Ch'en domain for ten years, the
order of 598 restricting the size of boats that could be built in the
south to about thirty feet so as to prevent water-borne dissidence,
and many more. Yang Kuang concentrated on what might be called a
cultural strategy meant to persuade southerners that their new rulers
were not barbarians but civilized men sharing and appreciating the

same heritage. In this strategy his personal sophistication was an asset; so no doubt were his increasing fluency in Wu, the principal southern dialect, and the presence of his high-born southern wife.

He moved into his post after the widespread armed revolt against the Sui conquerors had been put down with great savagery by Yang Su. Anti-Sui feeling was running high. The Ch'en Dynasty and aristocracy had long been generous patrons of Buddhism, and now the monks—many of whom had taken up arms in the anti-Sui uprisings—found themselves without patrons, eking out an existence in the ruined and half-empty temples at Nanking and elsewhere. Yang Kuang set about immediately to build a capital to replace Nanking, which for nearly three centuries had been the cultural and political hub of the south. It was from this capital, Chiang-tu, that he issued orders for the collection and recopying of Buddhist scriptures scattered in the war and subsequent civil disorder. There he built Buddhist temples and a library to house the holy books. And to his capital he summoned eminent southern monks to live in his temples and carry on religious and scholarly work. Perhaps the most noted among them was Chih-i, founder of the T'ien-t'ai school, who had long enjoyed the patronage of the Ch'en imperial house.

In Chiang-tu, late in the year 591, Yang Kuang gave a lavish vegetarian feast for a thousand southern monks. After the banquet the young prince knelt to receive from Chih-i the "Bodhisattva vows" for lay Buddhists and the religious sobriquet of Tsung-ch'ih p'u-sa, "Bodhisattva of Absolute Control." After Chih-i's return to his monastery at Mount T'ien-t'ai, Yang Kuang continued his patronage of the community there and corresponded regularly with the great prelate. Chih-i sent on to his patron petitions from southern clerics. One begged him to stop the razing of Buddhist temples along with everything else in the former Ch'en capital, to which Yang Kuang replied ambiguously; another requested that two local temples containing the holy remains of saintly monks be spared from noisy posthouse traffic—a request that was granted; a third was a report by Chih-i himself on Sui officials' dispersing—presumably for reasons of "security"—a gathering of a thousand monks who had come to hear him speak. When Chih-i sent him a Bodhisattva chaplet, the Prince wrote in his letter of thanks:

> The chaplet seems in its conception to be the work of a divine will, and its design comparable to something made by Maudgālyayāna [Buddha's disciple famed for his supernatu-

ral powers] . . . This chaplet does honor to its wearer. With formal solemnity I knelt and had it fitted to my head. As I looked in a hand mirror and walked back and forth, it seemed to flatter my homely face; adding grace, it altered my appearance.

In his considerable exchange of letters with Chih-i we see something of Yang Kuang's character at this time: a wide acquaintance with Buddhist scriptures and what appears to be genuine religious feeling, added to strong political instincts—the skilled mixture of flattery, cajolery, and patronage used to win over the leading southern monks, a mixture also likely to please his pious parents

Yang Kuang's cultural strategy in the south was by no means limited to Buddhism. Although this was by far the most influential tradition he invoked, he also built at his capital two Taoist monasteries to which he invited learned southern adepts. He issued invitations to noted Confucian scholars who had formerly served the Ch'en to come to his capital to teach and write under his patronage, and one of them compiled a huge collection of ritual texts in a hundred and twenty rolls. In addition to "representatives" of the two religions and of Confucianism, Yang Kuang assembled more than a hundred noted literary men of the south. It is obvious that this was not only a shrewd further move to allay anti-Sui sentiment among the southern élite, but an action very close to his own heart. He enjoyed literary companionship, and perhaps his favorite among these men was Liu Pien, sometime official of the Later Liang. Liu polished the young prince's prose and became a much-favored drinking companion. His talk was said to have been slanderous and hilarious. This relationship—which lasted the rest of his life—may also be viewed as one aspect of Yang Kuang's conversion to southern culture.

Chiang-tu and the southern literary culture it represented to him held a special place in his affections. It was a sensual landscape he celebrated often in his poetry, as in "The Joy of My Palace in Chiang-Tu":

Oh, to linger in my old haunts in Yang-chou
Terraced kiosks, high and bright, where
    I love to stroll.
To meet early summer in breeze-blown
    pavilions, under blossoming trees,
And say good-bye to autumn's end on tracts
    of marsh and grain-covered slopes.

> Cassia oars on clear pools, fishhawk
>   prows bobbing;
> A fruit falls on my golden saddle, the
>   dark steed startles.
> Amber wine and pale lees, we drink the
>   drifting clouds,
> Of long sleeves and clear song, a land
>   of pleasure and delight.

It may be that to a certain degree ruling the south involved Yang Kuang in the role of aristocratic aesthete and poet that was expected of a southern prince. At times he despised southern decadence, but he also maintained the southern tradition by writing new lyrics for a song composed by the last Ch'en ruler, "Spring River, Flowers, Moon, Night":

> The evening river, level, unmoving;
> Spring flowers full, just blossomed.
> The rolling waves carry the moon away,
> While tide waters come, bearing the
>   stars onward.

Although there is no comprehensive account of Yang Kuang's administration in the south, the absence of further rebellions and his long tenure at Chiang-tu suggest that it was a considerable success, and that the credit for many measures of cultural reunification should be his.

When, in the year 600, he was about to return to his Yangtze capital after a visit to the court, Yang Kuang paid a farewell visit to his mother the Empress. He found her in a towering rage about the behavior of her eldest son Yung, the Crown Prince; his principal consort had died with mysterious suddenness in 591, and he continued to be infatuated with his favorite concubine by whom he had four sons. His mother had set people spying on him, and their reports further outraged her puritanical and monogamous sentiments. The *Sui History* tells us that Yang Kuang saw in this growing estrangement his chance and that he returned to Chiang-tu to plot with his intimates for his brother's downfall. Such plotting meant secrecy and subterfuge; it involved great risks and also the chance of great rewards both for the principal and his confederates. One of the more blunt-spoken of the men who joined Yang Kuang's group said, in effect, "What have we got to lose? If the plot succeeds, you become Crown Prince; if not we can always fall back on the Huai Valley and the seacoast and return to the old pattern of a southern dynasty like the Liang and Ch'en."

It is impossible to know what credence to give the account of what followed, but it is plain that the wily and ruthless Yang Su was a principal conspirator. Sufficient "evidence" was eventually concocted to mislead the ever-suspicious emperor, and he finally proclaimed the edict deposing Yung as Crown Prince to an assemblage of ranking officials and imperial kinsmen gathered in one of the palace halls. Yang Kuang, who, it is said, had carefully engineered his "image" with his aging parents as a hard-working, pious, loyal, and monogamous young man—easier to accomplish at a considerable distance from the imperial capital—now won the coveted prize. In the eleventh month of the year 600 he was proclaimed Crown Prince and shortly thereafter moved his household north to the imperial capital.

By this time his father was completing the fifty-ninth year of his life—a particularly solemn anniversary in China where the sexagenary cycle was the most important large-scale measure of time. He was also preparing the empire-wide enshrinement of holy Buddhist relics described in Chapter Five, to be carried out simultaneously in thirty prefectural capitals on his birthday in the sixth month of 601. The newly elevated Crown Prince showed himself to be appropriately pious. In 601 he himself built a spacious temple in one of the southeastern wards of the city neighboring the elegant serpentine lake, inviting a large number of learned monks to live in it—one third of them from his own temple at Chiang-tu and all but three from the Huai and Yangtze valleys. By this means many southern Buddhist traditions were introduced into the north. When the Prince's mother died in 602, the eminent monks from his temple figured largely in the funerary observances.

After the Empress's death, the Emperor left more and more of the management of state affairs to the Crown Prince. When the imperial entourage moved for the summer to the Jen-shou Palace, a hundred miles or so northwest of the capital, the Emperor left Yang Kuang in charge. In 603, the Emperor was persuaded by alleged evidence of black magic to degrade his fourth son; the evidence was so presented as also to raise suspicions about the loyalty of the fifth son, Liang, Prince of Han. In the summer of 604, the Emperor fell ill. There is textual evidence that the Crown Prince and his confederates

Yang Su and Chang Heng hastened Wen-ti's end, and that they intercepted his deathbed message reinstating Yung as Crown Prince. There are grounds for doubting some of these texts, but although much of the evidence is tendentious, it seems possible. In any case, eight days later Yang Kuang ascended the throne as the second emperor of the Sui. His youngest brother Liang, Prince of Han, rose in revolt in the east, and advisors urged him to carve out a hegemony for himself in the rich North China Plain, the former territory of the Northern Ch'i. But he was indecisive and proved no match for Yang Su, who crushed his armies and took him prisoner. The new emperor graciously did not impose the death penalty, but Liang shortly afterwards "died in prison."

Characterization of the man known to history as Sui Yang-ti is exceedingly difficult, and one cannot hope for more than glimpses of the human reality behind the mass of doctored history and mythology that has gathered around him as a classic "bad-last" emperor. The historical texts contrast his father's prudence with Yang-ti's profligacy, but—as we shall see in the sections on building the eastern capital and on the completion of the canal system—the starkness of the contrast is overdrawn. The image of Yang-ti in popular literature paints him as licentious—as indulging his lusts in fantastic ways. But then one finds that even the hostile historians do not disguise the fact that his principal consort, a sensitive and educated woman, was never put aside for some palace favorite but was honored and, apparently, loved until the bitter end. Sui Yang-ti, who was, after all, a connoisseur of beautiful things, an accomplished poet, and a prose stylist, may have been something of a political aesthete who as a type was characterized in the following quotation: "Indeed, self-deception is perhaps the rule, for the political personality with a strong artistic component possesses a florid imagination which dramatizes his personal history and subordinates all reality to ambitious plans." He did indeed inherit a newly unified and prosperous empire from his hard-working father. And he planned and executed the armed expansion of its territory and of its influence. But these dreams and these expeditions were neither fantastic nor unprecedented. They were, rather, a filling out of the Han model of a Chinese empire which his father had adopted and which Yang-ti sought to complete. It was only the disastrous failure of his last adventure that casts a ghastly light backward and colors all the chronicles of his reign. Perhaps we can glimpse more of his complex character as we consider his political style and the men who were his ranking officials and close advisors. We should note at the outset that his Empress, although obviously in his confidence, did not assume—as his mother had—an active political role.

If one looks at the tables of the upper officialdom of the Sui, both civil and military, Yang-ti's appointments seem very similar to his father's. There is the same inclination, it would seem, to appoint kinsmen, people from their native place, and, in general, northwestern aristocrats of mixed ancestry. A few of the same men served both father and son in high office. Yü-wen K'ai, for example, was a great engineer. He worked on the planning and construction of the new Sui capital and was continuously engaged in building projects: canals, palaces, tombs, sections of the Great Wall, the mobile audience hall, and the vast tent palace with which Yang-ti impressed the Turks. He designed the bridge over the Liao River used in the first campaign against the Manchurian Kingdom of Koguryō (page 192), and at the time of his death in 612 he was serving as president of the Board of Works. Another faithful minister under both father and son was Niu Hung, the imperturbable northwesterner with a long beard and a speech impediment. He had an extraordinary career. At the beginning of the Sui he was the man who persuaded Wen-ti to embark on the systematic collection of the Chinese literary heritage, the books scattered in the upheavals of the centuries of disunion. (He recommended getting works from private collections by purchase or by confiscation; the imperial library became in turn the basis of the "Bibliography" chapter of the *Sui History*, our prime guide to the literature of the Period of Disunion.) He had been the chief voice in developing the Sui ritual code, served as president of the Board of Rites for at least three years, and probably had a major hand in compiling the Sui law codes. From 599 until his death in 610 he was president of the prestigious Board of Civil Office to which the Sui emperors delegated great powers over the selection, appointment, and promotion of officials. During Niu Hung's management of the selection system, the *Tzu-chih t'ung-tien* tells us, personal character was favored over literary ability. The powers of this office were somewhat eroded under Yang-ti, but the stolid, apparently incorruptible minister and Yang-ti were fast friends. They had exchanged poems when Yang-ti was Crown Prince, and Niu is said to have been invited to feast and drink in the inner palace in the presence of the Empress—a mark of special esteem. When Niu died at the Yangtze capital, the Emperor mourned him deeply and had his corpse sent back to Niu's native place, far in the west.

From about 609 the locus of power and critical decision making shifted away from the formal organs of government and the men who staffed them. Characteristically, Yang-ti was always on the move. He had three capitals—Ta-hsing ch'eng, the principal one, in the west; Loyang in the southern part of the North China Plain; and Chiang-tu, his beloved "Yangtze Capital." He traveled frequently by canal boat among the three capitals, taking a considerable entourage with him. On many occasions he traveled north to the Great Wall to inspect defenses or negotiate with the T'u-chüeh khans; in 608 he proceeded with an impressive entourage to Heng-shan, Hopei, one of the five sacred mountains of China, where he performed the imperial sacrifices. In 609 he personally led an expedition out from the Kansu corridor against the T'u-yü Hun. Yang-ti was a restless man; he apparently abhorred routine and enjoyed travel. His delight in this occupation appears in a number of fine landscape poems. Some of these are framed by attempts to justify imperial journeys, but all show a man who keenly appreciated the physical world. Here is one called "Morning Crossing of the Huai":

> The level Huai is a dark rolling flood
> That mists over in morning fog,
> But before the light outlines its domains,
> Its murky blackness shares dawn's radiance.
> Sunlit rose clouds turn round lone island peaks,
> Brocade sails emerge from the long shores.
> Fish of highwater often leap from the waves,
> Birds of the sands sing at the moment of flight,
> And if you wait till a high autumn evening,
> Sorrow will go off along with the passing waters.

Even more significantly, Yang-ti believed in showing the wealth and power of the dynasty to his subjects and in looking into local conditions himself. He is reported to have said, in 609: " 'From ancient times the Sons of Heaven have carried out the ritual of imperial tours of inspection. But the emperors in the south [during the Period of Disunion] mostly perpetuated womanly ways. They sat in the innermost palaces without ever meeting their people face to face. How would you interpret this?' " A courtier present replied, " 'This is precisely why their hold on power could not be prolonged.' " For Yang-ti the imperial progress was almost a way of life, and he built a number of detached palaces around the country where he might relax for a day or a week in the course of his tours.

This manner of existence meant that he could not conduct the business of government in the closely scheduled and orderly way so characteristic of his father—a style suited to the functionally zoned areas of the principal Sui capital. Indeed he is reported to have been advised by one of his courtiers to hold formal audiences only once every five days and to avoid "imitating Kao-tsu [his father] who wore himself out in toilsome labor." Yang-ti is said to have agreed with this advice. Whether we accept this account or not, the physical circumstances just noted, his own personality, and the connivance of skilled courtiers combined to make him increasingly dependent on a diminishing circle of intimate advisors. This group, of course, ultimately made him their captive, and meanwhile fed his ego, catered to his prejudices, and "took care of" those independent spirits who sought to offer advice.

Kao Chiung, the master statesman and general of the first Sui reign, had been rusticated by the jealous counsels of Wen-ti's empress. Yang-ti, at the beginning of his reign, restored the old man to office and gave him a high-sounding title. But in 607 Kao Chiung and others of his generation became outspokenly critical of the new emperor's policies and of the atmosphere of his court. The criticism was duly reported, and as a result Kao Chiung was condemned to death, and his sons exiled to the frontiers. Ho-jo Pi, one of the Sui's most gifted and successful generals, who, like Kao Chiung, had played a major role in the conquest of Ch'en, was indicted at the same time. He was executed, and his wives and children were made slaves of the state and transported to the frontier. Yü-wen Pi, another singularly talented and high-ranking official of the previous reign and, at the time, president of the Board of Rites, was also implicated and suffered a similar fate. The *Sui History*'s comment on his case may be applicable to other senior statesmen: "Having become famous for his talent and ability and having held a succession of exalted ranks and offices, his reputation was weighty indeed. In policy discussions his remarks were nearly always praised by others. As a result the Emperor conceived an envious dislike for him." The aged Hsüeh Taoheng, probably the greatest Confucian scholar of his time, was recalled from a provincial post early in Yang-ti's reign and given an important office. But he proved tactless in praising the previous reign and even invoked the name of Kao Chiung. Yang-ti went into a rage and turned Hsüeh over to the judicial authorities. After hoping against hope for either imperial justice or mercy, the old Confucian was strangled to death and his wives and children banished to Central Asia. All these men, whether for their intimate association with his father, or for their independent reputations combined with outspokenness, or for unknown personal reasons, incurred Yang-ti's disfavor and suffered accordingly. All, save possibly Yang Su—the *éminence grise* whose case, described in Chapter Three, falls somewhat outside the pattern—were the type of official who was skilled in the traditional style of remonstrance and discussion in open audience. Yang-ti, as we have suggested, favored another mode of reaching decisions, and this mode dictated the kind of official who shared the emperor's secrets and his power

It is significant that those who became the most powerful of the inner circle were both southerners. Yü Shih-chi was the son of a Ch'en official and had served that dynasty before its conquest by the Sui. The rise to power of this unimpressive man began with the accession of Yang-ti, and in a short time he became something like a confidential secretary, a role which *someone* had to fill, given Yang-ti's style of government. The *Sui History* speaks of this style and of Yü's role: "With Su Wei, Yü-wen Shu, P'ei Chü and P'ei Yün, he managed the court administration (*ch'ao-cheng*). Whereupon, as the affairs of the empire multiplied, the memorials coming in from all quarters reached a daily total of more than a hundred. The Emperor was then solemn and preoccupied, and matters were not subject to audience decision. Rather, after the Emperor had reached his council-chamber, he would first of all summon Shih-chi and orally indicate the disposition he wanted made of them. When Shih-chi reached his own office, he would turn these instructions into imperial orders. Although his daily output came to one hundred pages, they were without omissions or errors." From such an intimate relation with the supreme autocrat, Yü Shih-chi's power spread. The *Tzu-chih t'ung-chien* tells us that, although the Board of Civil Office was headed by Niu Hung, assisted by seven other ranking officials, "the brush that granted or took away was held by Yü Shih-chi alone; when he received a bribe, the candidate jumped in rank; when he did not, the candidate's name was simply entered on the official roster." That he took bribes is not confirmed by any other source, but his power was built into the arrangement. He was not incapable of giving good advice. The *Sui History* tells us, in one of the accounts of the siege of the Emperor by the Turks at Yen-men in 615, that after the imperial forces had failed to break out, Yü Shih-chi urged his master to encourage the troops and to offer them bounties; he drafted an edict for the Emperor announcing an end to the disliked campaigns against

Koguryō. The Emperor went along with these measures. But when
the soldiers broke the siege, Yang-ti went back on his word, failed to
distribute the promised bounties, and again proclaimed an invasion
of the Liao River Valley. This, the text tells, marked the end of the
Emperor's "credibility" in court and countryside; his confidential
secretary stayed with him to the end and died at the hands of the
same assassins who killed his master.

Yang-ti's style of government also required a chief of intelligence. The Emperor found him in P'ei Yün, grandson of a Liang official, son of a Ch'en official who had been taken prisoner by the Sui
and saw service under the Sui founder. "Because his father was in
the north," Yün secretly petitioned Wen-ti to be allowed to serve as
a Sui agent in the Ch'en domain, and, when the Ch'en fell, he was
rewarded by a succession of high offices. Yang-ti tested him in a series of assignments and eventually made him part of his inner circle.
Yün was utterly ruthless and, as his power increased, was made chief
censor and more and more encroached on the powers of the judi-
ciary. In 613, when Yang Hsüan-kan, the son of Yang Su, revolted,
the rising was quickly crushed, but the Emperor's confidence was
severely shaken. So he ordered Yün to ferret out all those in any way
implicated, and Yün hunted them down savagely. The *Sui History*
says that tens of thousands were executed and their property confiscated. Yün is said to have connived at the execution of the aged
Hsüeh Tao-heng, and he engineered the dismissal of a long-time
member of the inner circle, Su Wei, when that venerable statesman
tried indirectly to tell Yang-ti about the extent of rebellion in the
empire

Yü-wen Shu was a northerner of non-Chinese origin. He had
achieved military recognition under the Northern Chou and helped
the Sui founder in the consolidation of power. He had commanded a
unit of thirty thousand men in the campaign against Ch'en, saw
some hard fighting, and achieved notable success. During the campaign he met Yang Kuang, then Prince of Chin, and the latter was
much taken with this warrior whose background was so similar to
his own. He petitioned for his appointment to a post not distant from
his vice-regal capital at Chiang-tu and later involved him in the plot
to get the line of imperial succession altered. When this succeeded
he was richly rewarded, and rewarded again when Yang-ti came to
the throne. In 608 he drove the T'u-yü Hun from their ancestral
lands, took their leaders and some four thousand captives, who were
enslaved. From 609 on, he was a member of the Emperor's inner cir-

cle. Yü-wen Shu is said to have shamelessly abused his position; his
avarice was unlimited, and he was the terror of the court. He never
heard of a rare or costly object without trying to get it for himself. As
is often the case in the Chinese histories, his greed is linked to a total
sycophancy; from a look on his master's face, he knew what advice
was wanted (quite apart from what might be best for the monarch or
the empire), and he would then proffer it. Given the bias of the
sources, how much of this we should believe is a question. In fact,
Yü-wen Shu took on some difficult assignments. After a military disaster to his armies in the first campaign against Koguryō, he was
briefly cashiered and reduced to the rank of commoner. But a year
later, while en route to the northeast, he was ordered to proceed
against the first of those who rebelled against Sui rule, Yang Hsüan-
kan. He crushed Yang's armies, captured Yang, and sent his head to
the Emperor. Shu fell ill when the Emperor had already withdrawn
(on Shu's advice, it is said) to the Yangtze capital. He died there, after
begging his imperial master for clemency for his two sons, who were
then under house arrest. One of them shortly thereafter led the band
that assassinated Yang-ti. Yü-wen Shu was, first and last, a military
man, perhaps less of a master strategist—P'ei Chü had that role—
than a tough, relentless field commander. Such people often get an
undeservedly negative biography from bureaucratic historians.

Su Wei, already discussed as a member of Wen-ti's group of advisors, emerges again under Yang-ti, now in favor, now under heavy
censure, wily, ambitious, corrupt, carrying out a succession of difficult civil and military assignments, but probably considerably less
influential than other members of the inner circle. It is typical of him
that, having served both Sui emperors, he took service under Yang-
ti's assassin, later under other contenders for power, and died in his
mansion in Ch'ang-an at the age of eighty-two.

P'ei Chü was the member of the inner circle most concerned with
foreign and barbarian affairs. He appears to us, through the cloudy
glass of the sources, to have been a relatively honest official, somewhat less of a hatchet man than Yang Su or P'ei Yün, somewhat less
of the bloodless *alter ego* than Yü Shih-chi. He was a native of the
modern Shansi Province and grew up under the Northern Ch'i; he
met the future Sui founder when the latter arrived to take over a
prefecture after the Northern Chou conquest of the Ch'i. After the
establishment of the Sui, he held a series of lesser posts until Wen-ti
sent him south to relieve Kuang-chou (the modern Canton), then
under pressure from aboriginal rebels; he was successful, executed

the leaders, and, in the time-honored manner, settled the aborigines of "twenty-odd prefectures" under their own chiefs. When he returned north he was rewarded and promoted. From that time on his concern was mainly with the T'u-chüeh (Turks) and the northern and western frontiers generally. He both planned and executed military and diplomatic moves to check the Turks and he seems to have been quite successful. He was rewarded with important civil posts at the end of Wen-ti's reign.

When Yang-ti succeeded to the throne, P'ei Chü soon became his principal advisor on frontier problems and foreign peoples. In the course of his duties, P'ei went out to the border trading posts in what is now Kansu and there gathered intelligence regarding Inner Asia. He was an indefatigable geographer and ethnographer, and presented to his imperial master an "Illustrated Account of the Western Regions" (Hsi-yü t'u-chih), in which he described the characteristics of some forty-four "states" to the west of China and sketched the principal trade routes to the "Western Ocean" as well. His account was accompanied by a detailed map, which does not survive. His policy recommendations were to use peaceful means—mainly the wealth and prestige of China—to win over as many of these people as could be reached, or whose representatives could be impressed. But P'ei Chü also encouraged Yang-ti to establish garrison and trading towns beyond the frontiers and force the submission of certain ethnic groups. For example in 608 the land of the T'u-yü Hun, south of the Kansu corridor, was seized by the forces of Yü-wen Shu, divided into Chinese administrative units, and colonized with Chinese "convicted of minor crimes" and thus condemned to exile. Whether P'ei Chü was the principal advocate of foreign adventures, or whether Yang-ti would have embarked on them without his advice is an unanswerable question. The Tzu-chih t'ung-chien, in a particularly blatant piece of editorializing, says that in 607 Yang-ti, having listened to P'ei Chü, impulsively dreamed of emulating the achievements of Ch'in Shih Huang Ti and Han Wu-ti and of conquering the whole of Central Asia. And, after pointedly emphasizing the way that missions going to and fro from the Sui capital to Inner Asia exacted contributions from the local populace, Ssu-ma Kuang delivers the ultimate indictment: "That, in the end, the Central Kingdom was weakened and thereby brought to ruin was entirely because of the siren songs of P'ei Chü." That this is absurd seems beyond doubt.

Yang-ti's inner circle of advisors enabled him to deal with the business of government in his own style, and nearly all of these men accompanied him on his endless progresses up and down the land. With the exception of P'ei Chü and possibly Su Wei, they were functionaries, expediting officials, and not policy advisors with any of the function of "remonstrance" so necessary for Confucians in the balancing of imperial and bureaucratic powers over affairs of state. It is this configuration which may indeed have brought the empire to ruin. Whether it did or not, however, it certainly brought upon Yang-ti the harsh judgments of all subsequent historians, who were without exception Confucians.

CHAPTER 8

The
Dynasty at
Its Height

Yang-ti's reign stretched from 605 to 617. There are grounds for thinking that there is a break-point in this span of years, a point of change, and that it should be placed at about 609. Ssu-ma Kuang singles out this year as the "height of the Sui." He points to the existence of orderly and stable administrative units—190 prefectures and 1,225 counties; to the vast extent of the empire, which he estimated as 3,100 miles east and west and 4,938 miles north and south (taking a Chinese *li* as equivalent to one third of a mile); and, most significant of all, to its numerous population—approximately 9 million registered households, or about 50 million people.

But there are other grounds for believing that this same year, or near to it, marked a change in the political tone of the reign. Prior to 609, Yang-ti seems to have concentrated on such measures as would further solidify the empire inherited from his father, increase its power and prosperity, and elicit the consent of the governed. After 609 there is a growing preoccupation with foreign expansion (developing into an obsession with the conquest of the Manchurian kingdom of Koguryŏ), a relative neglect of domestic problems, and a growing dependence on his inner circle of advisors.

Many of the actions of the first years of Yang-ti's reign were part of the standard and expected performance of a new ruler: elevation of his wife to the status of empress, selection of a Crown Prince, an empire-wide amnesty, the choice of appropriate ceremonial colors and costumes, and so forth. But other early measures were far from usual. He remitted taxes for ten years to families who had members killed in the brief but sharp war against his brother, the Prince of Han. He ordered the abolition of the office of military commandant (*tsung-kuan*) which had existed in many of the prefectures of the empire. He announced his intention to sponsor on a large scale the revival of traditional Confucian learning (of which more below). He ordered the making of a new law code far less severe than his father's, and while it was being prepared, he ordered the suspension of the articles dealing with the "ten odious crimes" (as varieties of insubordination were termed). The grandiloquent phrases of the edict ordering the recodification of laws may catch something of the feelings of the new emperor as he first saw himself, as supreme autocrat, wise ruler, and cosmic pivot.

> We shall, with total abnegation of self, devote Ourselves to good government, and in Our thinking We shall follow the ancient standards. We shall renounce Our personal feelings the better to serve others, and We shall always follow a policy of leniency. . . . That, in my judgments, inadvertent errors would ever be allowed to obscure true virtue is utterly unthinkable.

In the second year of his reign he proclaimed from atop the south central gate of his eastern capital a general amnesty and a remission of taxes for the whole empire. Later in the year he issued an ordinance stating that all officials who did not attain their rank by examination had to be of outstanding ability to be proposed for promotion. In the same year he continued expanding the granaries begun by his father, completing huge installations in the vicinity of Loyang. At the end of the year he issued an edict saluting the rulers of the past who were worthy of posterity's respect and deploring the poor state of their tombs; he allocated the labor service of ten nearby families to the repair and protection of each and every tomb. This was also the year for a massive effort, carried through by P'ei Yün, to collect the music, instruments, and performers in the several musical traditions of the Period of Disunion. These traditions were lodged in hereditary families who had been supported by the several states; P'ei winnowed out the incompetents, selected the best performers, and gave them ranks and positions in the Court of Imperial Sacrifices (*T'ai-ch'ang ssu*). The Emperor was greatly pleased because, of course, music was not only pleasurable but also had its part in the organic harmony of the cosmos which, as Son of Heaven, he was obliged to maintain. In the eighth moon of 608, an imperial progress made its way north from T'ai-yüan to Heng-shan, the northernmost of the five sacred mountains of China, mentioned in the most ancient classics and taken into the imperial cosmology during the Han. There, in the presence of the prefects of the area north of the Yellow River and of representatives of ten or so kingdoms of Central Asia assembled by P'ei Chü, Yang-ti made the solemn sacrifices for the welfare of the realm—sacrifices whose traditions reached back to the mythological sage Emperor Shun. Then, having performed the sacrifices, he declared a general amnesty and on his return to the capital issued an order remitting one year's taxes in the districts through which the imperial progress had passed.

In these same early years the sources make much of his penchant for extravagance, pomp, and display. I am inclined to discount this. It is a fact, however, that his violent action against his three senior critics and their execution occurred in 607, the year of the promulgation of the new code with its generally lighter scale of punishments. These harsh measures prefigure a pattern of action which unhappily increases in subsequent years. But if, for a moment, we suppose that there may have been some substance to the charges that led to the execution of the three leading statesmen of the previous reign, the judicial murder of the aged Hsüeh Tao-heng in 609 for mild criticism of the *status quo* surely ushers in the second and darker phase of Yang-ti's reign.

The first emperor, in his later years, had become disillusioned with the schools established by his government for training young men for possible appointment to government posts. On his birthday in the sixth month of 601—the day he announced empire-wide Buddhist celebrations echoing Emperor Asoka's—he issued an edict greatly curtailing the Confucian schools. While reviewing his high hopes for such schools and the value of Confucianism for moral and practical training, he complained of the proliferation of students at the capital and local levels, and of their idleness and their failure to develop either into moral exemplars or potential officials, abolishing schools and reducing the number of state-supported scholars. There also was a falling off, in Wen-ti's later years, of support for Confucian projects of various other kinds.

Yang-ti came to the throne with something of a reputation as a literary man and with a record of patronage of Confucian scholars during his years at Chiang-tu. He was far too shrewd not to recognize the value of the tradition as the basis of a public morality of subservience to one's elders and betters and as the nexus of all the ramifying symbolism of the imperial order—seasonal sacrifices, prayers, invocations of ancestors and deities, and all the ritual procedures by which the Son of Heaven was to maintain harmony in the cosmos. In the first year of his reign he signaled the reversal of his father's policies in a high-flown edict that began: "For governing the people and building an enduring dynasty, teaching and learning have first place. Changing customs and altering traditional ways must all begin from this." He then reviewed the disruption of scholarly traditions in the Period of Disunion and contrasted the period of peace, prosperity, and unity over which he presided. He went on to order the appropriate commissioners throughout the empire to search out learned and talented people, select those suited for office, and provide other scholarly specialists with state stipends, "equitably according to the profundity of their professional skill and their family's standing." Finally he ordered the resumption of instruction in the capital schools (elsewhere we learn that the local schools were also reopened). "Let the students be instructed and drilled to prepare them for the procedure of examination which will complete the process of 'grinding and polishing' [an old metaphor for education]." Earlier in the same year the commissioners of inspection that he sent to the provinces were ordered, among their other duties, to search out men of noteworthy conduct, scholarly skills, or specialized competence, and to examine them and send them to the capital. As a result, the *Sui History* tells us, Confucian scholars came from near and far and were put to debating with one another on learned points. A high official established their rank order and reported this to the throne, whereupon many a destitute scholar was rehabilitated, and classical studies flourished, encompassing both northern and southern traditions. Commentaries were written to all the classics. But, the text continues, this rehabilitation was short-lived, failing as imperial attention shifted to foreign affairs and military concerns. The *Tzu-chih t'ung-chien*, in one of its few passages favorable to Yang-ti, says that late in his reign he enlarged the palace library secretariat by one hundred and twenty posts and filled them all with scholars.

That Yang-ti should gain praise in this area is in accord with what we know of his own scholarly predilections. Ssu-ma Kuang says that he was devoted to reading and to literary composition throughout his adult life. He had a hundred compilers working in his vice-regal office at Chiang-tu, and this interest continued throughout his reign. Great libraries were built in Ta-hsing ch'eng and Loyang, and the final result was a superb central imperial library, with the best editions kept in Loyang and amounting to more than 370,000 rolls. For use in the various palaces, ministries, and offices of the two capitals, he ordered abridged reference libraries to be prepared.

Yang-ti was frequently concerned with the ritual aspects of imperial Confucianism, the stately ceremonies that dramatized supreme power. On these the scholars were the recognized authorities. The choice of appropriate times for imperial sacrifices, the conferment in 608 of a new title on Confucius accompanied by an order to search out and list the descendants of the great sage, the proper performance of the Heng-shan sacrifice, and many other rituals—all of these occupied him from time to time. On the eve of the first advance against Koguryō, at his base camp near the modern Peking, the Emperor performed three of the ancient sacrifices traditionally made by a ruler before setting out on a campaign.

The second reign is thus one of far greater interest in all aspects of Confucian ritual, scholarship, and education than the period of Wen-ti's rule. Perhaps this was only natural; it has long been observed that Confucians are not useful in the forcible seizure of power but find their ideal role in helping a ruler hold on to what he has. For a time, Yang-ti's Confucians assumed that role to some degree, but violent events, beginning in 612, were to drive them from their projects and their posts to wait out once again a period of dynastic transition.

A month after Wen-ti's death, his youngest son Liang, Prince of Han, who by his father's favor had accumulated great power in the eastern plain, rose in revolt. He was crushed by the formidable Yang Su. At the end of the same year Yang-ti announced his intention of establishing his eastern capital at Loyang, which dominated the eastern plain. Early in the following year, 605, he appointed Yü-wen K'ai, working with Yang Su and Yang Ta (Yang-ti's cousin), to rebuild the city. Labor was recruited from among the people of the eastern plain, and work went on apace. When it was finished, the Emperor moved the residents of the former prefectural capital and "several tens of thousands" of families of rich merchants and traders into the rebuilt city to fill it up. In 607 he ordered the prefectures of the Honan area to send artisan families to reside in Loyang, thus doubling the available complement of skilled workers. He set up twelve special wards to accommodate them.

Yang-ti is condemned by moralists for his unconscionable extravagance in rebuilding this capital, but if one looks at his own arguments for it and at the geopolitical rationale, one finds ample justification. In his two edicts ordering the construction, he refers to the notable precedents for building at this site: the Duke of Chou's building of an eastern capital there (c. 1100 B.C.) and Han Kao-tsu's strong praise for the site. He might have mentioned that the Eastern Chou and Later Han had their main capitals here, as did the principal successors of the Han until the fall of the city to "barbarians" in 312. It had also been the site chosen for his new capital by the Sinicizing emperor of the Northern Wei in 494. Yang-ti mentions the Chou's need for a second base in the east from which to control the conquered Shang (c. 1100 B.C.), and refers to the recent example of his brother the Prince of Han's rising in the eastern plain as showing a parallel need: the Kuan-chung area was too distant a base from which to check dissidence in the east. Moreover Loyang was a natural hub of land and water transport and a key point in the storage and transshipment of grain tribute. The same factors were later to influence the T'ang to keep Loyang as an eastern capital for nearly three hundred years.

We know little about the Sui's second capital. In size—as shown by recent excavations of the outer walls—Sui and T'ang Loyang was roughly half the size of the western capital. It had the same division into three walled complexes: the palace city in the north, the administrative city to the south of the palace compound, and the rest of the city forming an uneven U-shaped area divided into wards and crossed about halfway to the south wall by the Lo River as it flowed eastward to its confluence with the Yellow River. The city was similar in general plan to its predecessor, the Northern Wei capital at Loyang. This was not built *de novo* as was the western capital of Ta-hsing ch'eng. It seems to have been a "capital" only when the Emperor chose to take his personal entourage and reside there for a time; there is no sign of the double staffing of the upper bureaucracy that was characteristic of the dual capital system of the Ming. But it was an important city, strategically and economically. More than this, it was an important symbol of imperial authority for the élite of the eastern plain at a site hallowed by myth and by history.

It is Yang-ti's canal building that became the object of the Confucian historians' most heated fulminations. The writers of fiction of

many centuries have taken the already biased work of the historians
and added layer upon layer of extravagant embroidery. We must
somehow read through these layers and describe the canal building
in more sober terms and account for its scale by reference to the economic and political strategies Yang-ti was pursuing. It was his father
Wen-ti who began construction of the canal network. In 584, when
he had barely occupied his new capital, he ordered Yü-wen K'ai to
design a canal from the capital eastward to the vital T'ung Pass, near
the confluence of the Wei and Yellow rivers. The building of this
canal, known as the Kuang-t'ung Ch'ü ("canal for expanded communication"), was made necessary by two pressures. One was that the
capital region was a food-deficit area (and was to become more so as
the population increased), and grain had to be shipped in regularly
from the fertile plain to the east. Secondly the Wei River, which
flowed eastward just north of the capital and joined the Yellow River
near its great bend, was subject to silting and was seasonally shallow.
The new canal provided a more reliable waterway. The Emperor's
edict, like that proclaiming the plan for a new capital, promised that
the fatigue of the corvée laborers in the short run would be more
than rewarded by the great convenience of the new canal, which he
promised would be available for private as well as official transport.
He also expressed the hope that the resources of Tai-pei (the modern
Shansi Province) could be sent by water down the Fen River, then
down the upper course of the Yellow River, and finally by canal to
the capital. The Kuang-t'ung Canal was rapidly completed, probably
because it followed, for the most part, the route of a Han Dynasty
canal that had been built for the same purpose seven hundred years
before. When the canal, which was a little under one hundred miles
in length, was completed in 589, the Emperor went out from the
capital to inspect the work, and gave suitable rewards of silk to the
supervisors of corveé labor. At the eastern end of the canal a granary
of the same name was built which served as a major grain storage
place whence supplies could be sent on to the capital area or to other
regions when there was a crop failure.

Yang-ti's first edict ordering the building of a canal was issued in
605, the first year of his reign. This was for the T'ung-chi ch'ü, which
linked Loyang with Ssu-chou on the Huai River and connected with
a very old canal route from Huai-yin south to the Yangtze at
Chiang-tu. Nearly all the links in this long canal followed the
courses of earlier canals. It should be noted that the building of this
and the rest of the system occurred in flat alluvial plains. No doubt a

great deal of dredging and new construction was needed, and if the canals were indeed bordered by imperial roads shaded by planted trees, as the sources tell us, the labor exactions must have been heavy. The *Sui History* says that for the northern and longer stretch of this canal Yang-ti in 605 mobilized a million or more workers and that later in the same year, for the stretch from the Huai to the Yangtze, he mobilized a hundred thousand or more workers. These figures become somewhat more credible if they count not the people engaged at any one time but the total number of corvée labor periods of twenty days each. There was yet another southern extension. In 610 Yang-ti ordered a canal from the Yangtze opposite Yang-chou south to the head of Hangchow Bay, a distance of about 270 miles. But here again, many stretches followed the courses of existing rivers or earlier canals.

By far the longest of all the canals was the Yung-chi ch'ü, which also began not far from the confluence of the Lo and Yellow River and struck off in a northeasterly direction. The Ch'in River, which rose in Shansi, was redirected to provide water for the canal, and it was fed along its course from other rivers normally tributary to the Yellow River. It ended, where later Grand Canals were to end, in the vicinity of modern Peking. Work was begun in 608 when "a hundred-odd tens of thousands" were mobilized for the work. The *Tzu-chih t'ung-chien* says that adult males were insufficient to supply the labor and so, for the first time, they conscripted women. The southern sections of this canal also followed the routes of ancient canals.

If one looks at a relief map of China and envisions the area of settled agriculture, it is clear that these canals plus the natural waterways assured for the Sui the resources of all the most productive land with the exception of Szechwan (which was linked to the capital by a well-established road). We have no figures on tax, grain, or cloth shipments in Sui times, but the great granaries were well stocked, and several became important prizes in the struggle for power at the end of the Sui. Much of the prosperity of the T'ang can be attributed to this network, which they inherited and improved. The Yung-chi ch'ü to the northeast was built not only to bring in the tax revenues of Hopei, but also partly with an important strategic purpose—namely, to supply the armies which, it was assumed, might be needed to defend the northern and northeastern regions. The canals also had a political use. China had only recently been forcibly reunified after a long period of disunion. The ability to display the wealth and majesty of the new monarch throughout the empire was an important advantage; obviously the ability to get armed men and supplies by boat to areas of potential dissidence was even more important. Southeastern China below the Yangtze was already in the process of being settled, and the extension of the canal system to Chiang-tu, for example, greatly stimulated its growth from a frontier outpost to a thriving commercial city.

If these strike us as the solid advantages of the canal system, such views are not reflected in Chinese historical writings. Here is a passage from the "Treatise on Economics" of the *Sui History* describing Yang-ti's progress from Loyang to Chiang-tu—his "Yangtze capital"—in 605, the year of the building of the T'ung-chi ch'ü:

> Moreover the emperor caused to be built dragon boats, phoenix vessels, war boats of the "Yellow Dragon" style, red battle cruisers, multi-decked transports, lesser vessels of bamboo slats. Boatmen hired from all the waterways . . . pulled the vessels by ropes of green silk on the imperial progress to Chiang-tu [Yangchow]. The Emperor rode in the dragon boat, and civil and military officials of the fifth grade and above rode in the multi-decked transports; those of the ninth grade and above were given the vessels of yellow bamboo. The boats followed one another poop to prow for more than 200 leagues [about 65 miles]. The prefectures and counties through which they passed were ordered to prepare to offer provisions. Those who made bountiful arrangements were given an additional office or title; those who fell short were given punishments up to the death penalty.

There follows a catalogue of the goods requisitioned from the whole empire and then this flight of hyperbole:

> Requisitioning was hurried and relentless; the morning's order had to be carried out by evening. The common people sought out food with snare and net to such an extent that on land and waters, the birds and the beasts were almost extinguished, and still they could not give what was demanded but found themselves buying from rich and powerful families which had amassed provisions. Prices leapt up, and in this year the tail of a pheasant cost ten rolls of fine silk.

How shall we explain the discrepancy between the almost leg-endary evil depicted in such passages as these and the solid advan-tages of a canal network seen by some contemporaries and by modern historians? Confucian officials who kept the records and wrote the histories in general did not favor great increases in central power and frowned on its flamboyant use by a reigning monarch; their physiocratic economic view saw no advantage in economic growth; their counsels as statesmen and their records as historians emphasized the high cost and the disadvantages of foreign military adventures. All emperors were, however covertly, the natural oppo-nents as well as the necessary allies of all officials. In the case of Yang-ti, who came to a bad end, this latent hostility expresses itself openly and nowhere more emphatically than in the condemnation of his foreign exploits.

CHAPTER 9

Military Disaster and Political Collapse

By focusing on the disastrous results of Yang-ti's foreign policy, later critics have neatly rounded out their view of Yang-ti as a profligate and irresponsible ruler, but have severely distorted our understanding of the process of Sui expansion. There was, in fact, no sharp break in the foreign policy of the two Sui emperors. The conventional judgment in Chinese histories has generally been that Wen-ti was prudent and wise in the conduct of foreign relations while Yang-ti was impetuous and profligate. In both emperors' reigns there were two kinds of operations beyond the borders: those started out of a desire for loot or out of personal curiosity, and those aimed at assuring the geopolitical dominance of the new empire in Eastern Asia. The former, often apparently on a small scale and not too costly, was in an old tradition going back to Ch'in Shih Huang Ti of an imperial autocrat indulging his curiosity or his taste for the exotic by state-financed expeditions. Not surprisingly, such a campaign could be subject to the whim or impetuosity of a ruler, and Yang-ti was particularly vulnerable. The latter type of operation was justified in terms of the old tradition of a central political and cultural order whose superiority in all realms excused not only its defense but the conquest of lesser peoples.

An eighth-century chronicler lists the arenas in which Sui military power prevailed over its enemies: in the south, the conquest of the Ch'en empire; in the north, successful strikes against the T'u-chüeh (Turks); in the west, the conquest of the T'u-yü Hun; in the far south, the seizure of Champa; in the east, the conquest of the islands known as Liu-ch'iu. He might have added relentless pressure on the aborigines of the south and southwest and the final effort to force Koguryō into submission—the one military operation that failed catastrophically.

The only one of these which does not represent the assertion of Chinese power beyond China proper is the conquest of Ch'en. The other major arenas in which Sui military power was deployed were places and peoples whose control Chinese policy makers, from early times, had regarded as vital for the empire's security and that had at times of great dynastic power been under Chinese control. Geography dictates many of these areas of concern, but history too was a powerful influence. Here, as in so many other policies, the Sui attempted to reenact the triumphs of the long-dead Han and to reassert Chinese centrality and omnipotence in Eastern Asia. The Sui succeeded remarkably well with this reassertion of regional power on the Han model. They had striking military successes on many fronts, and they revived and developed the tributary system, which should be viewed as a flexible set of policies and stratagems for the ordering of China's relations with its diverse neighbors. Let us consider how the Sui dealt with some of the more important peoples on China's periphery.

To the south and east, the foreign adventures of the Sui emperors included the invasion of Champa, which in fact began in the first reign and ended in the second; the expedition into the East China Sea; and the establishment of relations with Japan. The expansion westward and northward included the conquest and dispossession of the T'u-yü Hun from their ancestral grazing lands; the successes of Wen-ti against the Eastern Turks, who nonetheless continued to be a problem during Yang-ti's time; and finally the brief and unsuccessful expedition by Wen-ti in Koguryō some years later, followed by Yang-ti's ambitious, persistent, and disastrous campaign that was the Sui's ultimate undoing.

Chiao-chou, within the modern Hanoi-Haiphong region, had been in Han times a bustling port and an outpost of Chinese culture in the far south. But in the sixth century, the weak dynasties at Nanking no longer controlled the area, and a local satrap of mixed Annamese-Chinese stock set up his own dynasty. Wen-ti appointed the tough and experienced general Liu Fang to retake Chiao-chou, and the last ruler of the local dynasty surrendered in 602. The Kingdom of Champa (Lin-i) stretched along the coastal lands of what has in recent times been called Annam. Its capital was south of the modern Danang. It had discontinued all tribute relations with the enfeebled Ch'en state at Nanking. But the king, Çambhuvarman, prudently sent tribute to the Sui in 595. Unfortunately for him a myth, fostered by a successful Chinese raid in the fifth century, had grown up that Champa was a kind of El Dorado where fabulous riches were to be had for the taking. Wen-ti's well-known avarice overcame his accustomed caution, and he authorized an attack on Champa by Liu Fang, who, with experienced officers, led a land force and a naval squadron. Çambhuvarman deployed war elephants, but the Chinese forces broke through to the capital and managed to get away with the golden ancestral tablets of the royal house. On the route back to China the invaders were hit by an epidemic which carried off large numbers of the officers and men, including Liu Fang. The Sui effort to administer parts of Champa directly was short-lived. Çambhuvarman reasserted his power, sent an embassy to the Sui to "acknowledge his fault," and thereafter, we are told, "the tribute missions were uninterrupted." But the whole effort south of Chiao-chou, which continued into Yang-ti's reign, was a costly failure, and all the Chinese had to show for it were the stolen ancestral tablets, some cases of Buddhist scriptures, and a troupe of captured musicians.

In 610, Yang-ti sent an expedition to pacify the "Liu-ch'iu" Islands. The exact identification of these islands has been much debated. Japanese scholars generally believe that the term refers to Formosa; while an alternate view is that in Sui times "Liu-ch'iu" was a vague term for all the islands in the East China Sea. Be that as it may, the expedition was a failure, and in 610 Yang-ti appointed generals to recruit a new assault force in the area of modern Chekiang. The newly formed Sui force met stubborn resistance. Here there follow in the texts two conflicting versions of the outcome of the expedition. The first is the usual success story: triumph of Chinese arms, the defeat and execution of the King of "Liu-ch'iu," then the triumphant return of the Chinese forces with numerous captives, and the rewards and promotions for the successful generals. The second is a story of failure, in which the capture of prisoners is followed by an overextension of Chinese power in the islands: the onset of disease and death of 80 or 90 percent of the officers and men of the in-

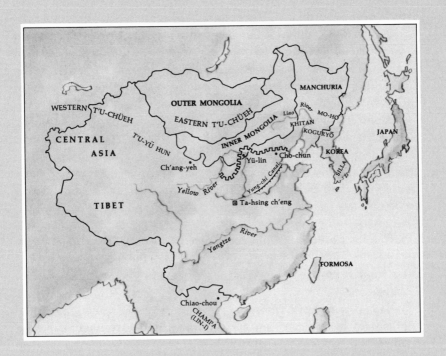

vading force. Whichever outcome one chooses, the sources in general do not indicate a significant or permanent establishment of Sui power in the islands of the East China Sea.

Another less than successful expedition was undertaken at the request of the T'u-yü Hun, who had long been vassals of the Turks during the great days of the Eastern Turkish empire. They had their grazing lands around Koko Nor, south of the string of garrison towns along the route to the Jade Gate—towns which they had harassed for centuries. When in 608 they came under attack by the Tölös their khan sent an emissary asking to submit to China and for China's help. Yang-ti sent out an army, under the redoubtable Yü-wen Shu, to "welcome" them into the fold. Seeing the size of the army, the T'u-yü Hun fled. The Chinese pursued and attacked, took several hundred heads, captured their leaders, and made slaves of some four thousand men and women. Thus, as the *Tzu-chih t'ung-chien* says, their old lands were emptied, and an area approximately 1,300 miles east-west and 600 miles north-south became a Sui possession; it was divided into Chinese administrative districts and settled with Chinese criminals convicted of "light" crimes. This "conquest," like some others, did not survive the Sui's downfall, and the T'u-yü Hun had to be dealt with afresh by the next dynasty, the T'ang.

Japan was a very different case. She had been receiving cultural influences from China since Han times, mostly by way of Korea, where she had considerable influence. During the Period of Disunion, Japanese principalities paid at least nominal tribute to the major North China dynasties. When they learned of the reunification of China, the Japanese were naturally interested in finding out more about the new order on the continent. There may have been a mission from Japan to China during the K'ai-huang period (581–600), but the first full embassy arrived in 607. The ambassador referred to Yang-ti as "the Bodhisattva Son of Heaven who gives the full weight of his support to the Buddhist teaching," and went on to say that he had brought with him a number of monks who wanted to study Buddhism. The envoy then produced a written communication from his monarch which began, "The Son of Heaven in the land of the rising sun sends this letter to the Son of Heaven of the land where the sun sets." The Emperor was displeased at this piece of unintentioned effrontery and said that the letter from these barbarians was discourteous, and that such letters should not again be brought to his august attention. Despite this gaffe, the Chinese sent a fairly low-ranking emissary to Japan the next year who brought back a fuller and more accurate account of Japan than had previously been available. The embassy apparently went off without a hitch, and the opening of relations at this time had highly important effects on the cultural history of Japan.

When the future Wen-ti was still an official of the Northern Chou, the T'u-chüeh (as the Chinese called the people known in the West as Turks) to the north loomed as a serious threat. They had emerged out of the kaleidoscopic pattern of tribal warfare in the steppe-land and by the 550s had attained loose but formidable control of a vast area stretching from the Liao River in Manchuria across to the borders of Persia. They grew strong and rich from successful raids on agricultural peoples and from their control of the silk routes between China and the West. Politically they were divided into two khanates, an eastern and a western, with the western one subordinate to the eastern. The eastern khanate had its center in the Orkhon region of what is now Outer Mongolia, and the western had its summer and winter encampments at seasonally favorable sites in Western Turkestan.

The western khanate increased its power and wealth by a series of complex moves involving the Ephthalites, Byzantium, and Sassanid Persia, while the eastern looked down upon a divided North China which it could manipulate to its advantage. The Northern Chou emperor humbly asked for a daughter of the eastern khan, and was granted this favor in 565; each year the Chou gave to the T'u-chüeh 100,000 pieces of silk, and Turkish residents at Ch'ang-an were lavishly feted and carefully courted. The Northern Ch'i state in the east nervously poured out treasure for fear the T'u-chüeh would side with their enemies, the Northern Chou. From his tents in the Orkhon, the T'u-chüeh ruler could contemplate the Chinese world with some complacency. He is alleged to have said to his entourage on several occasions, "My two children to the south [the emperors of the Northern Chou and Northern Ch'i] are always filial and obedient, so why should I fear poverty." In 582, after a large-scale T'u-chüeh raid into parts of the modern Shensi and Kansu, Wen-ti, in his usual trenchant manner, analyzed the situation:

> In days gone by the Wei's course declined, and disasters came thick and fast. The Chou and Ch'i contended and divided the land of China. The T'u-chüeh caitiffs trafficked equally with the two states. The Chou looked anxiously east-

ward, fearing that the Ch'i would get on better terms with the
T'u-chüeh, while the Ch'i looked anxiously westward, fearing that the Chou would get on more intimate terms with
them. This is what is called: the caitiffs' opinion tipping this
way or that, and the country as a consequence having peace
or war.

If the power of this great Turkish empire had continued to dominate the northern marches and all of Central Asia, the Sui could not
have reasserted Chinese power in those areas and might well have
had to take a defensive position such as that later taken by the Sung
in the face of the Khitan. But fortune favored the Sui. The khanate of
the Western Turks fell to an impulsive and quarrelsome man called
Tardu, and sometime between 582 and 584 he preempted the title of
khagan, previously reserved for the ruler of the Eastern Turks.
Thereafter the two Turkish empires were no longer united and were
often at war. More than this, the eastern empire, with the contested
accession of a new khagan in 582, offered the sort of opportunity
Chinese statesmen were long accustomed to exploit. They backed
now a khan, now an anti-khan, so that the political unity of the Eastern Turks was destroyed. At the same time, they saw to it that the
eastern empire did not so far disintegrate as to make possible the
forcible reunification of the two empires by Tardu. This Tardu essayed when in 601 he threatened the Sui capital and in 602 attacked
the Chinese puppet khan in the Ordos region. But suddenly, while
far from his base, his empire was riven by a revolt of one of its principal tribal components: the Tölös. We may suppose that the agents
of the Chinese had done their work well: Tardu disappeared from
the scene in 603. His grandson, Ch'u-lo, was able to assert power
over only the extreme western portion of his empire.

In the days of Yang-ti's prosperity, the Western Turks seem to
have been a minor problem, a nuisance to be manipulated at little
cost for the benefit of the Central Kingdom. Ch'u-lo, their khan, had
a Chinese mother who remained in the Sui capital where she served
both as hostage and as intermediary between the Chinese and the
Western Turks. When, in 610, Ch'u-lo showed signs of independence, Yang-ti, acting on the advice of P'ei Chü, set up an anti-khan,
Shih-kuei, who succeeded in driving Ch'u-lo, accompanied by some
of his cavalry, from his lands. Ch'u-lo's Chinese mother was sent out
to his place of refuge in the west and persuaded Ch'u-lo to come to
the capital, where he was received by the Emperor with fulsome

honors. He remained there with his own entourage until 612, kept as a kind of potential "anti-khan" in reserve to be used, possibly, against the Eastern Turks or as a challenge to the waxing power of Shih-kuei. He and his cavalry accompanied the Emperor on the first campaign against Koguryō and he was richly rewarded for his accomplishments. Yang-ti hoped to restore him to his ancestral lands, but the fall of the Sui intervened.

It is the empire of the Eastern Turks, occupying steppe territories roughly the same as modern Mongolia, that posed a threat to the central sector of China's northern frontier in Yang-ti's time. As we have noted, the Sui began early to repair and extend the Great Wall, and Yang-ti in 607 built or reconstructed a long L-shaped section; the longer part paralleled the north-south course of the Yellow River, along the border between the modern provinces of Shansi and Shensi; the shorter ran from west to east roughly along the northern border of Shansi, and was joined with long-existing parts of the Great Wall. But to keep the Turks in check required more than walls, and the second Sui emperor resorted periodically to one or several of the traditional Chinese stratagems: keeping sons and nephews of the Turkish khans resident in the Sui capitals (for "education"), settlement of tribes in Chinese territory, marriage diplomacy, investiture and deposition of khans, tribute missions and return gifts from China, barter at fixed places and times along the frontier (usually Chinese silk for Turkish horses), and political intrigue of all kinds. The frontier policy specialist on whom Yang-ti relied was P'ei Chü, who used his assignments to the far western towns of Chang-yeh (Kan-chou) and Tun-huang to gather intelligence for his imperial master, to intrigue successfully among the tribes, and to bribe and awe them into becoming subjects of the Chinese. Yang-ti's tours of the northwestern and western frontiers in 607–8 must here serve to illustrate the complexity of the Sui's relations with frontier peoples, and P'ei Chü's role.

Early in the year 607, P'ei Chü went ahead to Tun-huang while the Emperor began the first, northwestern, stage of his tour. This took him to Yü-lin inside the northwest elbow of the Great Wall. There, in his sumptuous traveling palace, the Emperor received the homage of the Khan Ch'i-min—previously won to China's side by P'ei Chü—and his consort the Chinese princess I-ch'eng. The Khan presented the Emperor with three thousand head of horses and received in return thirteen thousand lengths of silk. This high-level barter was accompanied by an exchange of courtesy visits (the Chinese Emperor proceeded to Ch'i-min's tent capital), gifts, and appropriate sentiments. In the year 608 Yang-ti was ready for a trip to the far west. P'ei Chü had made careful preparations and the imperial tour was a triumphal progress. At one point still in Shensi Province, he received the King of Turfan (long under T'u-chüeh influence), the Tutun Shad of Hami, and the representatives of twenty-seven "barbarian" tribes. According to the biography of P'ei Chü, all these properly submissive people "received decorations of gold and nephrite as well as garments of brocade and other fabrics. There were musical performances, noisy feasts with singing and dancing, burning of incense." Then the whole male and female population of two garrison and trading towns "was ordered to dress up in splendid clothes and show themselves to the barbarians. Horsemen and carts were ordered to crowd together in a space several tens of *li* in circumference, so as to display the prosperity of the Central Kingdom." P'ei Chü was, of course, the successful stage manager of this and other shows of Chinese opulence, and the foolish herdsmen, we are told, were suitably impressed, the Emperor greatly pleased.

Behind all these measures lay one of the solid objectives of Sui *Realpolitik*. This was further to weaken the Turks, to prevent their forming alliances with other tribal groups to the east or west of them, and, when possible, to use them as a striking force against the Sui's other potential enemies. For example, in 605, after the Khitan had raided China, the Emperor sent a Chinese general to lead a cavalry force of twenty thousand Eastern Turks against them. The Khitan were badly defeated, and their women and livestock were given to the Turks as a reward. In 608 Turks were to join forces with the Chinese in an attack on the Central Asian oasis of Hami, at one time a Han garrison town on the northern route across Inner Asia. In this case the Turkish allies apparently did not appear, but the Sui army captured the place, built a new fortress, and left troops to defend it. There was a bland rationale given for this aggressive action: now the Inner Asian peoples would no longer need to travel great distances in order to trade with the Chinese.

During the Emperor's visit to Ch'i-min Khan's capital in 607, the Khan had been greatly embarrassed by the presence of an embassy from the state of Koguryō and had tried to make the best of it by formally presenting the emissary to his imperial visitor. Such evidence of what was intended to be secret intercourse between potential enemies always alarmed the Chinese. P'ei Chü advised his master to instruct the Koguryō ambassador that he was to return to his country and tell his king to present himself forthwith to pay homage at the Sui court; if he did not do so, he was to be told, the Chinese would lead a Turkish army to chastise his contemptible country. Niu Hung was promptly ordered to make this plain to the ambassador. The ambassador returned with the message, but his king refused to make the appropriate gestures of submission. The authority of the Central Kingdom had been flouted, and sooner or later the response would have to be the application of overwhelming force against the miscreant.

P'ei Chü's advice to his master is susceptible to two interpretations. One is that he thought Koguryō would quickly submit, and thus allow an entire civilized area to return to its appropriate tributary status. The other is that he expected them to put up resistance, which could however be quickly overcome by the use of Turkish mercenaries; then Koguryō could be made an integral part of the empire. He noted that the Han had conquered this same area and had divided it into three prefectures. He reminded the Emperor that his father had attempted a conquest but had failed because of the incompetence of his field commander. He pointed out that Koguryō was "civilized" and thus ready for incorporation into the empire, but here were their representatives paying court to the wretched nomad Ch'i-min Khan! What he did not say, because his experience, wide as it had been, included no firsthand knowledge of the northeast, was that victory might not be easy. P'ei Chü was intelligent, steeped in the accepted values, deeply knowledgeable about some areas of tension and conflict, but totally uninformed about the area where he was now promising a cheap and easy victory.

The first thing to go wrong with his scheme was the failure of the Eastern Turkish mercenaries to materialize. The submissive Ch'i-min Khan died in 609 while paying court at Loyang. His son Shih-pi was elevated to succeed him, loaded with gifts, and given a Chinese princess to wed. But Shih-pi was far more shrewd than his father, and when P'ei Chü began the oft-repeated game of building up his younger brother as rival khan so as to weaken the Eastern Turks, Shih-pi turned hostile and soon stopped coming to the Sui court. Thus the chastisement of Koguryō fell to the Chinese alone at the moment when uncertainties were developing about the security of their own north and northwest frontiers.

In the early seventh century, the kingdom of Koguryō lay to China's northeast, occupying that part of Manchuria east of the Liao River plus the northern section of the Korean peninsula. Its capital was at the modern Pyong-yang. This northern kingdom had paid tribute to the Northern Wei and its successor states in North China, but in the 590s began edging across the Liao. In 598 Wen-ti launched a brief but disastrous land and sea campaign against Koguryō, settling in the end for a *pro forma* submission by the Koguryō ruler. Yang-ti was more ambitious and persistent in this quarter than his father. The course was to bring ruin to the dynasty.

At the turn of the century, Koguryō was militarily strong, and its potential threat to China was multiplied and complicated by other elements (in addition to the threat of its alliance with the Eastern Turks). North of it was a militant coalition of Tungusic tribes called the Mo-ho who joined with Koguryō in territorial incursions across the Liao River. In the lower reaches of the Liao Valley were the Khitan, who in 605 had invaded Hopei but, as we have seen, were then defeated by an Eastern Turkish force under Chinese command. They remained a threat, alone or in alliance with one of their restive neighbors. Perhaps too, the court in its distant capital in the west feared the possible influence of a militarily strong Koguryō in the Hopei area where separatist sentiments dating from the Northern Ch'i period were far from dead.

It may have been Yang-ti's intention to wait for the completion of the long Yung-chi ch'ü—the great length of the grand canal linking the heart of China to Peking—before launching a "punitive expedition" against Koguryō. In any case, this canal was completed in 609. In 610 special war taxes were levied on the rich, and military preparations went on apace; a large force (said by the *Sui History* to be the largest ever assembled) with massive logistic support was assembled at Cho-chün in the neighborhood of what is now Peking. A flood of the Yellow River plain which inundated forty prefectures disrupted planning and caused desertions among the conscripts. Nonetheless, in the first moon of 612, the Emperor, his generals, and a sizable force were ready to strike by land while a naval force was to strike by sea. Sacrifices were duly performed, and a grandiloquent edict appropriate for the occasion was issued. In it the Emperor insisted on the virtue, the cosmic ordering force, and the great accomplishments of the Sui, with appropriate allusions to sage rulers and great emperors of the past. He castigated the King of Koguryō for his failure to submit, for his cunning, and his nefarious collusion with the Khitan and the Mo-ho in violating Sui territory, etc. P'ei Chü was with him as strategic advisor; the great engineer Yü-wen K'ai bridged the Liao River; the enormous force advanced. The plan had been for a quick thrust to the Koguryō capital, but the walled cities along the east bank of the Liao held out until the late summer rains made further military operations impossible. At the end of August, Yang-ti withdrew. He had suffered heavy losses and returned to Loyang. Back in the capital, he disciplined several of his defeated generals and tightened up his administration.

In the first moon of 613 he announced a second mobilization, and moved north in the early summer for a second attempt against Koguryō. There was an ominous increase in the number of domestic rebellions during the early part of this year, seven of them concentrated in the areas affected by the Yellow River flood of 611. The Emperor again crossed the Liao River, but in the midst of the campaign word reached him of the serious revolt of Yang Su's son, Yang Hsüan-kan, then president of the Board of Rites and the man in charge of the supply center at the southern end of the Yung-chi ch'ü. Hsüan-kan's revolt was the first defection of a major political figure. It occurred near the very heart of the empire, not far from Loyang. Yang-ti sent his best general, Yü-wen Shu, back from the northeastern campaign to crush the rebellion. A short, sharp civil war ensued, and Yang Hsüan-kan's forces were defeated, his head sent as evidence to the Emperor in the field; but the social fabric, the tax, militia, and supply systems had been badly disrupted.

In view of this and of the outbreak of eight widely distributed rebellions in the second half of the year, it is strange to find the Emperor announcing a third campaign for 614. He did so after asking his officialdom to present their views, but, the *Sui History* tells us, "for several days, no one dared speak out." So, in the second moon, he issued an edict, this time in a self-justifying tone. He said he had always devoted himself wholeheartedly to his kingly task and to military matters. He invoked the precedent of the fifty-two battles of the (mythical) founder of the Shang; to these he added the military exploits of the founder of the second Han. He spoke of his hatred of war and of his distress at the loss of life in the previous campaigns. He ordered that the remains of the war dead be collected and properly buried and that a Buddhist shrine be erected where masses would be performed to confer grace on the souls of the departed and allay the suffering of the unhappy ghosts. Preparations were begun and, despite shortages of supplies and horses and the failure of many conscripts to report for duty, the Sui armies again crossed the Liao. Again the strong points along the river held, but the Sui forces penetrated the outskirts of Pyong-yang. Later in 614, the King of Koguryō, sorely beset, sent an emissary with his offer of submission, and the emissary brought with him a Sui general who had defected to Koguryō. The Sui vanguard wanted to take Pyong-yang and capture the king, but they were summoned back by imperial order. Yang-ti once again ordered the King of Koguryō to appear at the imperial court to pay homage. When he did not come, the Emperor ordered the armies to stand by for a fourth expedition, but by this time the country was seething with rebellion. Foreign adventures were at an end.

Yang-ti was driven to these repeated campaigns, which were ruinously expensive in manpower and material, by his conception of the majesty and cosmic centrality of the empire, his urge to restore the glory of the Han, and his image of himself as destined to great victories against all who resisted the benevolent transforming influence of the Central Kingdom, and by considerations of *Realpolitik* persuasively put to him by P'ei Chü and his other military men. He had a clear vision of what the outcome of the campaigns should be. After failure, he would poetically declare victory and return.

> RECORD OF LIAO-TUNG
> At Liao-tung north of the Ocean
>   we've cut up great Leviathan,
> Cleared the clouds and winds for a thousand miles.
> And now we must melt down our spearheads,
>   disperse horses and cattle back to their homes.
> Return the army and feast in our capital.
> First the songs and then the dances
>   to show the army's might,
> Drink victory libations, take off our campaign robes.
> In our judgment we have not uselessly gone
>   on a thousand-mile campaign,
> Nor have we returned in vain, from Five Plain Pass.

Why he persisted in the face of repeated disaster seems clear. Why he failed has long been a matter of speculation. Several explanations have been put forward recently: (1) The terrain and climate favored the defenders. The area attacked was forbidding, densely forested in parts, where heavy summer rains were quickly followed by long severe winters; the fighting season for invaders was only from April to the beginning of the rains in July. (2) Koguryō strategists, knowing their terrain and having most of the year to prepare themselves, were formidable in defense. The nodes of their defense were the walled towns stretching north from An-shih near the mouth of the Liao all the way up the east bank. Time after time they tied down the besieging armies until the onset of winter forced withdrawal. (3) The distance of the campaign base from the capital of the Chinese empire was formidable, close to a thousand miles; it took nearly a month, for example, for the news of Yang Hsüan-kan's revolt to reach Yang-ti in the field. Koguryō enjoyed a compensating advantage. (4) The Sui use of naval forces was costly but inept, and Koguryō's coastal defenses were good.

These factors continued to be decisive in the disastrous campaign of T'ang T'ai-tsung during the following dynasty, and the balance was only changed when the Chinese persuaded and "assisted" Koguryō's southern neighbor Silla to open a second front.

When the Emperor returned first to Loyang and then to the capital in the west in the tenth moon of 614, he had the general who had defected to Koguryō dismembered outside the west central gate of the city. Thereafter, an attempt was made to conduct imperial business as usual. At the new year, 615, Yang-ti feasted his officials, and, the *Sui History* tells us, received tributary emissaries from the Turks, Silla, the Mo-ho, the Khitan, and a number of Inner Asian states. Later in the same month he entertained representatives of the southern and eastern aborigines and made them gifts. In the second moon he reviewed in an edict the strains and disruptions of the campaigns but urged his people back to their settled peacetime pursuits. After all their troubles, he tells them, "the empire is pacified and united, all within the four seas quiescent." In fact, however, all sections of the empire were in turmoil, and the imperial troops were engaged on a dozen fronts in an effort to contain or exterminate the rebels. The Emperor spent the summer season at the Fen-yang Palace which he had built near T'ai-yüan. Late in the summer, while on a progress to the north, he was almost captured by a force of Eastern Turks under Shih-pi Khan and took refuge in the walled city of Yen-men. There are various accounts of panic and disaffection among the defenders, of brash proposals to escape or drive off the enemy. But an order was apparently got out to prefects in the vicinity to bring troops to their emperor's aid. The siege was lifted, but the Emperor had been severely alarmed, his confidence badly shaken; later he became more and more depressed.

We cannot tell how much he knew at this time about the state of the empire which was increasingly in the grip of numerous local rebels. His particular style of governing made it inevitable that his inner circle would try to keep the whole bitter truth from him. According to one account, his advisors indulged in delphic utterance, double-talk, and outright lying to do so. One man who spoke out was beaten to death in the audience hall. In the autumn of 616, at the urging of Yü-wen Shu, the Emperor sailed with his newly built canal fleet for the Yangtze capital. He left officials in charge of the north, the center of empire, but he himself never returned. His last days in Chiang-tu were melancholy. He was wracked by fear and self-doubt, unable to tolerate news of the empire, much less take any action upon it. By 617 two of his grandsons had been enthroned as his successors by rival rebels in the north, and he had been given by one of them the exalted but empty title of "Retired Emperor" (T'ai-shang huang). In 618, he was murdered in his bathhouse by Yü-wen Hua-chi, descendant of the house his father had so ruthlessly displaced and the son of his most trusted general, Yü-wen Shu.

The moral judgments on Yang-ti by the Confucian historians have been harsh indeed. They made of him a minatory stereotype of the bad last emperor. His popular image in folklore, theater, and story is extravagantly colored by the wish-fulfillment fantasies of writers and audiences alike—people who could live only vicariously in a world of unlimited power, magnificent palaces, and boundless opportunities for sensual indulgence. Among Chinese emperors he was by no means the worst, and in the context of his own time he was no more tyrannical than others. He was a very gifted man, well suited to consolidate—as he had first intended—the great work his father had begun. Yet his visions of what the history of his reign would say of him and his taste for pomp and glory soon came to outweigh his judgment. Such extravagances could only thrive in the hothouse of a sycophantic circle and this, fatally for him, is what he had. The conquest of Koguryŏ, attempted, I believe, with a rational if traditional end in mind, became after each defeat more and more of an obsession, and obsessions tend to be fatal for supreme autocrats and for the people they govern.

Despite this graphic debacle and the period of civil war which followed, the Sui reunification of China after its longest period of disunion was a formidable achievement. So was the Sui elimination of the outworn and ineffective institutions of their predecessors, the creation of the fabric of a centralized empire, the development of a sense of common culture in areas long politically separated. No one studying any aspect of the structure and life of the great T'ang empire which followed can fail to see at every turn one or another dimension of the Sui's achievement—surely one of the most impressive in China's history.

CHAPTER 10

The Sui
Legacy
by
Robert M. Somers

When Yang Chien, the man who would found the Sui Dynasty, proceeded from his prime minister's office to the Imperial Palace sometime during the day of March 4, 581, he was aware of having reached a great turning point in his own life and sensed, perhaps, that this was an important turning point for China as well. Now, just four months short of his fortieth birthday, he was taking the most fateful step of a career already crowded with challenges met and opportunities seized. Three years earlier, his daughter Li-hua had become Empress, suddenly boosting the fortunes of the already influential Yang family, though the woman's husband, Emperor Hsüan of the Northern Chou Dynasty, was a sadist and a fool. That ruler's abdication in 579, which remains unexplained, and his subsequent premature death the next year, offered Yang Chien *de facto* power at court if he assumed the regency for the seven-year-old child who was now Emperor of China. Yang Chien fully understood the implications of this fateful step, knew, as his wife allegedly reminded him, that he would be "riding a tiger, with no way to get off." Whatever doubts he may have held, Yang nevertheless embraced this opportunity.

Yang's regency began, it seems, about June 8, 580, and during the next nine months he weathered a series of challenges to his pretensions, carried through manifold and complex acts to legitimate his claims, and determined that the ultimate opportunity lay within his grasp. And so, on March 4, 581, he left his prime minister's office in ordinary clothes, a sign that he was about to don the gauze cap and yellow robe worn only by the emperor, and an inescapable portent that a new dynasty was about to be proclaimed. The dynasty could only be called the Sui, for that was the family's entitlement and Yang Chien intended it to be his legacy. Triumphs and disasters lay ahead for him and his family, but he knew, correctly, that this was a true point of departure. Neither Yang Chien nor his son Yang Kuang was ever able to get off that tiger they were riding, but they did bring China through a whirlwind period of innovation and transformation.

The Sui Dynasty lasted merely three decades, from A.D. 581 to 617, but those years were among the most decisive and eventful in the entire history of China. During that brief span, a complex process that normally occupied several centuries—the rise and fall of a major centralizing dynasty—was compressed into the space of a single generation. If the Sui failed to achieve the long period of stable rule we find in major Chinese dynasties, and if they lacked the durability of the Hapsburgs in the West, the regime had the concentrated impact of Europe's Napoleonic era. Thus we miss something essential in the Sui if we overlook the sheer headstrong energy of the regime, the high level of risk undertaken by its rulers and their ultimately disastrous impatience with obstacles. Those elements eventually combined to produce a profound reaction against the regime, as every class in Chinese society joined in a jolting overthrow of the Sui.

We must not, of course, conclude that the Sui goal of imperial centralization was impossible. Chinese history is dominated by a series of great centralizing dynasties, each of which dedicated its energies and strategy to the same imperial purpose. The Sui had simply attempted that immense task too quickly and with insufficient restraint to have had any real chance of lasting success. A fully stable and politically integrated regime never took form in China in less than two full generations. China's great consolidators—Han Wu-ti (r. 140–87 B.C.), T'ang T'ai-tsung (r. 627–650), and K'ang-hsi of the Ch'ing (r. 1661–1722)—typically came to power at some distance from the founding period, and no dynasty reached the summit of its strength and prosperity until the passage of a century or more. By then the legacy of contention from the founding had dissipated, and a wary acceptance of the new regime had been transformed into

proud and even coveted participation in an all-encompassing structure of power. To secure political stability of that degree in a country
the size of China takes considerable time, but the Sui rulers were
impatient with the restraints imposed by such a lengthy process.

In A.D. 617 a new regime seized the Sui capital and, after a brief
interval, compelled Sui abdication. The usurping dynasty was called
the T'ang, after the hereditary fief of the founder's family. The founder, Li Yüan, had served for more than a decade as a senior general
of the Sui, but showed little reluctance to join the avalanche of rebellion which had begun, four years earlier, to roll down on the Sui.
Few who experienced the chaos of those years could have imagined,
however, that the T'ang Dynasty would not only secure but indeed
build on the foundations laid down by the Sui and develop into the
preeminent political system of the medieval world. The capital that
the Sui had called "City of the Great Ascendancy" was renamed by
the T'ang "Eternal Peace" (Ch'ang-an), and within a century it had
become an enormous metropolis, dwarfing any other city in the
world, just as the T'ang Dynasty vastly overshadowed any contemporary regime.

The life-span of the T'ang Dynasty encompassed not three decades but three centuries, from A.D. 617–906, and is rightly honored
as one of the great epochs of Chinese history. During T'ang times the
frontiers of China stretched east and west from the China Sea to remote Central Asia, and north and south from the steppe-lands of
Mongolia to the sweltering tropics of Canton and its hinterlands.
T'ang strength and prosperity stimulated a great cultural efflores-
cence. Art, architecture, and literature thrived, highlighted by the development of a series of superb poetic styles for which the life at
court was a main subject, as well as by major achievements in prose,
notably the essay and short story. The names Li Po, Tu Fu, and Han
Yü, all outstanding writers of the T'ang, are as honored in China as
are Shakespeare, Milton, and Montaigne in the West. In addition to
its conspicuous literary accomplishments, the material culture of the
age was endlessly rich, fascinating, and influential. T'ang books, ornaments, musical instruments, and other treasures are preserved,
sometimes in T'ang-style buildings, in Japan, only one of several foreign lands to have come under massive Chinese influence during
T'ang times.

The great success of the T'ang and its prestige both within China
and beyond has, in the eyes of later Chinese, considerably overshadowed the importance of the Sui. The Sui appears at first glance to

have made a series of crucial misjudgments and to have been saddled with rulers either too cautious or excessively flamboyant. The Sui regime is thus seen as merely a prelude to the T'ang Dynasty, its contributions to T'ang success often overlooked. It is those contributions that we must examine and judge, for nothing else will indicate so clearly the strength and character of the Sui legacy. We shall see, however, that the Sui legacy was by no means uniform and straightforward, for it involved both striking continuity and sharp breaks. Those mixed effects, at first glance contradictory, were in truth equally essential to the creation and survival of the T'ang state. It is only through an over-all judgment, an assessment considering both continuity and departure, that we shall understand the influence of the Sui experience on succeeding generations in China.

The positive contributions of the Sui appear most readily within the broad panoply of rule which they developed and passed down to their successors. The T'ang inherited a comprehensive set of institutions already shaped and essayed during Sui times, social and political devices which the T'ang simply applied more broadly and systematically than their predecessors. In no major institution do we find important T'ang innovations. The legal system established by the Sui persisted not only through T'ang times but even down to much later imperial periods. Similarly, the "equal field" system of land redistribution was practiced under the T'ang much as it had been under the Sui. The T'ang structure of field administration was, in its fully developed form, the same two-tier pattern employed by the Sui. And the decentralized *fu-ping* militia system of the T'ang similarly followed Sui practice. Thus in each major institution of empire the T'ang simply followed lines of organization established by their Sui forerunners.

These larger institutions of empire were controlled and monitored from the capital, which had its own complex set of institutions, and here too the T'ang was the direct heir of the Sui. Their capital of Ch'ang-an had been built by the Sui to contain an immense population and to awe visitors. It was an intensely cosmopolitan city, concentrating within its enormous walls elements from the entire empire. Under the T'ang, the population of this great metropolis reached an estimated 2 million persons, half contained within the city and half in sprawling suburbs which grew up around it. No other city of the medieval world covered even one-half of Ch'ang-an's thirty square miles; Baghdad, a third the size, was the closest at an estimated 11.6 square miles. Within the capital, the T'ang emperors had at their disposal a substantial body of officials organized and ranked according to a complex structure developed during Sui times from an even earlier heritage. Each principal governmental department of the Sui—State Affairs, the Secretariat, and the Chancellery—remained a center of ministerial responsibility under the T'ang. Their own subdivisions nearly all had Sui precedents and many bore Sui names. Other crucial governmental functions, such as surveillance and remonstrance, were carried out by T'ang censors and counselors whose functions had already been well-established during Sui times. In each of these vital areas of governmental structure and function—and we could name more—we see clear continuities between Sui and T'ang imperial institutions, and any measurement of the success of the T'ang state must make considerable allowance for the vital contributions made by the Sui.

In addition to the formal structure of government, the Sui had not neglected to develop a comprehensive ideological code to underpin and justify their rule. Perhaps no other emperor could match Sui Wen-ti's systematic manipulation of Chinese normative social codes and belief systems—Confucianism, Taoism, and Buddhism—each of which he supported and even patronized to maintain social order and bolster the authority of his regime. Surely no T'ang ruler so persistently pursued normative sanctification, further testimony to the effectiveness of Wen-ti's syncretic ideology. This ideological superstructure, when joined with the comprehensive institutions designed by the Sui rulers and with the great capital city which served as the hub of their empire, provided the T'ang Dynasty with a mature system of rule, and one which they never hesitated to employ.

Nor can any assessment of Sui-T'ang continuity ignore the extraordinary carry-over of senior government personnel from one dynasty to the next. A substantial proportion of the most eminent officials of the early T'ang had served the Sui as well, and these were men ready to bring their experience and abilities to the task of re-centralization that the T'ang gradually undertook. Even those officials who had never served the Sui came, most of them, from those same regions of North China that produced most high Sui officials; just as many represented a similar racial heritage, some of them pure Chinese, others having a strong admixture of Inner Asian blood. In character and physique they were, over-all, the same robust, outdoor types who had served the Sui with such notable courage and determination.

If the institutional, ideological, and political continuities between the Sui and T'ang regimes are striking, the differences between the two regimes are just as significant. These divergences are no less important in explaining the longevity of the T'ang as against the brief span of the Sui and are equally a part of the Sui legacy. What we observe here is the notable caution of T'ang policy, so different from the headstrong and dramatic application of Sui designs. The T'ang rulers were acutely aware that the wrenching stresses and deprivations precipitated by the Sui would require in the healing a substantial period of relaxation and recovery. Edicts from the early T'ang speak of the "era of Sui, when all within the Four Seas boiled over." Lest the T'ang emperors forget, their ministers were ready to point out to them the hardships suffered during Sui times, the devastation and depopulation of large regions through continual warfare. "Yang-ti scorned the Chou and Ch'i [the Sui predecessors]," the minister Ma Chou reminded T'ang T'ai-tsung in 637. "We cannot allow posterity to scorn us as we now scorn Yang-ti!" In spite of all their positive contributions to T'ang rule, then, the Sui served equally as a cautionary and even minatory example for the rulers of the T'ang, who took considerable care to avoid the extreme and ill-advised coercions of the Sui, though the goal of imperial centralization was never abandoned.

We can explore the differences between the two regimes in many areas, but perhaps the most obvious divergence is in the pattern of imperial behavior itself. Here the contrasts stand out boldy. Sui Wen-ti was a tough, canny man whose aloof and suspicious personality allowed little room for relationships based on trust and whose impatience with ministers and fits of imperial temper were legendary. His son Yang-ti was a talented and flamboyant figure who disdained restraint of any sort. There is little to suggest that either man was close to those around him, though Yang-ti clearly relished the deference of his minions and innumerable entertainers. For all their differences in personality, then, both Sui emperors were alike in their imperial remoteness.

The chasm that separated the Sui emperors from their entourage is in striking contrast to the close relationship that the T'ang rulers developed and maintained with their supporters. That intimacy was never more apparent than during the reign of T'ang T'ai-tsung, perhaps the greatest of the T'ang rulers and surely one of the most admired figures in Chinese history. One might expect, from his mighty reputation, a figure of immense proportions, held in awe by his officials. But he comes down to us less as the remote despot than as a kind of senior figure in a government oligarchy—indeed, for much of his career as little more than *primus inter pares*. T'ai-tsung, we are startled to discover, remained on something surprisingly close to equal terms with his high ministers, who were more his colleagues than the Emperor's servants. We possess extensive collections of T'ai-tsung's court discussions with his ministers, who advise him on every conceivable issue of high government policy, both civil and military. The Emperor, in turn, listens with care, asks further questions, solicits more information, considers options and alternatives. The tone is cautious and restrained. As often as the Emperor acted, so too did he frequently decide against action. These long court dialogues and debates offer an unequivocal picture of an emperor weighing alternatives, an emperor wary of precipitate and reckless policies, an emperor who knew the risks. Those risks he knew from the experience of the Sui Dynasty, for Sui history would have been fresh and powerful in his mind as he plotted the course for his own fledgling regime. If he knew the sources of danger, T'ai-tsung knew also that he could not rule alone, that the support and confidence of his ministers would be an essential ingredient of T'ang success. Without faithful supporters, the T'ang emperors would be no less vulnerable than their Sui predecessors.

If the Sui emperors were more distant from their officials than were the T'ang rulers from theirs, they also treated their officials with a punitive severity that was sometimes simply vindictive. Wen-ti, in particular, was capable of a harshness bordering on sadism. Wen-ti's court was often the scene of whippings and beatings of offending officials. One advisor protested, unsuccessfully, that "the Court is not the place to kill people, and the Palace is not the place to judge guilt." Wen-ti asked another official, "Are my beatings heavy?" and was told that they were. The Emperor demanded an explanation. The official held up his hand and said, "Your Majesty's bastinado is as large as a finger. When you have a man struck thirty times it is like several hundred blows of an ordinary whip. Thus many die." The Emperor, disturbed, had the bastinado removed from court. But he soon brought it back after a high regional official dared suggest that the Emperor had shown excessive favor to the trusted Kao Chiung, criticism that drove the Emperor to beat that incautious official to death with an ordinary horse whip. Though Wen-ti's fits of black rage alternated with extreme remorse, his officials came to fear the worst, and it was to no avail that he ordered them to speak their minds.

The effect of such brutal and capricious behavior was considerable, setting in motion a cycle of fear and mistrust which produced
plots and rumors of plots, all of which fed the boundless apprehen-
sions of the Sui emperors. Both Sui rulers were thus driven to mete
out to their own closest supporters the same harshness they normally reserved for enemies of the dynasty. The catalogue of their
victims is comprehensive, and includes nearly every member of the
dynasty's inner circle: the Emperor's father-in-law Tu-ku Hsin,
forced to commit suicide; the trusted Kao Chiung, reduced to commoner status and barely saved from execution; Yang Su, Wen-ti's
flamboyant and once-mighty confidant, involved in plots against the
government and an eventual suicide. There is some rough justice in
the harsh and vindictive treatment meted out to these fallen officials,
for they were themselves tough and often ruthless. Yang Su is especially notorious for having devised the policy of beheading any soldier retreating from the ranks of a Sui army.

Collectively, these episodes suggest a fierce and unstable regime
that consumed all those it touched. Yang Kuang became in time
scarcely less suspicious and hostile than his father, and it was ru-
mored in 617 that the Emperor was executing all officials named
Li—perhaps the most common surname in China—because a popular ballad prophesied an overthrow of the Sui by a new dynasty
whose rulers bore that name. Thus did Li Yüan, the Emperor's most
powerful general, finally move against the Sui and inaugurate his
own dynasty, the T'ang.

Having been the intended victims of imperial capriciousness of a
savage variety, the early T'ang rulers dispelled at their own court
that lethal atmosphere of fear and hatred. The contrast between Sui
and T'ang treatment of officials is striking. Where the Sui rulers
were harsh and unforgiving, the emperors of the early T'ang were so
indulgent as to seem, on occasion, simply amiable. In 637, for example, Emperor T'ai-tsung planned to send a palace eunuch on a distant provincial assignment, but this plan was stymied when an
official refused to grant the needed passport. The matter was reported to the throne and the offending official was demoted for his
effrontery. But another court minister intervened, remonstrating
with the Emperor that it was an unwise policy to use eunuchs in far-
flung responsibilities. T'ang T'ai-tsung accepted this cautionary advice, restored the official to his former position, and agreed not to
use eunuchs in future political responsibilities.

One will search the entire record of the Sui Dynasty in vain for a similar account. In the place of T'ang T'ai-tsung, either Sui emperor would have severely disciplined, perhaps even killed, any official who dared to flout imperial intentions. Nor would they have tolerated ministerial remonstrance on any aspect of their conduct. But this contrast does not in itself touch the actual extent of difference between the two regimes. For the simple fact is that no Sui official would have dared in the first place to consider subversion of the imperial will.

We have only begun to explore here the force of the Sui legacy in T'ang times, but we have seen that it was both complex and powerful. The T'ang would survive for a full three centuries and leave its own heritage for succeeding generations. But for the small group of hardened and experienced men who began in the early decades of the seventh century to establish the foundations of the T'ang empire, the immediate, inescapable task was to master the lessons of the Sui so that the mistakes of the regime would not be repeated. Thus we must see in T'ang history the confirmation of a policy of imperial centralization set in motion by a predecessor regime of extraordinary energy and determination. After the Sui experience, Chinese history could never be the same, because the effects of that brief but crucial era, and its memory, would never fade.

*Chinese Terms
and
Names*

Notes

Bibliography

Index

Chinese Terms and Names

a-she-li 阿闍梨
an 安
An-hsi 安熹
An-shih 安市

ch'ang 長
Ch'ang-an 長安
Chang'yeh 張掖
ch'ao-cheng 朝政
ch'ao-chi shih 朝集使
Chao, Prince of
    Chao-ts'an 趙僭王招
Ch'en (Dynasty) 陳
Ch'en Ch'ing-chih 陳慶之
chen-jen 直人
Chen-kao 直誥
Ch'en Pa-hsien 陳霸先
Ch'en Shu-pao 陳叔寶
Ch'en Yin-k'o 陳寅恪
ch'eng-hsiang 承相
Ch'i-chou 岐州
Ch'i-ch'un 蘄春

ch'i-chü chu 起居注
ch'i-i 起義
Ch'i-min 啓民
chia-tzu 甲子
Chiang-ling 江陵
Chiang-tu 江都
Chiao-chou 交州
Ch'ien-chien 乾鏗
Ch'ien-hsiu, Duke
    of Yüeh-hsi 越攜公乾銑
Chien-k'ang 建康
Chien-ling 乾鈴
Chien-te 建德
chih (treatise) 志
chih (knowledge) 知
Chih-hsien 智仙
Chih-i 智顗
Chin (Dynasty) 晉
Ch'in (Dynasty) 秦
Ch'in-ling Mountains 秦嶺
chin-shih 進士
Ch'in Shih Huang-ti 秦世皇帝

Ching Prefecture 荊州

Ch'ing-lung ssu 青龍寺

Chiu-ssu 九寺

chou 州

Chou (Dynasty) 周

Chou-li 周禮

Ch'u (State) 楚

Chu-ch'iao men chieh 朱雀門街

Chu-kuo 柱國

Ch'u-lo 處羅

ch'ü-pi 曲筆

chün 郡

Ch'un-ming men 春明門

Chung-cheng 中正

Ch'ung-jen fang 崇仁坊

Chung-nan shan 終南山

chung-yüan 中原

Duke of Ch'in-ho 清河公

Duke of Chou 周公

Fang Kung-i 房恭懿

fang-lüeh 方略

fang-sheng 放生

fu 府

fu-ping 府兵

General Han Ch'in-hu 韓擒虎

General Ho-jo Pi 賀若弼

General Liu Jen-en 劉仁恩

General Yen Jung 燕榮

Hai-chou 海州

Han (Dynasty) 漢

Han-k'ou 漢口

Han River 漢江

Han Wu-ti 漢武帝

Han Yü 韓愈

Hangchow Bay 杭州灣

Heng-shan 恆山

Ho-fei 合肥

Ho Yung-k'ang 何永康

Honan 河南

Hou Ching 侯景

Hsi-yü t'u-chi 西域圖志

Hsiang-chou 相州

Hsiang-yang 襄陽

Hsiao-ching 孝經

Hsiao Yen 蕭衍

Hsiao Yü 蕭瑀

hsien 縣

Hsien-pei 鮮北

hsin 信

Hsin-chou 信州

Hsin-lin 新林

hsin-lü 新律

hsing-pu 刑部

hsiu-ts'ai 秀才

Hsüan-cheng 宣政

Hsüan-ning 玄凝

Hsüeh Tao-heng 薛道衡

Hu-pu 戶部

Hua-shan 華山

Hua-yin 華陰

Huai River 淮河

huang-ch'eng 皇城

Huang Sui Ling-kan chih 皇隋靈感誌

hui 諱

Hui-yü 惠鬱

Hupeh 湖北

i 義

jen 仁

jen-ch'ing 人情

Jen-shou Palace 仁壽宮

K'ai-huang 開皇

K'ai-huang Code 開皇律

K'ang-hsi 康熙

Kao Chiung 高熲

Kao Huan 高歡

Kao Yang 高洋

Khitan 契丹

Kiangsu 江蘇

King Ch'eng of the Chou 周成王

Koguryō 高句麗

K'ou Ch'ien-chih 寇謙之

Kuan 觀
Kuan-chung 關中
Kuan-yin 觀音
Kuang-chou 廣州
Kung-pu 工部
kuo-shih 國史
Kuo-tzu chien 國子監
Kuo-tzu ssu 國子寺

Lady of Ch'iao-kuo 譙國夫人
Lake T'ai-hu 太湖
Lao-tzu 老子
li (⅓ mile) 里
li (norms) 禮
Li-ch'uan fang 醴泉坊
Li Po 李白
Li-pu (Board Rites) 吏部
Li-pu (Civil Office) 禮部
Li Te-lin 李德林
Li Yüan 李淵
Liang (Dynasty) 梁
Liang, Prince of Han 漢王諒
liang-shih 良史
Liang Wu-ti 梁武帝
Liang Yen-kuang 梁彥光
Liao River 遼河
lieh-chuan 列傳
ling 令
Ling-kan ssu 靈感寺
Ling-ts'ang 靈藏
Liu-ch'iu 流求
Liu Cho 劉焯
Liu Chün 劉駿
Liu Hsüan 劉炫
Liu Pien 柳卞
Liu Shao 劉劭
Lo-chou 羅州
lun 論
Loyang 洛陽
Lung-men 龍門

Ma Chou 馬周
Men-hsia sheng 門下省
Min 閩

Min-pu 民部
Ming-ching 明經
Ming-te men 明德門
Mo-ho 靺鞨
Mount Sung 嵩山
Mount T'ai 泰山

Na-lo-yen 那羅延
nan-jen 南人
Nanking 南京
Nei-shih sheng 內史省
Niu Hung 牛弘
Northern Ch'i (Dynasty) 北齊
Northern Chou (Dynasty) 北周

Paekche 白濟
Pao-p'u tzu 抱朴子
P'ei Cheng 裴政
P'ei Chü 裴矩
P'ei Shih-yüan 裴世元
P'ei Yün 裴蘊
Peking 北京
pen-chi 本紀
p'i-p'a 琵琶
p'in 品
p'ing 平
P'ing-ch'eng 平乘
Ping-pu 兵部
Po-ling 博陵
Prince of Chin 晉王
Princess I-cheng 義成公主
P'u-liu-ju 普六茹
Pyong-yang 平壤

Sa-fu 薩甫
San Kung 三公
San-sheng 三省
San Shih 三史
Seng-yün 僧暈
Shan-yin (Princess) 山陰
Shang (Dynasty) 商
Shang-shu sheng 尚書省
Shanhaikwan 山海關
Shansi 山西

Shantung 山東
She-kuei 射匱
Shih-pi 始畢
Shou-hsien 壽縣
Shun 舜
Shou-chou 朔州
Silla 新羅
Soochow 蘇州
ssu 寺
Su-ma Hsiao-nan 司馬消難
Ssu-ma Kuang 司馬光
Su Ch'o 蘇綽
su-lu 索虜
su-seng 俗僧
Su Wei 蘇威
Sui 隋
Sui-kuo kung 隋國公
Sui-shu 隋書
Sui Wen-ti 隋文帝
Sui Yang-ti 隋煬帝
Szechwan 四川

Ta-hsiang 大象
Ta-hsing 大興
Ta-hsing ch'eng 大興城
Ta-hsing-shan Ssu 大興善寺
Ta-hsing tien 大興殿
Ta-li ssu 大理寺
Ta-ting 大定
T'ai-ch'ang-ssu 太常寺
T'ai-chi tien 太極殿
T'ai-hang Mountains 太行山
T'ai-ho 太和
T'ai-hsüeh 太學
T'ai-shang huang 太上皇
T'ai-yüan 太原
T'ang (Dynasty) 唐
T'ang T'ai-tsung 唐太宗
T'ao Hung-ching 陶弘景
tao-i 島夷
Tao-te ching 道德經
Tao-te fang 道德坊
T'ien-hsia 天下
Ting-chou 定州

T'ien-t'ai 天台
Toba 拓跋
Ts'ao Ts'ao 曹操
Ts'ao Wei (Dynasty) 曹魏
Ts'ui's of Ch'ing-ho 清河崔
Ts'ui Tzu-shih 崔子石
Tsung-ch'ih p'u-sa 總持菩薩
tsung-kuan 總管
Tu Cheng-hsüan 杜正玄
T'u-chüeh 突厥
Tu Fu 杜甫
Tu-ku Hsin 獨孤信
Tu-shui chien 都水監
Tu-shui t'ai 都水臺
T'u-yü Hun 吐谷渾
t'un 屯
Tun-huang 敦煌
T'ung-tao-kuan 通道觀
T'ung-tien 通典
Tzu-chih t'ung-chien 資治通鑑
tz'u-shih 刺史

wan-sui 萬歲
Wang Mang 王莽
Wang Shao 王劭
Wei (Dynasty) 魏
Wei Cheng 魏徵
Wei-ch'ih Ch'iung 尉遲迥
Wei River 渭河
Wu (State) 吳
Wu-chiao 五教
Wu-chou 吳州
Wu-hu 蕪湖
Wu-t'ai shan 吾台山

yang 陽
Yang Chien 楊堅
Yang-chou 揚州
Yang Chung 楊忠
Yang Hsüan-kan 楊玄感
Yang Kuang 楊廣
Yang Li-hua 楊麗華
Yang Shang-hsi 楊尚希
Yang Su 楊素

Yang Ta 楊達
Yang-t'i 陽翟
Yao 堯
Yeh 鄴
yeh-seng 野僧
Yen Chih-t'ui 顏之推
Yen-men 鴈門
Yü 禹
Yü-lin 榆林
Yü-wen Yung 宇文邕
Yü Hsin 庾信
Yü Shih-chi 虞世基
yü-shih ta-fu 御史大夫
Yü-shih t'ai 御史臺

Yü-wen Hua-chi 宇文化及
Yü-wen K'ai 宇文愷
Yü-wen Pi 宇文弼
Yü-wen Pin 宇文贇
Yü-wen Shu 宇文述
Yü-wen T'ai 宇文泰
Yüan, Duke of Te-kuang 德廣公員
Yüan (surname adopted by Hsien-
    pei imperial family) 元
Yüeh (State) 越
Yümen (Jade Gate) 玉門
Yün-kang 雲岡
Yung-an 永安
Yung-chi ch'ü 永濟渠

Notes

ABBREVIATIONS USED IN THE NOTES

(For full data on the following references, see the alphabetical listings in the Bibliography.)

CKCY Chen-kuan cheng-yao, comp. by Wu Ching

SS Sui-shu, comp. by Wei Cheng

TCTC Tzu-chih t'ung-chien, comp. by Ssu-ma Kuang

TFYK Ts'e-fu yüan-kuei, comp. by Wang Ch'in-jo

CHAPTER 1: THE SUI CHALLENGE

12 DECLINE Heinrich Fichtenau, *The Carolingian Empire,* p. 187.

15 LOST RECORDS *SS* 32.908.

18 DEMEANING TREATMENT *Pei Ch'i-shu* 37.488–89.

18 VALUABLE BOOK This is the *Chen-kuan cheng-yao,* compiled about 706 by Wu Ching.

19 DENUNCIATION *SS* 69.1613.

CHAPTER 2: SIXTH-CENTURY CHINA

23 KUAN-CHUNG Pan Ku, "Rhyme-prose on the Western Capital," in *Wen-hsüan* 1.3a.

24 SOGDIAN LETTER Quoted in Waley, *The Secret History of the Mongols,* pp. 54–55.

27 LOYANG DIALECT Richard Mather, "A Note on the Dialects of Lo-yang and Nanking During the Six Dynasties," in Chow, ed., *Wen-lin,* p. 251.

28 LAND EXPLOITATION *Liang-shu* 686–87.

29 NOMADIC LIFE *Chin-shu* 126.3145.

32–33 DIATRIBE Lo-yang chia-lan chi 2.117–18.

34 LITERARY SCENE IN THE NORTH Quoted by Mou, "The Differences of Academic Ap-

proach," p. 57, from a gossipy collection, part of which may date from a T'ang work of the same title, *Ch'ao-yeh chien-tsai* 6.28a–b.

34 FAMILY INJUNCTIONS Teng, tr., *Yen-shih chia-hsün*, p. 22. In some of the quotations from Prof. Teng's valuable translation I have slightly altered the wording. For insights into the north–south problem I am particularly indebted to the late Moriya Mitsuo, whose fine study of northerners and southerners was republished in a volume of his collected essays, *Chūgoku kodai no kazoku to kokka*, pp. 416–60.

34 STORY FROM YEN Teng, pp. 63–64.

34 CONTRAST IN MANNERS Teng, p. 31.

35 PROPER RITUALS Teng, p. 44.

35 NORTHERN WOMEN Teng, p. 19.

36 COLLABORATION D. C. Lao, tr., "Advice to My Sons" by Yen Chih-t'ui (A.D. 531–after 597), *Renditions*, No. 1, Autumn 1973, pp. 94–98.

38 MONSTROUS SADISM *SS* 25.704. Cf. Balazs, *Le Traité juridique*, p. 56.

39 NORTHERN CH'I WEAKNESS *Pei-Ch'i shu* 24.247–48. Cf. Balazs, *Le Traité économique*, pp. 258–59.

39 DECREE Emperor Wu's decree appears in the *Ch'üan shang-ku san-tai Ch'in-Han San-kuo Liu-ch'ao wen*, Vol. 3, p. 2958. For this translation and for many insights into Liang history I

am indebted to my former student James Lee.

40 OLDER ARISTOCRATIC CLANS Teng, pp. 53–54.

41 BITTERLY CENSORIOUS Teng, pp. 116–17.

41 LIANG REBELLIONS *TCTC* 160.4966. For details on rebellions I am indebted to Mr. James Lee.

46 STERN CODE Teng, p. 18.

46 WISDOM OR PRUDENCE Teng, p. 130.

47 READING AND STUDYING Teng, p. 59.

49 YEN'S BELIEFS Teng, p. 148.

50 BUDDHIST BUILDING *Wei-shu* 22.

51 BUDDHIST PEASANT REBELLIONS Paul Demiéville, "Philosophy and Religions from Han to Sui," draft chapter (1973) for the *Cambridge History of China*, ms. p. 86.

51 BUDDHIST FORMULA *Wei-shu* 114.3021 and Tsukamoto Zenryū's translation in Japanese, which appears as an appendix to vol. XVI of Mizuno and Nagahiro, *Unko Sekkutsu no kenkyū*, p. 531.

CHAPTER 3: THE RISE OF YANG CHIEN

56 REBUKING AN OLD FRIEND *TCTC* 175.5436.

58 PATHOLOGICAL EMPEROR *Chou-shu* 1.5–9.

58 YANG CHIEN'S POSITION *SS* 1.3.

59 IMPASSIONED PLEA *TCTC* 174.5407.

59 OLD PROVERB *TCTC* 174.5412.

60 WEI-CH'IH'S ADDRESS TO CITIZENS *TCTC* 174.5414.

61 WEI-CH'IH'S SUICIDE *TCTC* 174.5424–25.

62 FLORID EDICT PRAISING YANG CHIEN *SS* 1.4.

63 CHILD EMPEROR'S DEATH *Chou-shu* 8.136.

63 DUKE AND FIVE SONS *Chou-shu* 10.158.

63 EXECUTIONS OF CHAO AND FAMILY *Chou-shu* 13.203.

65 ASSOCIATE INDICTED FOR UNFILIAL CONDUCT *TCTC* 175.5444.

67 FLOODED THE PALACES *Ch'ang-an chih* 12.10a; the full interpretation is from *Hsi-an li-shih shih-lüeh*, p. 72.

67 A VICE-PRESIDENT NEARLY EXECUTED *SS* 62.1486.

67 EMPEROR LATER FILLED WITH REMORSE *TCTC* 177.5528–29.

68 WANG MANG COMPARISON *TCTC* 177.5527.

68 WANG SHAO'S CABALISTIC TEXT *SS* 69.1608.

68 IF KAO CHIUNG WERE PUT TO DEATH *SS* 41.1183.

69 COMMEMORATIVE STELE *SS* 45.1240.

69 PUNISHMENT OF THIRD SON *SS* 45.1240.

70 YANG CHIEN BENDING THE LAW TO HIS FEELINGS *SS* 38.1143.

71 WHAT SORT OF RULER *CKCY* 1.28a–b.

71 EMPRESS'S REFUSAL OF CLEMENCY *SS* 36.1108.

73 AFTER HER DEATH *SS* 36.1108–09.

77 YANG SU'S HONORS *SS* 48.1281–88.

77 YANG SU'S DEATH *SS* 48.1292.

78 YANG SU'S POEM The text appears in the collection *Ch'üan*

Han San-kuo Chin Nan-pei-ch'ao shih, vol. 6, p. 1941; translation by Stephen Owen.

79 SU WEI'S TASKS *SS* 41.1185.

80 FIVE TEACHINGS *TCTC* 177.5530.

80 SU WEI'S DISMISSAL *SS* 41.1187.

CHAPTER 4: REUNIFICATION

84 YANG CHIEN'S LONG EDICT *SS* 1.17–18; *Pei-shih* 11.407.

85 CAPITAL PLANNING On the planners and planning, cf. Ch'en Yin-k'o, *Sui-T'ang chih-tu*, pp. 62–81.

85 CORVÉE LABORERS *TFYK* 487.5828a. This passage states that, in mobilizing labor, the Sui still used the corvée regulations of the previous Northern Chou dynasty.

85–86 BUILDING THE OUTER WALLS Details on the measurements of the city's walls and much other detail are derived from a preliminary survey of the site of T'ang Ch'ang-an, "T'ang Ch'ang-an ch'eng ti chi," published in 1958 by the Shensi Provincial Cultural Commission.

87 WALLS OF WARDS AND MARKETS DISINTEGRATED *TFYK* 105.26a.

89 KUAN-YIN FIGURE On this figure and its location, cf. Jan Fontein and Tung Wu, *Unearthing China's Past*, pp. 152–54.

90 GATE HOUSES BUILT BY YÜ-WEN K'AI This detail, along with much else about the city, has been drawn from the great eighteenth-century work of

Hsü Sung, *T'ang liang-ching ch'eng-fang k'ao*; for Sui Buddhist temples, the best source is the *Liang-ching hsin-chi*, the first descriptive work on Sui and T'ang Ch'ang-an. For a general description, see my article "Ch'ang-an" in Arnold Toynbee, ed., *Cities of Destiny*.

90 JUDGMENT OF A NOTED AUTHORITY The authority is Naba Toshisada, whose classic article "Shina shuto keikaku shijō" was published in 1930.

91 NORTHERN CHOU OF NON-CHINESE DESCENT Yamazaki Hiroshi, "Zuichō kanryō," p. 17.

91 SUI PROPORTION OF CHINESE TO NON-CHINESE Yamazaki, "Zuichō kanryō," pp. 17–23.

92 NINE RANKS Tabulated in Ts'en, *Sui-T'ang shih*, p. 7.

94 MAKE-UP OF CORE GROUP Yamazaki, "Zuichō kanryō," pp. 15–25.

95 NORTHERN CHOU POWER GROUP Yamazaki, "Zuichō kanryō," p. 17.

95 NIU HUNG His biography is in *SS* 49.1297–1310.

96 GIVING REWARDS *SS* 2.54.

96 BEST GOVERNOR *TCTC* 178.5550.

96 YANG TA CHOSEN *SS* 49.1218.

96 PROFILE OF BUREAUCRACY Yamazaki, "Zuichō kanryō," pp. 26–44.

98 323 OFFICIALS *SS* 28.783.

98 A HAMLET PROCLAIMED A PREFECTURE *Pei-Ch'i shu* 4.62–3; the edict refers particularly to the vast lands between the Yangtze and Huai rivers that

the Wei had annexed from the Southern Ch'i.

99 SHUO-CHOU PREFECTURE Ts'en, *Sui-T'ang shih*, pp. 3–4.

99 SIX-AND-A-HALF-FOLD Yen, *Chung-kuo ti-fang*, Vol. 4, p. 896.

99 NINE SHEPHERDS FOR TEN SHEEP *SS* 46.1253.

101 INTERCHANGE BETWEEN TWO SIXTH-CENTURY OFFICIALS *Pei-Ch'i shu* 43.576.

101 NO MORE CORRUPT OFFICIALS *T'ung-tien* 14.81a.

101 LI TE-LIN'S MEMORIAL *SS* 42.1207.

102 SU CH'O ON GOOD MEN *Chou-shu* 23.386.

102 PERSONAL QUALITIES OF THREE WORTHY MEN *T'ung-tien* 14.81a.

103 TU CHENG-HSÜAN *SS* 76.1747; his younger brother also took this examination.

103 DECREE OF 594 *SS* 2.39

104 FANG KUNG'I'S PERFORMANCE *TCTC* 175.5449.

104 EMPEROR, IN A FURY *SS* 1.25.

105 WITHOUT BENDING OR FLINCHING *T'ung-tien* 14.81a.

105 EMPEROR HAS CENSORS EXECUTED *SS* 25.715; Balazs, *Le Traité juridique*, pp. 87–88.

107 NO MORE LITIGANTS *SS* 73.1575–76; *TCTC* 175.5447–48.

CHAPTER 5: THE RESTORATION OF CULTURAL HEGEMONY

109 PATCHWORK OF BELIEFS AND PRACTICES *SS* 75.1706.

110 AUDIENCE OF LOCAL RESIDENTS *Ta-T'ang K'ai-yüan-li*, section

130; Edwin Reischauer, tr., *Ennin's Diary*, pp. 180–82.

111 USURPATION OF HAN POWER *SS* 1.3; *TCTC* 174.5408.

111 VERBAL FORMULA *SS* 1.7; *San-kuo chih* 1.37.

112 NINE GIFTS *SS* 1.10–11; for the Han procedures, cf. Dubs, *History of the Former Han Dynasty*, Vol. III, pp. 208–10, and *San-kuo chih* 1.39.

112 CHILD EMPEROR'S EDICT OF ABDI-CATION *SS* 1.11–12.

112–13 TZU-CHIH T'UNG-CHIEN DE-SCRIPTION OF SUI INAUGURA-TION *TCTC* 175.5433.

113 CEREMONIAL SPRING PLOWING *TCTC* 175.5438.

114 DEATH OF EX-EMPEROR, AGE EIGHT *Chou-shu* 8.136.

114 WANG SHAO READING ALOUD *TCTC* 178.5547.

115 AXIOM FROM ANCIENT RITUAL CLASSIC *Li-chi*, Legge's translation, p. 90. My amplification.

116 SUI MODEL The Ritual Treatise of the *Sui History*, chs. 11 and 12, provides abundant detail. A splendid review appears in the eighth-century encyclopedia *T'ung-tien* 41.132. I am indebted to Dr. David Mc-Mullen for allowing me to read his draft chapter on the *li* for the *Cambridge History of China, Vol. III: Sui–T'ang* (forthcoming).

116 IMPERIAL EDICT OF PROMULGA-TION *SS* 25.712; Balazs, *Le Traité juridique*, p. 77.

118 EXECUTIONS IN MARKETPLACE *SS* 25.716; Balazs, *Le Traité juridique*, p. 89.

119 REVERSING OF PENALTY REDUC-

TIONS *SS* 25.716–17; Balazs, *Le Traité juridique*, pp. 92–3.

119 PERORATION *SS* 47.1277–78.

120 INSTRUCTION, ESPECIALLY IN BE-HAVIORAL NORMS *SS* 47.1278.

120 SCHOLAR REWARDED *SS* 75.1708.

122 OBJECTION TO LIU CHO'S TREA-TISE Yabuuchi, *Zui-Tō no Rihōshi no kenkyū*, pp. 256–60.

122 LIU HSÜAN'S PETITION *SS* 75.1718–19.

122 NIU HUNG'S MEMORIAL *SS* 49.1300.

123 CONVICTED BROTHER *SS* 32.908, 75.1720.

124 EDICT ON LITERARY STYLE *TCTC* 176.5424–25.

125 REVIVAL OF CONFUCIANISM The essay is by Wei Cheng (580–643), in his introduction to the section of biographies of Confucian scholars, *SS* 75.1706.

126 DISTRIBUTION OF BUDDHIST RELICS *SS* 2.46–7.

128 RESCIND CHOU PROSCRIPTION *TCTC* 174.5413; *Hsü Kao-seng chuan* 8.491a, 19.581b.

128 DECREE OF THIRD MONTH *Li-tai san-pao-chi* 12.107b. This Bud-dhist chronicle was completed in 597 by an ex-monk who had been laicized in the Northern Chou proscription. There are other versions of this edict.

129 ACTS PROMOTING BUDDHISM, IN 581 AND 583 For an under-standing of this sequence of official acts I am indebted to Tsukamoto Zenryū's article on the Japanese Kokubunji compared with Sui and T'ang

policies toward official temples; this is contained in his *Nisshi Bukkyō kōtsūshi kenkyū*, pp. 1–47.

130 TING-HSIEN INSCRIPTION The inscription is partially translated by Tsukamoto in his *Nisshi Bukkyō kōtsūshi kenkyū*, p. 43. He remarks that he had been shown and allowed to copy an actual rubbing of the stone inscription in the possession of the famous writer Lu Hsün. The text used here is in the *Local History of Ting Hsien*, originally published in 1934, Taiwan facsimile reprint of 1969, Vol. 3, pp. 996–98.

132 FUNCTIONING NUNNERY *Liang-ching hsin-chi* 3.3.

132 OTHER DONORS All materials on donors from fragments of the *Liang-ching hsin-chi*.

133 WEN-TI'S REMARK TO LIN-TSANG *Li-tai san-pao-chi* 12.102–03; *Hsü Kao-seng chuan* 21.610b.

133 ÉLITE CORPS OF MONKS I am indebted to the writings of Yamazaki Hiroshi for this interpretation of the "Community of Twenty-Five"; see his *Shina chūsei Bukkyō no tenkai*, pp. 298–308.

134 EDICT ON DISTRIBUTING BUDDHIST RELICS *Kuang Hung-ming chi* 17.213b.

135 CAPITAL CEREMONY *Kuang Hung-ming chi* 17.214a–b.

137 COMMEMORATIVE PIECE FOR LAO-TZU A translation is to be found in Legge, *The Texts of Taoism*, Vol. II, pp. 311–19.

137 NUMBER OF CLERGY The Taoist

figure comes from the *Li-tai ch'ung-tao chi* contained in the Taoist canon, in the T'ung-hsüan section, subsection on chronicles. The Buddhist figures are from the *Pien-cheng-lun*, by Fa-lin (572–640).

CHAPTER 6: CONQUEST OF THE SOUTH

140 SUI MILITARY GARRISONS Details in *SS* 2.29 seq; *TCTC* 176.5490 seq.

141 EDICT OF DENUNCIATION *TCTC* 176.5496.

142 WROTE POETRY UNCEASINGLY *TCTC* 176.5502.

143 FRESH HORSES *SS* 73.1681.

148–49 WITCHES GORGE Mennie, *The Grandeur of the Gorges*, text to Plate IX.

149 GOD OF THE YANGTZE *TCTC* 176.5500.

150 REASSURE THE POPULATIONS *SS* 48.1283. There are difficulties in reconciling the *SS* and *TCTC* accounts of Yang Su's operations. For a fuller discussion of his battleships, see Needham, *Science and Civilization in China*, Vol. IV, Part 3, pp. 690–92; an illustration of a "Five-Toothed" warship appears on p. 691.

152 LADY CH'IAO-KUO REWARDED *SS* 80.1801. Material on Lady Ch'iao-kuo is drawn mainly from her biography, *SS* 80.1800–03.

153 GIFTS DISPLAYED AT GREAT RECEPTION *SS* 80.1803.

153 TAKEN CONTROL OF CH'EN DOMAIN *SS* 2.32.

154 HOMECOMING *TCTC* 177.5516.

154 FILLED WITH SHAME *TCTC* 177.5516; some details from *Nan-shih* 10.309–10.

154 THIRTY MILLION LENGTHS *TCTC* 177.5517.

155 MOST THOROUGH SURVEY Ts'en, *Sui-shu ch'iu-shih,* pp. 134–332.

156 DISEMBOWELED NEWLY AP- POINTED OFFICIALS *TCTC* 177.5530–32.

CHAPTER 7: THE SECOND EMPEROR

158 FONDNESS FOR THE SOUTH Cf. Arthur F. Wright, "Sui Yang- ti: Personality and Stereo- type," pp. 49–56.

159–60 BODHISATTVA CHAPLET *Kuo-ch'ing pai-lu* 2.807b.

160–61 "THE JOY OF MY PAL- ACE" Owen, *The Poetry of the Early T'ang,* pp. 24–25.

161 "SPRING RIVER" Owen, *The Po- etry of the Early T'ang,* p. 25.

161–62 BLUNT-SPOKEN MEMBER OF YUNG-KUANG'S GROUP *SS* 61.1470.

162 LEARNED MONKS Yamazaki, "Yōtei no shidōjō," pp. 22–35.

163 SUI YANG-TI AS POLITICAL AES- THETE Lasswell, *Psychopathology and Politics,* p. 50.

164 SUI LAW CODES Balazs, *Le Traité juridique,* pp. 162–63.

164 MANAGEMENT OF SELECTION SYSTEM *T'ung-tien* 14.81a.

165 "MORNING CROSSING" Owen, unpublished translation.

165 COURTIER'S REPLY ON IMPERIAL POWER *TCTC* 180.5644.

166 ADVICE ABOUT FORMAL AUDI- ENCES *SS* 61.1470.

166 CASE OF YÜ-WEN PI *SS* 56.1391.

167 YÜ SHIH-CHI'S ROLE *SS* 67.1572; the composition of the inner circle is confirmed in *SS* 41.1188.

167 YÜ SHIH-CHI'S POWER *TCTC* 180.5624.

167–68 YANG-TI AND YÜ SHIH- CHI ASSASSINATED BY TURKS *SS* 67.1573–74.

169 P'EI CHÜ'S CHARACTER Cf. Fritz Jäger, "Leben und Werk des P'ei Kü," pp. 81–115, 216–31.

170 SSU-MA KUANG'S INDICTMENT OF P'EI CHÜ *TCTC* 180.5653.

CHAPTER 8: THE DYNASTY AT ITS HEIGHT

172 POPULATION The interpretation of these population figures has been much discussed; see Bielenstein, "The Population of China," pp. 160–61, and Pulleyblank, "Registration of Population," pp. 289–301.

173 EDICT ORDERING RECODIFICA- TION *SS* 25.716; Balazs, *Le Traité juridique,* p. 91.

175 GRINDING AND POLISHING *SS* 3.64–5.

175 SCHOLARS' REHABILITATION SHORT-LIVED *SS* 75.1707.

176 ABRIDGED REFERENCE LIBRARIES *TCTC* 182.5694.

178 YÜ-WEN K'AI TO DESIGN CANAL TO T'UNG PASS Cf. Chang K'un-ho, "Sui Yün-ho k'ao," pp. 201–11; Balazs, *Le Traité économique,* p. 48.

179 CANAL WORKERS Cf. Yang,

"Economic Aspects of Public Works," pp. 203–4.

179 CONSCRIPTED WOMEN *TCTC* 181.5636.

180 CHIANG-TU Maspero, "Rapport sommaire," p. 5.

180 YANG-TI'S PROGRESS *SS* 24.686–87; Balazs, *Le Traité économique*, pp. 54–55.

CHAPTER 9: MILITARY DISASTER AND POLITICAL COLLAPSE

182–83 SUI MILITARY POWER PREVAILED Li Fan, *Yeh-hou chia-chuan*, quoted in Ts'en, *Fu-ping chih-tu yen-chiu*, p. 43.

186–87 EFFECTS ON JAPAN *SS* 81.1825–28; Tsunoda and Goodrich, *Japan in the Chinese Dynastic Histories*, pp. 28–36.

187 MY TWO CHILDREN *SS* 84.1865.

187–88 WEN-TI ANALYZED THE SITUATION *SS* 84.1866.

190 PROPERLY SUBMISSIVE PEOPLE *SS* 67.1580; Jäger, "Leben und Werk des P'ei Kü," p. 97.

192 THREAT TO CHINA John C. Jamieson, "The *Samguk Sagi* and the Unification Wars," University of California dissertation, 1969, pp. 20–32; Pulleyblank, *The Background of the Rebellion of An Lu-shan*, p. 77.

192 READY TO STRIKE *SS* 4.79–82.

193 DOMESTIC REBELLIONS Bingham, *The Founding of the T'ang Dynasty*, p. 43.

193 EMPEROR ASKED FOR HIS OFFICIALS' VIEWS *SS* 4.86.

193 SELF-JUSTIFYING EDICT *SS* 4.86–87; Yamazaki, "Zui no Koguryō ensei to Bukkyō," pp. 1–10.

194–95 EXPLANATIONS FOR FAILURE Jamieson, "The *Samguk Sagi* and the Unification Wars," pp. 32–34.

195 PEACETIME PURSUITS *SS* 4.89.

CHAPTER 10: THE SUI LEGACY

198 LI-HUA HAD BECOME EMPRESS *Chou-shu* 9.145.

200 ENORMOUS METROPOLIS Cf. Arthur F. Wright, "Symbolism and Function," pp. 667–79.

201 PANOPLY OF RULE See the discussion in Denis Twitchett and Arthur F. Wright, "Introduction" to *Perspectives on the T'ang*, pp. 25ff.

203 EDICTS FROM EARLY T'ANG *T'ang Ta chao-ling-chi* 65.369.

203 MA CHOU'S REMINDER *TCTC* 195.6132–33.

203 CLOSE RELATIONSHIP T'ai-tsung's relationships with his ministers are fully explored in Wechsler, *Mirror to the Son of Heaven*.

204 COURT WHIPPINGS *TCTC* 177.5528–29.

205 DISTANT PROVINCIAL ASSIGNMENT *TCTC* 195.6158; this incident is discussed in Wechsler, *Mirror to the Son of Heaven*, p. 182.

Bibliography

BALAZS, ÉTIENNE. *Le Traité économique du "Souei-chou."* Leiden: E. J. Brill, 1953.

————. *Le Traité juridique du "Souei-chou."* Bibliothèque de l'Institut des Hautes Études Chinoises, Vol. IX. Leiden: E. J. Brill, 1954.

BIELENSTEIN, HANS. "The census of China during the period 2–742 A.D." *Bulletin of the Museum of Far Eastern Antiquities* 19 (1947), 125–63.

BINGHAM, WOODBRIDGE. *The Founding of the T'ang Dynasty: The Fall of Sui and Rise of T'ang.* Baltimore: Waverly Press, 1941.

Ch'ang-an chih 長安志 (*Gazetteer of Ch'ang-an*). Comp. by Pi Yüan 畢沅 (1729–97). Facsimile edition in Hiraoka Takeo 平岡武夫, ed., *Chōan to Rakuyō: Shiryō* 長安と洛陽：資料 (*Ch'ang-an and Loyang: Texts*), T'ang Civilization Reference Series, Vol. 6. Kyoto: Jimbun Kagaku Kenkyūjo, 1956.

CHANG K'UN-HO 張崑河. "Sui Yün-ho k'ao" 隋運河考 (An Examination of the Sui Canal System), in *Yü-kung* 禹貢 7 (1937), 201–12.

Chen-kuan cheng-yao 貞觀政要 (*Essentials of Government of the Chen-kuan Period, 627–650*). Comp. ca. 707–9 by Wu Ching 吳競. *Ssu-pu ts'ungk'an* 四部叢刊, 2nd series. Shanghai: Commercial Press, 1929.

CH'EN YIN-K'O 陳寅恪. *Sui-T'ang chih-tu yüan-yüan lüeh-lun-kao* 隋唐制度淵源略論稿 (*A Draft Outline of the Origins of Sui-T'ang Institutions*). Peking: Sheng-huo tu-shu hsin-chih san-lien shu-tien, 1956.

Chin-shu 晉書 (*History of the Chin Dynasty*). Comp. by Fang Hsüan-ling 房玄齡 (578–648) et al. Peking: Chung-hua shu-chü, 1974.

Chou-shu 周書 (*History of the Chou Dynasty*). Comp. by Ling-hu Te-fen
令狐德棻 (583–661) et al. Peking: Chung-hua shu-chü, 1971.

Ch'üan Han San-kuo Chin Nan-pei-ch'ao shih 全漢三國晉南北朝詩 (*Complete Poetry of the Han, Three Kingdoms, Chin and Northern and Southern Dynasties*). Comp. by Ting Fu-pao 丁福保 (1874–1952). Shanghai:
Wu-hsi Ting shih, 1916.

Ch'üan shang-ku san-tai Ch'in-Han San-kuo Liu-ch'ao Wen
全上古三代秦漢三國六朝文 (*Complete Prose of Ancient and Medieval
China*). Comp. by Yen K'o-chün 嚴可均 (1762–1843). Peking:
Chung-hua shu-chü, 1965.

DEMIÉVILLE, PAUL. "Philosophy and Religions from Han to Sui." Draft
chapter (1973) for the *Cambridge History of China*, Vol. II. Cambridge,
England: Cambridge University Press, forthcoming.

Dubs, Homer H. *History of the Former Han Dynasty*, Vol. III. Baltimore:
Waverly Press, 1955.

Fichtenau, Heinrich. *The Carolingian Empire: The Age of Charlemagne*, trans.
by Peter Minz. New York: Harper Torchbooks, 1964.

Fontein, Jan, and Tung Wu. *Unearthing China's Past*. Boston: Museum of
Fine Arts, 1973.

Han-shu 漢書 (*History of the Former Han Dynasty*). Comp. by Pan Ku
班固 (A.D. 32–92), et al. Peking: Chung-hua shu-chü, 1962.

Hsi-an li-shih shih-lüeh 西安歷史史略 (*A Brief History of Sian*). Sian: Jen-
min ch'u-pan-she, 1959.

Hsü Kao-seng chuan 續高僧傳 (*Continuation of the Lives of Eminent Monks*).
Comp. by Tao-hsüan 道宣 , c. 645. In *Taishō Tripitaka*, Vol. 50.
Tokyo: Taishō Shinshū Daizōkyō kankōkai, 1927.

Hurvitz, Leon, trans. "Wei Shou Treatise on Buddhism and Taoism, An
English Translation of the Original Chinese Text of Wei-shu CXIV
and the Japanese Annotation of Tsukamoto Zenryu," in Mizuno Seii-
chi 水野清一 and Nagahirō Toshiō 長広敏雄, *Unkō sekkutsu no
kenkyū* 雲岡石窟の研究 (*Studies in the Cave Temples of Yun-kang*),
Vol. XVI, pp. 23–103. Kyoto: Kyoto University Research Institute for
the Humanistic Sciences, 1951–56.

Jäger, Fritz. "Leben und werk des P'ei Kü," *Ostasiatische Zeitschrift* 9
(1920–22), 81–115, 216–31.

Jamieson, John C. "The *Samguk Sagi* and the Unification Wars." University of California, Berkeley, dissertation, 1969.

Kuang Hung-ming chi 廣弘明集. Comp. by Tao-hsüan 道宣
(596–667). *Taishō Tripitaka*, Vol. 52. Tokyo: Taishō shinshū Daizōkyō
kankōkai, 1927.

Kuo-ch'ing pai-lu 國清百錄. Comp. by Kuan-ting 灌頂 (561–632) in
Taishō Tripitaka, Vol. 46. Tokyo: Taishō shinshū Daizōkyō kōkankai,
1927.

Lasswell, Harold. *Psychopathology and Politics*. Chicago: University of Chicago Press, 1930.

Legge, James. *Sacred Books of China: The Texts of Taoism*. Oxford: The Clarendon Press, 1891.

Li-chi 禮記 (*Record of Ritual*), trans. by James Legge in Max Müller, ed., *Sacred Books of the East*, Vols. 27–28. Oxford: Clarendon Press, 1885.

Li-tai san-pao chi 歷代三寶記 (*Buddhism's Three Treasures Through the Ages*). Comp. by Fei Ch'ang-fang 費長房, c. 597. In *Taishō Tripitaka*, Vol. 49. Tokyo: Taishō shinshū Daizōkyō kankōkai, 1927.

Liang-ching hsin-chi 兩京新記 (*A New Account of the Two Capitals*). Comp. by Wei Shu 韋述 (d. 757). Hiraoka Takeo 平岡武夫 includes several facsimile editions in *Chōan to Rakuyō: Shiryō* 長安と洛陽：資料 (*Ch'ang-an and Loyang: Texts*), *T'ang Civilization Reference Series*, Vol. 6. Kyoto: Jimbun Kagaku Kenkyūjo, 1956.

Liang-shu 梁書 (*History of the Liang Dynasty*). Comp. by Yao Ch'a 姚察 (533–606) and Yao Ssu-lien 姚思廉 (d. 637). Peking: Chunghua shu-chü, 1973.

Lo-yang chia-lan-chi 洛陽伽藍記 (*Memories of Lo-yang*), by Yang Hsüan-chih 楊衒之, c. 530. Shanghai: Ku-tien wen-hsüeh, 1958.

Maspero, Georges. *Le Royaume de Champa*. Paris and Brussels: G. van Oest, 1928.

Maspero, Henri. "Rapport sommaire sur une Mission Archéologique au Tchö-kiang," *Bulletin de l'École Française d'Extrême Orient* 14 (1914), pp. 1–25.

Mather, Richard. "A Note on the Dialects of Lo-yang and Nanking During the Six Dynasties," in Chow Tse-tsung, ed., *Wen-lin: Studies in the Chinese Humanities*. Madison: University of Wisconsin Press, 1968, pp. 247–56.

Mennie, Donald. *The Grandeur of the Gorges*. Shanghai: A. S. Watson & Co., 1926.

Moriya Mitsuo 守屋美都雄. "Nanjin to Hokujin" 南人と北人 (Southerner and Northerner), in his collection *Chūgoku kodai no kazoku to kokka* 中國古代の家族と國家 (*Family and State in Ancient China*). Kyoto: Tōyōshi kenkyūkai, 1968.

Mou Jun-sun 牟潤孫. "T'ang-ch'u nan-pei hsüeh-jen lun-hsüeh chih i-ch'ü chi ch'i ying-hsiang" 唐初南北學人論學之異趣及其影響 (The Difference in Northern and Southern Scholarship in the Early T'ang and Its Influence). *Hsiang-kang Chung-wen ta-hsüeh Chung-kuo wen-hua yen-chiu-so hsüeh-pao* 香港中文大學中國文化研究所學報 (*The Journal of the Institute of Chinese Studies of the Chinese University of Hong Kong*), 1 (1968), 50–86.

Naba Toshisada 邪波利貞, "Shina shuto keikakushijō yori kōsatsu shita Tō no Chōanjō" 支那首都計劃史より考察した唐の長安城 (T'ang Ch'ang-an Considered in the Light of Chinese Metropolitan

Planning), in *Kuwabara Hakushi kanreki kinen Tōyōshi ronsō*
桑原博士還暦記念東洋史論叢 (*Essays in East Asian History in Honor
of the Sixtieth Birthday of Prof. Kuwabara Jitsuzō*). Kyoto: Kōbundō, 1930,
pp. 1203–69.

Needham, Joseph. *Science and Civilization in China. Vol. IV: Physics and Physical Technology. Part 3: Civil Engineering and Nautics.* Cambridge, England:
Cambridge University Press, 1971.

Owen, Stephen. *The Poetry of the Early T'ang.* New Haven: Yale University
Press, 1977.

Pei Ch'i-shu 北齊書 (*History of the Northern Ch'i*), comp. by Li Pai-yao
李百藥 (565–648). Peking: Chung-hua shu-chü, 1972.

Pei-shih 北史 (*History of the Northern Dynasties*), comp. by Li Yen-shou
李延壽 (c. 629). Peking: Chung-hua shu-chü, 1974.

Pien-cheng-lun 辯正論. Comp. by Fa-lin 法琳 (572–640). *Taishō Tripitaka,*
Vol. 52. Tokyo: Taishō shinshū Daizōkyō kankōkai, 1927.

Pulleyblank, Edwin G. "Registration of Population in China During the
Sui and T'ang Periods." *Journal of the Economic and Social History of the
Orient* 4 (1961), 289–301.

Reischauer, Edwin. *Ennin's Diary: The Record of a Pilgrimage to China in Search
of the Law.* New York: Ronald Press, 1955.

San-kuo chih 三國志 (*History of the Three Kingdoms*). Comp. by Ch'en
Shou 陳壽 (233–97). Peking: Chung-hua shü-chu, 1962.

Shensi Provincial Cultural Commission (Shan-shi sheng wen-wu kuan-li wei-
yüan-hui 陝西省文物管理委員會). "T'ang Ch'ang-an ch'eng ti chi
ch'u-pu t'an-tse tse-liao" 唐長安城地其初探測資料 (Materials from
a Preliminary Survey of the Site of T'ang Ch'ang-an). *Jen-wen tsa-chih*
人文襍志 58.1 (February 1958), 85–95.

Sui-shu 隋書 (*Sui History*). Comp. by Wei Cheng 魏徵 (580–643),
K'ung Ying-ta 孔穎達 et al. Peking: Chung-hua shu-chü, 1973.

Ta-T'ang K'ai-yüan Li 大唐開元禮 (*The T'ang Ritual Code of the K'ai-yüan
Period,* A.D. 713–25). Comp. by Hsiao Sung 蕭嵩 et al. In facsimile
edition, edited by Ikeda On 池田溫. Tokyo: Koten Kenkyūkai,
1972.

T'ang liang-ching ch'eng-fang k'ao 唐兩京城坊考 (*A Study of the Wards of
the Two T'ang Capitals*). Comp. by Hsü Sung 徐松 (1781–1848).
Facsimile edition in Hiraoka Takeo 平岡武夫, ed., *Chōan to Rakuyō:
Shiryō* 長安と洛陽：資料 (*Ch'ang-an and Lo-yang: Texts*), *T'ang Civilization Reference Series,* Vol. 6. Kyoto: Jimbun Kagaku Kenkyūjo,
1956.

T'ang Ta chao-ling chi 唐大詔令集 (*Collected Imperial Edicts of the T'ang*).
Comp. by Sung Min-ch'iu 宋敏求 (1019–79). Peking: Commercial
Press, 1959.

Teng Ssu-yü 鄧嗣禹, trans. *Yen-shih chia-hsün: Family Instructions for the
Yen Clan.* Leiden: E. J. Brill, 1968.

Ts'e-fu yüan-kuei 册府元龜 (*Outstanding Models from the Storehouse of Literature*). Comp. 1005–13 by Wang Ch'in-jo 王欽若 et al. Taipei: Ch'ing-hua shu-chü, 1967 (reprint of 1642 edition).

Ts'en Chung-mien 岑仲勉. *Fu-ping chih-tu yen-chiu* 府兵制度研究 (*A Study of the Fu-ping Military System*). Shanghai: Jen-min ch'u-pan-she, 1957.

———. *Sui-T'ang Shih* 隋唐史 (*Sui-T'ang History*). Shanghai: Kao-teng chiao-yü ch'u-pan-she, 1957.

———. *Sui-shu ch'iu-shih* 隋書求是 (*Investigations in the Sui History*). Peking: Commercial Press, 1958.

Tsukamoto Zenryū 塚本善隆. *Nisshi Bukkyō kōtsushi kenkyū* 日支佛教交通史研究 (*Studies in Relations between Japanese and Chinese Buddhism*). Tokyo: Kōbundo, 1947.

Tsunoda Ryusaku and L. C. Goodrich. *Japan in the Chinese Dynastic Histories: Later Han Through Ming Dynasties*. South Pasadena: P. D. and Ione Perkins, 1951.

T'ung-tien 通典 (*Conspectus of Institutions*). Comp. by Tu Yu 杜佑, c. 801. *Shih-t'ung* edition. Shanghai: Commercial Press, 1935.

Tzu-chih t'ung-chien 資治通鑑 (*Comprehensive Mirror for Aid in Government*). Comp. by Ssu-ma Kuang 司馬光 (1019–86) et al. Peking: Chung-hua shu-chü, 1956.

Waley, Arthur. *A Secret History of the Mongols*. London: George Allen & Unwin, 1963.

Wechsler, Howard J. *Mirror to the Son of Heaven: Wei Cheng at the Court of T'ang T'ai-tsung*. New Haven: Yale University Press, 1974.

Wei-shu 魏書 (*History of the Wei Dynasty*). Comp. by Wei Shou 魏收 (506–72). Peking: Chung-hua shu-chü, 1974.

Wen-hsüan 文選 (*Literary Anthology*). Comp. by Hsiao T'ung 蕭統 (501–31). Taipei: I-wen reprint of Sung Ch'un-hsi 宋淳熙 (1174–90) ed.

Wright, Arthur F. "Sui Yang-ti: Personality and Stereotype," in A. F. Wright, ed., *The Confucian Persuasion*, 47–76. Stanford: Stanford University Press, 1960. Reprinted in A. F. Wright, *The Civilization of Imperial China: Traditional Culture, Religion and Rule*. New Haven: Yale University Press, 1979.

———. "Symbolism and Function: Reflections on Ch'ang-an and Other Great Cities," *Journal of Asian Studies* 24.4 (August 1965), 667–97. Reprinted in A. F. Wright, *The Civilization of Imperial China: Traditional Culture, Religion and Rule*. New Haven: Yale University Press, 1979.

———. "Ch'ang-an," in Arnold Toynbee, ed., *Cities of Destiny*, pp. 143–49. New York: McGraw-Hill, 1967.

Wright, Arthur F., and Denis Twitchett, eds. *Perspectives on the T'ang*. New Haven: Yale University Press, 1973.

Yabuuchi Kiyoshi 藪內清. *Zui-Tō rekihōshi no kenkyū* 隋唐曆法史の研究

(*A History of Calendrical Technique in Sui and T'ang China*).
Tokyo: Sanseido, 1944.

Yamazaki Hiroshi 山崎宏. *Shina chūsei Bukkyō no tenkai*
支那中世佛教の展開 (*The Development of Medieval Chinese Buddhism*).
Kyoto: Hōzōkan, 1942.

————. "Yōtei no shidōjō" 煬帝の四道場 (Sui Yang-ti's Four Temples), *Tōyō gakuhō* 東洋學報 34 (1952), 22–35.

————. "Zui no Koguryō ensei to Bukkyō" 隋の高句麗遠征と佛教
(Buddhism and the Sui Campaigns to Koguryō). *Shichō* 史潮 58
(1953), 1–10.

————. "Zuichō kanryō no seikaku" 隋朝官僚の性格 (The Character
of Sui Officialdom). *Tōkyō kyōiku daigaku bungakubu kiyō*
東京教育大學文學部紀要 6 (1956), 1–59.

Yang Lien-sheng 楊聯昇. "Economic Aspects of Public Works in Imperial China," in author's collection *Excursions in Sinology*, pp. 191–248.
Cambridge, Mass.: Harvard University Press, 1969.

Yen Keng-wang 嚴耕望. *Chung-kuo ti-fang hsing-cheng chih-tu shih*
中國地方行政制度史 (*A History of Chinese Local Administrative Systems*), 4 vols. Taipei: Academia Sinica, 1961–63.

Index

A Note About the Author

Arthur F. Wright was born in Portland, Oregon, in 1913. Educated at Stanford, Oxford, and Harvard, he began his teaching career at Stanford in 1947 and in 1959 came to Yale University. He was named Charles Seymour Professor of History in 1961. Dr. Wright was Chairman of the Council on East Asian Studies, a fellow of the American Academy of Arts and Sciences, and a Guggenheim Fellow. He died in 1976.

A Note on the Type

The text of this book was set in a film version of Palatino, a type face designed by the noted German typographer Hermann Zapf. Named after Giovanbattista Palatino, a writing master of Renaissance Italy, Palatino was the first of Zapf's type faces to be introduced to America. The first designs for the face were made in 1948, and the fonts for the complete face were issued between 1950 and 1952. Like all Zapf-designed type faces, Palatino is beautifully balanced and exceedingly readable.

Composed by American-Stratford Graphics, Inc.

Maps of China by David Lindroth

Typography and binding design
by Holly McNeely